HARVARD ORIENTAL SERIES

Edited by MICHAEL WITZEL

VOLUME EIGHTY-TWO

AN EARLY TEXT ON THE HISTORY OF RWA SGRENG MONASTERY

THE *RGYAL BA'I DBEN GNAS RWA SGRENG GI BSHAD PA NYI MA'I 'OD ZER* OF 'BROM SHES RAB ME LCE

By

MAHO IUCHI

**PUBLISHED BY THE DEPARTMENT OF SOUTH ASIAN STUDIES
HARVARD UNIVERSITY
DISTRIBUTED BY HARVARD UNIVERSITY PRESS,
CAMBRIDGE, MASSACHUSETTS
AND LONDON, ENGLAND**

2016

Printed in the United States of America

For information write to Editor, Harvard Oriental Series, Department of South Asian Studies,
1 Bow Street, Cambridge MA 02138, USA
617-495 3295; email: witzel@fas.harvard.edu

Library of Congress Cataloguing in Publication Data
An Early Text on the History of Rwa sgreng Monastery. The *Rgyal ba'i dben gnas rwa sgreng gi bshad pa nyi ma'i 'od zer* of 'Brom shes rab me lce

Harvard Oriental Series; v. 82 ISBN 9780674975569

I. Maho Iuchi 1978-
II. Title
III. Series: Harvard Oriental Series; 82
CIP

An Early Text on the History of Rwa sgreng Monastery

The *Rgyal ba'i dben gnas rwa sgreng gi bshad pa nyi ma'i 'od zer* of 'Brom Shes rab me lce

Maho Iuchi

Contents

ACKNOWLEDGEMENTS

Firstly, I would like to thank Prof. Leonard. W. J. van der Kuijp of Harvard University for reading the Tibetan text with me. He has been an unfailing source of support during my three years as a Post-Doctoral Associate at Harvard University. Also, I would like to thank Prof. Em. Khangkar Tsultrim Kelsang, Otani University, Kyoto, and Khenpo Ngawang Dorje, Tashi Choeling Buddhist Center, Charlottesville, VA. Both helped proofread the Tibetan text of Part Two and gave me invaluable advice. My thanks also go out to Mr. Rory Lindsay, Ph.D. Candidate, Harvard University, and Mr. Andy Francis, Wisdom Publications, Somerville, for their generous help proofreading the English text. Also, I would like to thank Mr. Lobsang Shastri, TBRC, Cambridge, Dr. Dorje Nyingcha, Minzu University, Beijing, and Mr. Dorje Tseten, Ph.D. Candidate, Minzu University, for their helpful advice. With regard to the list of sacred objects at Rwa sgreng, Part One, I would like to thank Prof. Em. Taidō Kitamura, Shuchi'in University, Kyoto, Prof. Konomi Nakashima, Bukkyo University, Kyoto, Dr. Ryūta Kikuya, Tohoku University, Sendai, and Prof. Kazuo Kano, Kōyasan University, Wakayama. All four were of immense help in identifying the Sanskrit terminology, when relevant. Also, with regard to the facsimile of the *Rgyal ba'i dben gnas rwa sgreng gi bshad pa nyi ma'i 'od zer* manuscript, I would like to thank the Dpal brtsegs bod yig dpe rnying zhib 'jug khang, Lhasa. They allowed me to use the facsimile of the manuscript. Last but not least, I thank Prof. Michael Witzel for his readiness to accept this booklet for publication in the Harvard Oriental Series, of which he is the editor. Needless to say, whatever faults remain, they are mine and mine alone.

This study was supported by the Japan Society for the Promotion of Science (JSPS, April 2011–August 2013) and Bukkyo Dendo Kyokai (BDK, September 2013–August 2014).

Part One

Introduction

1. Overview

It is generally accepted that Rwa sgreng monastery, the mother monastery of the ancient Bka' gdams tradition,[1] was founded by 'Brom ston pa Rgyal ba'i 'byung gnas (1005–1064) in 1057 (the fire-female-bird-year) following the passing of his master, the great Bangladeshi Paṇdit Atiśa (Dīpaṃkaraśrījñāna, 982–1054). Since the eighteenth century Rwa sgreng has been known as the home monastery of the Rwa sgreng sprul sku-s, a line of reincarnate lamas that, for a time, produced the governor (*srid skyong*) of the Dga' ldan pho brang, the religious government of Tibet.[2] Although Rwa sgreng monastery played a key role in Tibetan religious and political life from the eighteenth until the twentieth century, curiously, despite its association with one of the founders of the sect, it seems to have not had much of a presence as a monastic college during the height of the Bka' gdams period (eleventh–thirteenth centuries) compared to other monasteries of the sect, such as Gsang phu sne'u thog and Snar thang Monastery.[3] Consequently, reliable, early sources on the history of the monastery are rare.

In recent years, thanks to the Dpal brtsegs Institute's publication of rare texts concerning the Bka' gdams school—such as the series of texts under the title *Bka' gdams gsung 'bum* (*The Collected Works of the Bka' gdams*)—it has become possible to gather new information on the Bka' gdams tradition.[4] Within the pages of another series, the *Bod kyi lo rgyus rnam thar phyogs bsgrigs* (*Collection of Tibetan Historical Works and Biographies*), compiled by the Dpal brtsegs Institute and published by the Mtsho sngon mi rigs dpe skrun khang in 2010, one finds a text entitled *Rgyal ba'i dben gnas rwa sgreng gi bshad*

---

[1] In general, the meaning of "*bka' gdams*" is understanding every word of the Buddha (*bka'*) as an instruction (*gdams ngag*), without excluding a single letter. *Gsal ba'i sgron me*: 3b4–5. *Gsal ba'i sgron me*: 4a3–6 gives three other explanations of its meaning: (1) At the time Jo bo (Atiśa) was in Snye thang, [his] disciples respected the word of Jo bo. Therefore, one Lama says, it is called "*bka' dam pa*" because it appeared that they recognized the word of the Lama (*bka'*) as superior (*dam pa*). It is thought that this is an interpretation of "*bka' dam*. (2) Because the former Bka' gdams pa people such as Bshes gnyen Ston pa ('Brom ston pa) sustained the tradition of the Tripitaka, and [they sustained] the word (*bka'*) strictly (*dam dog*) in the secret mantra of the greater vehicle, although they practiced the profound tantric [practice] on the inside. (3) Most of lamas say it is "*bka' gdams*" because the father of the Bka' gdams [pa school], 'Brom ston selected (*gdam nga*) "*Lha chos bdun ldan*" (the seven having the divine dharma) according to the word (*bka'*) of Jo bo, "*lha bzhi chos gsum*" ("*lha bzhi*"; thub pa, spyan ras gzigs, sgrol ma, mi g.yo ba, "*chos gsum*": sde snod gsum). Also see Thupten Jinpa (2008: 7– 8), Iuchi and Yoshimizu (2011: 20).

[2] See Roesler (2007). The first Rwa sgreng Tulku was a teacher (*yongs 'dzin*) of the seventh Dalai Lama Bskal bzang rgya mtsho (1708–1757), Dga' ldan khri pa Ngag dbang mchog ldan (1677–1751). See Lhun grub chos 'phel (1994: 210–212) and *Bod kyi rig gnas lo rgyus dpyad gzhi'i rgyu cha bdams bsgrigs*, 4 (Bod rang skyong ljongs chab gros rig gnas lo rgyus dpyad gzhi'i rgyu cha u yon lhan khang, Bod ljongs mi dmangs dpe skrun khang, Lhasa (1981: 133–144). After the death of the sixth Rwa sgreng Tulku Bstan 'dzin 'jigs med mthu stobs dbang phyug (1948–1997), Blo gros rgya mtsho (1997–), who was born in Nag chu, was recognized as the seventh Rwa sgreng Tulku.

[3] Roesler (2007: 126–127) also points this out.

[4] So far, the Dpal brtsegs bod yig dpe rnying zhib 'jug khang, a private institute in Lhasa, has published three collections of rare works by early Bka' gdams pa masters; these are the *Bka' gdams gsung 'bum phyogs bsgrigs*, parts 1, 2, 3 (2006, 2007, 2009).

pa nyi ma'i 'od zer [henceforce *Rwa sgreng nyi ma'i 'od zer*] (*Rays of the Sun: A Statement about Rwa sgreng Monastery, Hermitage of the Victor*), by 'Brom Shes rab me lce (13th–14th c.),[5] which forms the subject of this work. The manuscript is written in an *dbu med* script and consists of thirty-two folios. Its title page is marked with the word "outside" (*phyi*), which indicates that the manuscript was a text from an "outside" library kept in the personal collection of the Fifth Dalai Lama Ngag dbang blo bzang rgya mtsho (1617–1682), perhaps in the Chapel of the Sixteen Elders (*gnas bcu lha khang*), on the second floor of the assembly hall (*tshogs chen*) of 'Bras spungs monastery in Lhasa.[6]

The fact that most of the large-scale works dealing with the historical and social development of the Bka' gdams school, the histories of the Bka' gdams school (*Bka' gdams chos 'byung*), were written in a period spanning from the late fifteenth up to the early seventeenth century,[7] places *Rwa sgreng nyi ma'i 'od zer* relatively early in the development of Bka' gdams histories. It is the only work that we presently know of that is solely devoted to Rwa sgreng monastery. Until its recent publication by the Mtsho sngon mi rigs dpe skrun khang, the existence of this text was only known via the *Mdo smad chos 'byung*, a nineteenth century regional religious history written by Brag dkar Zhabs drung Dkon mchog bstan pa rab rgyas (1801–after 1866), in which is mentioned the existence of a text called *Rwa sgreng dkar chag* written by 'Brom Me lce 'phreng ba,[8] a title and authorship represented that differ slightly

---

[5] *Bod kyi lo rgyus rnam thar phyogs bsgrigs kyi dkar chag* (2010: 28) gives to this text the title *Rwa sgreng dgon gyi gdan rabs, The Abbatial Succession of Rwa sgreng monastery*, but this title does not appear in the text. Also, the Dpal brtsegs bod yig dpe rnying zhib 'jug khang (2004: 1532) lists this text under catlogue number 017285 and Dpal brtsegs Institute gives a title, *Rwa sgrengs [sgreng] bzhengs pa'i lo rgyus, An Account of the Foundation of Rwa sgreng*.

[6] According to the introduction and preface of Dpal brtsegs bod yig dpe rnying zhib 'jug khang (2004), in general, the title pages of each manuscript in the 'Bras spungs catalog were marked with the word "home" (*nang*) or "outside" (*phyi*) to indicate that the texts were part of the "home" library housed at 'Bras spungs monastery during the period of the Fifth Dalai Lama or that they were texts from "outside" libraries, such as the Sne gdong pho brang (Lho kha) and Bsam grub rtse (Gzhis ka rtse), that were brought to 'Bras spungs. The collection housed in the Chapel of the Sixteen Elders makes up the largest part of the 'Bras spungs catalogue, and most of what the Dpal brtsegs Institute has published have been manuscripts from the collection marked "outside." Also see Iuchi (2006: 20–22).

Gsal ba'i sgron me is the most extensive history of the Bka' gdams school. It comprises four hundred seventeen folios and ten chapters. Three publications are available: the block-print version (*Bod kyi lo rgyus rnam thar phyogs bsgrigs*, set 1, vol. 3); a handwritten manuscript (B. Jamyang Norbu (comp.), *A Detailed Account of the Spread of the Kadampa Sect in Tibet*, vol. 2, New Delhi 1972); and a western book-style version (Mig dmar rgyal mtshan (ed.), Bod ljongs mi dmang dpe skrun khang, Lhasa 2003). According to the colophon (block-print version: 417a5–6), the wood blocks were created upon the order of the Fifth Dalai Lama. It is assumed that the handwritten and western book-style versions are based on this block-print version. Also, Toh. 7038 is the block print printed using the same wood blocks. Hadano (1954) is the earlier and important study for Bka' gdams school using *Gsal ba'i sgron me*. See Iuchi and Yoshimizu (2011: 15–19).

[7] There are several works of the *Bka' gdams chos 'byung* genre, such as Bsod nams lha'i dbang po (1423–1496), Las chen Kun dga' rgyal mtshan (1432–1506), Paṇ chen Bsod nams grags pa (1478–1554), A myes zhabs Ngag dbang kun dga' bsod nams (1597–1662), and Yongs 'dzin Ye shes rgyal mtshan (1717–1793). Dung dkar blo bzang 'phrin las (2002: 164–165) mentions *Dbus pa blo gsal gyi chos 'byung* (MHTL 10845) by Dbus pa blo gsal (b. 13th c.) and *Paṇ chen ye shes rtse mo'i bka' gdams chos 'byung* (MHTL 10849) by Paṇ chen Ye shes rtse mo (1433–?) as representing the *Bka' gdams chos 'byung* genre. See Roesler (2008: 396), Iuchi and Yoshimizu (2011: 16).

[8] *Mdo smad chos 'byung*: 7. Mr. Tashi Tsering, a director of Amnye Machen Institute (Dharamsala, India),

from those of our text.

Although the *Rwa sgreng nyi ma'i 'od zer* is the only early history to deal strictly with Rwa sgreng that we know of, there have been three modern publications that have focused exclusively on the monastery and its history.[9] A text called *Rwa sgreng dgon pa'i dkar chag*, compiled by the modern Tibetan scholar Lhun grub chos 'phel,[10] is the most detailed among the modern works to deal with the monastery.[11] Lhun grub chos 'phel mentions a "catalog by 'Brom shes rab me lce" that is almost certainly *Rwa sgreng nyi ma'i 'od zer*,[12] quotes portions of that text (albeit without proper attribution),[13] and indicates in his conclusion the existence of an old handwritten catalogue of Rwa sgreng monastery of unclear provenance.[14] Although the details he provides about his sources are obscure, it seems clear that Lhun grub chos 'phel had access to both an old, unpublished catalogue and a catalogue attributed to 'Brom Shes rab me lce, presumably the *Rwa sgreng nyi ma'i 'od zer*.[15]

Although Rwa sgreng was the mother monastery of the Bka' gdams school, it was eventually integrated into the Dge lugs school and administered by that sect.[16] Despite its position of political

---

kindly provided me with this reference.

[9] Lhun grub chos 'phel (1994), Gzigs pa sprul sku Blo bzang bzod pa, Phun tshogs rab rgyas (2006), and Gzim sprul Bstan 'dzin ye shes (2012). Also, Rwa sgreng monastery self-published a small yellow booklet for visitors edited by 'Jam dpal dge 'dun, titled *Dpal gyi 'byung gnas rwa sgreng chos sde chen po'i lo rgyus skal ldan dang ba 'dren pa'i pho nya*. It seems that the other three publications used this work as a reference. Gzigs pa sprul sku Blo bzang bzod pa and Phun tshogs rab rgyas (2006: 10, 12) cite Lhun grub chos 'phel (1994).

[10] According to one current monk of Rwa sgreng monastery, Lhun grub chos 'phel was a monk of Chab mdo byams pa gling. He was a disciple of Thub bstan dam pa, who was a teacher of the 11th 'Phags pa lha Dge legs rnam rgyal (1939–).

[11] The full title of this work is *Dpal gyi 'byung gnas rwa sgreng rgyal ba'i dben gnas dang/ gtsug la khang gi rten dang brten par bcas pa'i dkar chag mthong don ldan dge legs nor bu'i bang mdzod*. See Lhungrub chos 'phel (1994: 9). The author makes mention of the *Bu ston chos 'byung* (11) and the *Bka' gdams glegs bam* (43) as sources, as well as the *Rwa sgreng gi gnas yig dang skor tshad dag snang skor* (179–184) by Rwa sgreng khri sprul Bstan pa rab rgyas (1759–1815). We do not, at present, have any information regarding the person of Lhun grub chos 'phel, beyond his name, and we cannot say how he had access to the texts that he relied upon to compile the work.

[12] Lhun grub chos 'phel (1994: 90) mentions the *Rwa sgreng nyi ma'i 'od zer* only once: "...one should know the details of these matters from [texts] such as the catalogue by 'Brom Shes rab me lce..." (*'di dag gi zhib cha ni 'brom shes rab me lces mdzad pa'i dkar chag sogs las shes par bya zhing*).

[13] The quotations in Lhun grub chos 'phel (1994) are as follows (the folio number of *Rwa sgreng nyi ma'i 'od zer* is in brackets: 7–8 (1b4–7), 8–9 (1b7–2a5), 15–16 (2a6–2b3), 16–17 (2b3–6), 88 (19b1–8), 89 (20a4–5), and 90 (22a4–7).

[14] "*sngar gyi dkar chag rnying pa mdzad byang mi gsal ba bris ma.*" See Lhun grub chos 'phel (1994: 209). Unfortunatelly, I could not see this old catalogue, but according to one current monk of Rwa sgreng monastery, this catalogue exists in the monastery even now. The monk mentions that Lhun grub chos 'phel copied this catalogue and the content of his book is the same as the catalogue.

[15] Lhun grub chos 'phel (1994: 208–209) mentions in his conclusion that the work was written at the urging of two of his teachers, Grags pa snyan grags and Blo bzang brtson 'grus. He finished writing the book near the Sprul pa'i gtsug lag khang (Sprul snang/ Jo khang Temple) on the twenty-fifth day of the eighth Tibetan lunar month (*hor zla*) in the earth–snake–year in the seventeenth *Rabjung* (1989). Grags pa snyan grags was a sponsor for the thousand images (*stong sku*), which were completed in 1988. See Kano (2012: 144–145, n.73) for a Japanese translation of this section. Also, Lhun grub chos 'phel (1994) includes a catalogue on the new supports at Rwa sgreng monastery that were completed in 1988. See Lhun grub chos 'phel (1994: 184–203). It seems that Lhun grub chos 'phel (1994) wrote in reaction to these reconstrutions after the Cultural Revolution.

[16] Tsong kha pa Blo bzang grags pa (1357–1419) stayed and wrote his *Lam rim chen mo* at Yang dgon ri

importance in later centuries, many of the details of the early history of Rwa sgreng remain obscure. The *Rwa sgreng nyi ma'i 'od zer*, however, offers details concerning the early activities of Rwa sgreng monastery during the Bka' gdams period, such as the construction buildings at the monastery and the monastery's relationships, not only with local sponsors, but with the outside world as well, including Mi nyag (Xixia, 西夏). These descriptions are quite significant in that they provide insight into political and social aspects of the Bka' gdams school between the eleventh and thirteenth century.

---

khrod in the foot of Brags seng ge. See *Bai ḍūrya gser po*: 183. It is located in the behind of Rwa sgreng monastery.

For more on the present status of Bka' gdams pa monasteries, see my "Changes in Early Bka' gdams pa monasteries with Shifts in the Structure of the Buddhist Community in Tibet," published via the 12th IATS (Vancouver, 2010), as well as Iuchi (2010). Given that monasteries that were Bka' gdams in origin are no longer Bka' gdams in affiliation and the sect no longer extant, we must adopt the more accurate nomenclature of "monasteries with Bka' gdams roots," between around the fourteenth and fifteenth centuries, with the rise of the Dge lugs School, sometimes called "New Bka' gdams" (*Bka' gdams gsar ma*), most of the monasteries with Bka' gdams roots were absorbed into the Dge lugs school, or became partly affiliated with the Sa skya school.

2. DATE AND AUTHORSHIP OF THE TEXT

The colophon of the *Rwa sgreng nyi ma'i 'od zer*, as we have it, presents the possibility that 'Brom Shes rab me lce composed the work in either 1299 (242 years after the founding of Rwa sgreng) or 1335 (wood-pig-year).[17] The colophon states:[18]

> *rgyal ba'i dben gnas rwa sgreng gi bshad pa nyi ma'i 'od zer ces bya ba 'di ni//rgyal ba'i dben gnas de nyid bzhengs nas/ lo nyis brgya dang bzhi bcu rtsa gnyis lon pa'i tshe/ yongs kyi dge ba'i bshes gnyen chen po rnal 'byor byang seng gi gdan sar/ dad pa dang shes rab phun sum tshogs pa dang ldan pa'i dge slong dge 'dun dbang phyug la sogs pa 'ga ['ga'] zhig gis bskul nas: shing mo phag gi lo la 'brom shes rab me lce bya bas yi ger bkod pa'o/*
>
> Having been asked by some at the seat of the great perfect spiritual teacher (*dge bshes*), Rnal 'byor Byang seng (byang chub seng ge),[19] beginning with the monk Dge 'dun dbang phyug, who is full of excellent faith and wisdom, the one named 'Brom Shes rab me lce composed this work called *Rays of the Sun: A Statement about Rwa sgreng Monastery, Hermitage of the Victor* in the wood-pig-year, when 242 years had passed since the founding of that very hermitage of the Victor.

The Tibetan wood-pig-year mentioned here is the year 1335. However, the hermitage itself was founded in 1057, which, when the two hundred forty-two intervening years are introduced, brings us only to the year 1299 (the earth-pig-year in the Tibetan reckoning). The discrepant dates in the colophon prevent identification of the date of the composition of the text with certainty, but based on evidence within the pages of the text itself, we have reason to believe that it is more likely that text was composed in 1299.

The single most compelling point of evidence to this end lies in the point at which the line of abbatical succession at Rwa sgreng terminates in the pages of the text. Slob dpon Gur ston (13th c.), the last abbot mentioned in the *Rwa sgreng nyi ma'i 'od zer*,[20] served fifteen years as the eighth abbot of

---

[17] The *Rwa sgreng nyi ma'i 'od zer* does not mention the episode described in the *Deb ther sngon po* where Rwa sgreng monastery was burned by the Mongol army (*hor dmag*) in the iron-male-mouse-year (1240). See *Deb ther sngon po*: kha, 13a1 and Roerich (1949: 90–91).

[18] *Rwa sgreng nyi ma'i 'od zer*: 32a5–8.

[19] A disciple of Sha ra ba Yon tan grags (1070–1141); date of birth and death unknown. *Gsal ba'i sgron me*: 245b1.

[20] *Rwa sgreng nyi ma'i 'od zer*, 21b4–5. Slob dpon Gur ston seems to have been one of the disciple of Spyan snga pa Tshul khrims 'bar (1038–1103). See *Gsal ba'i sgron me*: 168b3. For details on Spyan snga pa and Lo monastery, which was founded by Spyan snga pa, see Iuchi (2010).

Rwa sgreng, following Slob dpon Sna ra ba, who held the post for fourteen years before he passed away in 1283 (water–female–ox–year). Based on this timeline, Slob dpon Gur ston would have assumed the abbacy of Rwa sgreng by 1298. Given that the text does not mention another abbot after Slob dpon Gur ston, it is quite possible that 'Brom wrote the work while Gur ston still held that office.

As for the identity of the author of the *Rwa sgreng nyi ma'i 'od zer*, 'Brom Shes rab me lce, to whom Lhun grub chos 'phel attributes the text, is not discussed in the manuscript or in any other available histories of the Bka' gdams. The editor from the Dpal brtsegs Institute who oversaw the publication of *Bod kyi lo rgyus rnam thar phyogs bsgrigs* identified 'Brom Gzhon nu blo gros, alias 'Brom Ku mā ra ma ti (1271–?),[21]—an important person in the formation and tradition of the *Bka' gdams glegs bam*[22]—as the author of our text. This attribution seems to be made on the strength of the author's reference to himself as "a monk of Rwa sgreng by the name of Gzhon nu" in the concluding verses of the text. It should be noted, however, that the full name 'Brom Gzhon nu blo gros does not appear in the text. The concluding verses read as follows:[23]

dam bas [pas] bsngags pa'i dben gnas de'i [//] bzhengs tshul lo rgyus sngar yang mang snang mod//
[upper inter lineally: 'on kyang de dag dbang don bye brag/] go bar dka' zhing ma 'brel ma 'gribs par//
phyogs su bsdebs la go bar sla ba gcig// bdag la gyis ces mkhas pa'i skye bo dang//
dad ldan skye bus bskul bar gyur bas na// sngon kyi [gyi] yi ge rgan po'i gsung rnams dang//
rang gi [gis] mthong dang thos tshod la brten nas// gzhon nu ming can dge sbyong rwa sgreng pas//
yi ger bkod kyi 'gal 'khrul [under inter lineally: mchis] srid na// jo bo yab sras bla ma rgyud [brgyud] pa dang//
yi dam lha dang chos skyong bsrung mar bcas// mkhas pa'i tshogs la bzo ba mdzad par rigs//
gzhan gyis bskul nas bdag gis bris [under inter lineally: pa] yis// bsod nams de yis skye ba thams cad du//
jo bo yab sras chos la longs spyod cing/ 'gro don [under inter lineally: lhun grub] byang chub thob par shog//

There have appeared in the past many histories about the founding of the hermitage

[21] Dpal brtsegs bod yig dpe rnying zhib 'jug khang (2010: 62–65).

[22] Iuchi and Yoshimizu (2011: 63). Another work by 'Brom Gzhon nu blo gros, *Bstan pa rin po che lha chos phun sum tshogs pa'i lo rgyus ngo mtshar rmad du byung ba'i lo rgyus* is also contained in the *Bod kyi lo rgyus rnam thar phyogs bsgrigs*, set 1, vol.4, 395–611.

[23] *Rwa sgreng nyi ma'i 'od zer*: 32a1–5.

that is praised by the holy.
However, the specifics of their details are difficult to understand and incoherent.
Since scholars and devoted people have asked me to create a compilation that is easy to understand and unobscured,
I, a monk of Rwa sgreng by the name of Gzhon nu, composed this, relying on old documents by past authors and whatever I have seen and heard.
If there are contradictions and errors herein, I pray the line of gurus of the Jo bo father and son tradition,
along with the deities, Dharma protectors, and the scholarly community bear with them.
As I have written at the behest of others, due to the merit [of doing so] may I enjoy the Dharma of the Jo bo father and son tradition in all my lives
and attain the enlightenment that spontaneously fulfills the aims of sentient beings.

Regarding 'Brom Gzhon nu blo gros, *Gsal ba'i sgron me* includes a short biography of this figure, according to which he was born in Shi'u sna of Ngar, Klungs shod area,[24] in 1271 (the iron-female-sheep-year). At the age of seven, 'Brom was sent to study reading and writing (*klog sbyong*) under Slob dpon Nam mkha' rin chen (1214–1286)[25] in Stabs ka monastery,[26] which was probably located in the Klungs shod area. He took novice ordination at age twelve under Gzhon nu tshul khrims and Gzhon nu blo gros, and went on to study such works as *Madhyamakāvatāra* (*Dbu ma 'jug pa*) and *Bodhisattvacaryāvatāra* (*Spyod 'jug*) under Jo sras Bkra shis rgyal at Thang sag monastery.[27] At the age of twenty, 'Brom became fully ordained under Ye shes seng ge and Bsod ston in Jog po dgon gsar.[28] In 1294 (the wood-male-horse-year), when he was twenty-four, he went to Snar thang monastery, where he studied for six years under the eighth abbot, Skyo ston pa Smon lam tshul khrims (1219–1299), who was a disciple of Mchims Nam mkha' grags (1250–1285).

Since 'Brom Gzhon nu blo gros went on to develop a strong connections with Snar thang monastery, comparing the *Rwa sgreng nyi ma'i 'od zer* with comments on the history of Rwa sgreng found in the works of Mchims Nam mkha' grags, the great scholar of Snar thang, may help to

---

[24] Klung shod is an area in around the present-day Mal gro kun dkar. See Dung dkar Blo bzang 'phrin las (2002: 123). Many Bka' gdams pa masters were from Klung shod area along with 'Phan yul.

[25] There is a brief biography of Nam mkha' rin chen in the *Gsal ba'i sgron me*: 282a2–286b3.

[26] Stabs ka was a monastery of Dge bshes Stabs ka ba (Dar ma grags, 1103–1174), a disciple of Sha ra ba. *Gsal ba'i sgron me*: 240a5–241b1.

[27] Thang sag, or Thang sag Dga' ldan chos 'khor, was founded by Zhang Thang sag pa Ye shes 'byung gnas (11th–12th c.), who was a disciple of Pa tshab Nyi ma grags (1055–?). See Roesler (2004: 36–37), Iuchi and Yoshimizu (2011: 33, n.82)

[28] This monastery is unspecified.

corroborate that this 'Brom Gzhon nu blo gros of Snar thang was indeed the author of our text. Among of the works of Mchims, the recently published *Dge bshes ston pa'i rnam thar* (*The Biography of Dge bshes Ston pa*), which was first introduced by Eimer in 2008,[29] devotes much of its third chapter to the founding of Rwa sgreng monastery. The content of the text is as follows:[30]

1. ['Brom ston pa's] excellence on account of the lineage in which he had been born (167b4–168a4)
2. ['Brom ston pa's] excellence on account of the virtue of the purified [person] (168a4–179b5)
3. ['Brom ston pa's] excellence on account of the deeds performed (179b5–202a1)
   3–1. The reason for building the temple (Rwa sgreng) (179b6–185a5)
   3–2. How it was built (185a5–187b2)
   3–3. How it was maintained (187b2–202a1)
      3–3–1. How it was supported by ['Brom ston pa] himself (187b2–196a6)
      3–3–2. How it was maintained by others (196a6–201a6)
      3–3–3. How it became the basis of the teachings (201a6–202a1)

Looking to the *Rwa sgreng nyi ma'i 'od zer,* we find identical descriptions, as in the case of the prophecy for Rwa sgreng monastery. The prophecy appearing in both texts is as follows:[31]

> *'jam dpal bstan pa rol pa'i rgyud las//*

---

[29] *Dge bshes ston pa'i rnam thar* is included in the *Bod kyi lo rgyus rnam thar phyogs bsgrigs*, set 3, vol.2, Xining: Mtsho sngon mi rigs dpe skrun khang, 2012. Tibetan Buddhist Resource Center (TBRC, www.tbrc.org) has a scan of this manuscript (W2CZ7888, 343–416).

[30] Also see Eimer (2008: 383–386).

[31] *Rwa sgreng nyi ma'i 'od zer*: 2a6–7. There is a parallel description in the *Dge bshes ston pa'i rnam thar*: 184b2–4. The other prophecies for Rwa sgreng monastery appear in both texts, and are different. The *Rwa sgreng nyi ma'i 'od zer*: 2b1–3 gives the prophecy by Srong btsan sgam po (c. 617–650) as follows:

> [*Rwa sgreng nyi ma'i 'od zer*: 2b1–3]
> The prophecy by Srong btsan sgam po (c. 617–650):
>
> After five hundreds years,
> The teachings of the Buddha will spread
> To the mountain center in the northern region, the snowy land,
> The region that has a variety of medicine,
> The place of extensive fragrant wood and forests.
> The place where people gather and worship,
> Will be announced by the stainless king.
> This place was prophesied by the marvelous king.

On the other hand, *Dge bshes ston pa'i rnam thar*: 184b5–6 mentions the prophecy in the *Mdo sde rgyan.* For the English translation of the prophecy in the *Dge bshes ston pa'i rnam thar*, see Roesler (2007: 131).

lnga brgya dus kyi tha ma la// sangs rgyas bstan pa gar [dar] rgyas pa//
byang phyogs kha ba can gyi ri'i dbus// sman sna sna tshogs yod pa'i gul [khul]//
spos shing nags tshal rgyas pa'i gnas// yi ge dang po ra la de 'og sgreng//

According to the *'Jam dpal bstan pa rol pa'i rgyud:*[32]
Five hundred [years] into the final age the teachings of the Buddha will have spread:
to the north, amid the snowy mountains, on a hillside where there are a variety of medicinal plants—
a place with an extensive forest of aromatic trees—*sgreng* following the initial letter *ra*.

The above prophecy for Rwa sgreng monastery also appears in the *Rnam thar rgyas pa yongs grags*, another work compiled by Mchims Nam mkha' grags.[33] We may presume that 'Brom Shes rab me lce referred to the works of Mchims Nam mkha' grags when writing the *Rwa sgreng nyi ma'i 'od zer*. 'Brom also provides descriptions of the landscape around Rwa sgreng[34] and of the donors for the construction of each of the buildings at Rwa sgreng that are very similar to Mchims' works, although 'Brom does not identify Mchims as his source.[35]

On the other hand, the *Dge bshes ston pa'i rnam thar* provides an interpretation of the name "Rwa sgreng" that does not appear in the *Rwa sgreng nyi ma'i 'od zer:*[36]

me pho spre'u'i lo ra sgyeng [sgreng] du chgas [phyag] phab bo/ de yang dang po ldan ma'i yul yin pas ldan skad du ra sgyeng [sgreng]/ bod skad du chu mig ring mo zhe bya ba yin skad/

...they proceeded to Rwa sgyeng (*sgreng*)[37] in the male-fire-monkey-year (1066). Because this was formerly the region of Ldan ma,[38] it is called Ra sgyeng (*sgreng*) in the

---

[32] This quote is unidentified. See Eimer (1979): Teil 1, 337, Roesler (2007: 131, n.19).

[33] *Rnam thar rgyas pa yongs grags*: 221–222.

[34] Roesler (2007) translated into English this part of *Dge bshes ston pa'i rnam thar*: 182a5–185b6. Roesler (2007: 128) writes: "It is presumably not only the oldest extant source which contains an extensive description of the symbolic geography of Rwa sgreng, but also is an interesting source on geomancy."

[35] For the descriptions of the landscape of Rwa sgreng, the *Rwa sgreng nyi ma'i 'od zer*: 15a5–15b6 is parallel with the *Dge bshes ston pa'i rnam thar*: 182a6–183b4.

[36] *Dge bshes ston pa'i rnam thar*: 182a5–6. This part is translated by Roesler (2008: 129).

[37] In the *Dge bshes ston pa'i rnam thar*, Rwa sgreng appears with a different spelling, "Rwa sgyeng," throughout the text.

[38] Ldan ma (/'Dan ma), also known as 'Dan khog, which is located in Ljong mda' rdzong, TAR and Ser shul rdzong, Ganzi Autonomous Region, Sichuan Province, is an important place related with Bka' gdams school. 'Brom ston pa spent twenty years there, studying under Se btsun Dbang phyug gzhon nu and Smṛtijñānarkīrti (Dran pa ye shes, 10th–11th c.) before the arrival of Atiśa. Khu ston Brtson 'grus g.yung drung (1011–1075), Rngog Legs pa'i shes rab, and Bang ston Byang chub rgyal mtshan also studied under Se btsun. For the 'Dan ma and Bka' gdams pa masters, see Iuchi (2013).

> Ldan [ma] language. In Tibetan it means "perennial spring" (*chu mig ring mo*),[39] thus it is said...

In addition, the relationship between the monks of Rwa sgreng and the king of Mi nyag (Xixia) mentioned in the *Rwa sgreng nyi ma'i 'od zer* (see chapter 7 below) is not mentioned in the *Dge bshes ston pa'i rnam thar* or the *Rnam thar rgyas pa yongs grags*.

So, considering the close similarities shared between the *Rwa sgreng nyi ma'i 'od zer* and the works of Mchims, the great scholar of Snar thang, we cannot completely deny the possibility that 'Brom Gzhon nu blo gros and 'Brom Shes rab me lce may have been one and the same. In addition, the two possible dates given for the composition of the text in the colophon, 1299 and 1335, coincide with dates for 'Brom Gzhon nu blo gros.

[39] According to Gzim sprul Bstan 'dzin ye shes (2012: 96), at present, there exists a spring called "*Bstan pa'i chu mig ring mo*" (the spring of teaching) in the Dbu rtse ka gnyis ma of Rwa sgreng monastery. There are pictures of the spring. There is no mention of "*chu mig ring mo,*" but the *Rwa sgreng nyi ma'i 'od zer*: 16b4 mentions that there are two springs at the base (*sa gzhi*) of Dbu rtse ka gnyis ma. It seems that *chu mig* (spring) is a key term for the Rwa sgreng. The *Rwa sgreng nyi ma'i 'od zer*: 1b6–7 states, "...the precious monastery, the great helmitage of the victor, Rwa sgreng which is like the springhead of one hundred eight springs..." (*...chu mig brgya rtsa brgyad kyi mgo' lta bur gyur pa'i gdan sa rin po che rgyal ba'i dben gnas chen po rwa sgreng ...*).

3. DESCRIPTION OF THE MANUSCRIPT

The manuscript of *Rwa sgreng nyi ma'i 'od zer* is handwritten in an *dbu med* script,[40] consists of thirty-two folios that range from seven to nine lines,[41] and measures 8 x 46 cm.[42] The available black and white photographs of the manuscript is mostly clear, but the interlinear and marginal notes written in very small letters are often unreadable. As with other handwritten manuscripts, the *Rwa sgreng nyi ma'i 'od zer* contains many abbreviations (*bsdud yig* and *skung yig*). Characteristic abbreviations that appear throughout the manuscript are as follows:

	dkon mchog gsum
	rgyal mtshan
	dngos grub
	lnga bcu rtsa bdun
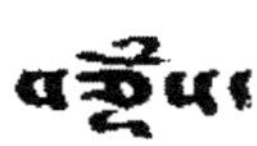	bcom ldan 'das
	gnyis su
	nyi shu
	jo bo
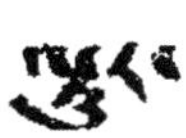	lta bur
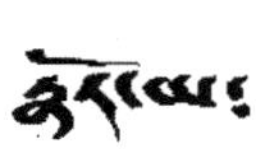	rnal 'byor ma

[40] Dpal brtsegs bod yig dpe rnying zhib 'jug khang (2004: 1532) mentiones the writing style of the manuscript is *dpe tshugs* style. The most of the manuscript marked as *phyi*, is written in the writing style of *dpe tshugs* or *'Bru tsha zhabs thung*. This topic was discussed by me at the Palaeography Workshop, Khyentse Center for Tibetan Buddhist Textual Scholarship, University of Hamburg (Hamburg, Germany 2015), in a paper titled "Punctuation signs and some particular spellings in the collection of the Gnas bcu lha khang, 'Bras spungs monastery."

[41] Mostly eight lines.

[42] See Dpal brtsegs bod yig dpe rnying zhib 'jug khang (2004: 1532).

 sna tshogs

 pho brang

 byon nas

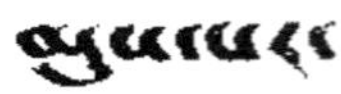 ma lus par

 yid bzhin

 rin po che

 rwas sgreng[43]

 la sogs pa

 lags skad

 longs spyod

 sangs rgyas

 gzigs

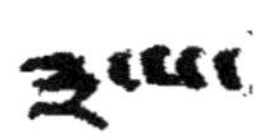 gsum pa

 slob dpon

 bsod nams

The following four types of punctuation also appear in the manuscript (transcriptions of punctuation marks as used in Part two: Text Transcription, displayed in center column):

---

[43] In the *Rwa sgreng nyi ma'i 'od zer*, Rwa sgreng appears with a different spelling, "Rwas sgreng," throughout the text.

	/	*shad*
	¦	broken *shad*
	:	double dot
	⁝	triple dot

The first punctuation sign is an ordinary *shad*. The second sign, a "broken *shad*" (¦), appears frequentry throughout the manuscript. Hugon (2004) assumes that this sign has the same function as an ordinary *shad*.[44] The third sign, a "double dot" (:), resembling a colon, appears less frequently than the broken *shad*.[45] The fourth sign, a "triple dot" (⁝), appears thirty-three times in the manuscript.[46] Some, but not all of the marks, appear after sentence final particles (e.g. *to, do, so*). Nishida (1987) points out that the double dot appears in manuscripts before the eleventh century and it is one of the features of an Old Tibetan writing system.[47] So these punctuation signs may also indicate something about the age of the manuscript.[48]

Another feature of our manuscript that resembles Old Tibetan writing is the *'a*-suffix, which appears in the manuscript as follows:

[8a8]	mtho' lding
[9b2, 5]	gnye' thang
[16a6, 17a6]	bzo' khyad
[16b3, 17a3]	phyag dpe'
[16b7]	mdo'
[17a2]	shing bzo' ba
[17a4]	bzo' bo

The Tibetan writing system was revised three times upon imperial decree (*bkas bcad*). Nishida (1987) explains that the *'a*-suffix was revised upon the second imperial decree (*bkas bcad gnyis pa*), around the year 826.[49] As Takeuchi (2002) has pointed out, however, Classical Tibetan, which is the writing

---

[44] See Hugon (2004: xxi). As Harter (2008) points out, Hugon (2004) did not mention the date of the manuscript itself. Interestingly, there are some common feautures on the punctuation signs within the manuscript of *Tshad ma shes rab sgron ma*.

[45] Hugon (2004) names this sign as "Two vertical dots."

[46] Hugon (2004) names this sign as "Three vertical dots."

[47] The similar sign, the double dot sign, appears in Old Tibetan writing systems found in Dunhuang manuscripts and inscriptions. See Nishida (1987: 165).

[48] So far, it seems there is no detailed study on punctuation signs in *dbu med* texts. Further investigation into Tibetan writing systems involving examples from each period is needed.

[49] See Nishida (1987: 122). Scherrer-Schaub (2002) discusses on the date of the imperial decree. According

system found after the second imperial decree, was established after the third imperial decree (*bkas bcad gsum pa*) in the eleventh century. Unfortunately, we do not know when this particular manuscript was copied, how the original may have appeared, or whether the writing style that appears in this manuscript coincides precisely with the style of the original manuscript or if it reflects the writing style of the period in which it was copied. In any case, further research comparing manuscripts will be required to solve this issue definitively. Surely our manuscript can serve as an example of a particular old system of writing.

The manuscript also contains unique spellings of some Tibetan words. The following are examples of unique spellings that appear throughout the manuscript (standard modern spellings in parentheses):

lo tshtsa ba	(lo tstsha ba)
spyan mnga'	(spyan snga)
sdzogs[50]	(rdzogs)
'jal	(mjal)
gnye [/gnye'] thang	(snye thang)

Also, there is some confusion in the spellings, particularly in connection with homophones (standard modern spellings in parentheses):

[7b8]	cin	(phyin)	*went*
[8b8]	dbus rtsang	(dbus gtsang)	*the provinces of Dbus and Gtsang*
[20b1]	ja'i zla ba'i	(bya'i zla ba'i)	*the eighth month*
[22b7]	grang	(drang)	*in front of*

to it, the first decree was in 763 or a little later, the second was in 783, and the third was in 814.

[50] The spelling, *sdzogs* is appeared not only the *Rwa sgreng nyi ma'i 'od zer*, but also the other text from the Gnas bcu lha khang, such as the *Tshad ma shes rab sgron ma.*

4. Outline of the Text

The text consists of two chapters. Chapter one is a description of the construction of Rwa sgreng monastery that consists of three sections: (1–1) Prophecies, (1–2) History of Atiśa and 'Brom ston pa, and (1–3) Construction of the Rwa sgreng monastery. Chapter two is an account of the "sacred objects" (*rten*) that were housed at the monastery that consists of two sections: (2–1) external sacred objects and (2–2) internal sacred objects. The complete outline of the text is as follows:

Introduction (1b1–7)
Chapter 1. An explanation of how Rwa sgreng was constructed (1b7–22a8)
  1–1. Prophecies (2a2–2b6)
    1–1–1. Prophecy by the Buddha (2a2–8)
      1–1–1–1. The prophecy: in general, how the precious teaching was spread in the country (2a2–6)
      1–1–1–2. The prophecy: in particular, on Rwa sgreng (2a6–8)
    1–1–2. Prophecy by the incarnated king (2a8–2b3)
    1–1–3. Prophecy by the teaching linage of Jo bo (Atiśa) (2b3–6)
  1–2. Letting good qualities descend (*spu phab pa*)[51] (/History of Jo bo and 'Brom ston pa) (2b6–14a5)
    1–2–1. The history of Jo bo, who let good qualities descend (2b6–9b5)
      1–2–1–1. The great history of [when Jo bo] was at home (2b8–3a7)
      1–2–1–2. The great history of [when Jo bo] departed for liberation (3a7–5a7)
        1–2–1–2–1. The school in which [Jo bo] was ordained (3b1–2)
        1–2–1–2–2. The lineage of the Lama (2b2–5a5)
        1–2–1–2–3. The place in which [Jo bo] worked for the benefit of others in Tibet (5a5–7)
      1–2–1–3. How [Jo bo] acted for the benefit of the Buddha's teaching (5a5–9b6)
        1–2–1–3–1. The reason [Jo bo] needed to go to Tibet (5a8–6b7)
          1–2–1–3–1–1. In general, how the increase and decrease of the Buddha's teaching appeared in Tibet (5b1–6b3)
          1–2–1–3–1–2. How the teaching appeared at that time (6b3–6)
          1–2–1–3–2. How [Jo bo] was invited to Tibet (6b8–8a7)
            1–2–1–3–2–1. The king who supported [Jo bo] (6b8–7a4)
            1–2–1–3–2–2. The envoy who invited [Jo bo] (7a4–8a2)

[51] Literally, *spus phab* means "letting the qualities descend." *Bod rgya tshig mdzod chen mo*: 1660 explains that *spus phab pa* is an archaic word (*brda rnying*) and the meaning is the same as *rung ba* (appropriate) and *blo la bab pa* (descend into the mind).

1-2-1-3-2-3. The process: what [Jo bo] did for the benefit of others on his way [to Tibet] (8a2–7)

1-2-1-3-3. How [Jo bo] worked for the benefit of others after arriving Tibet (8a7–9b6)

1-2-1-3-3-1. Where [Jo bo] gave teachings on the Piṭakas (scriptures) (8a8–9a3)

1-2-1-3-3-2. The kinds of disciples who appeared (9a3–8)

1-2-1-3-3-3. The number of years [Jo bo] stayed in Tibet (9b1)

1-2-1-3-3-4. Where [Jo bo] finally demonstrated nirvana (9b1–3)

1-2-1-3-3-5. The names by which [Jo bo] was called during that period (9b3–5)

1-2-2. The history of Dge bshes Ston pa who was a person who let good qualities descend (9b6–13b4)

1-2-2-1. Where his incarnation was born (9b7–10a7)

1-2-2-1-1. The family lineage (9b8–10a3)

1-2-2-1-2. The lineage: bone (10a3)

1-2-2-1-3. Father and mother (10a3–4)

1-2-2-1-4. Name (10a3–4)

1-2-2-1-5. The actual birthplace (10a4–7)

1-2-2-2. How ['Brom ston pa] relied on Jo bo Se btsun (10a7–11a4)

1-2-2-3. How ['Brom ston pa] met with 'Phrang kha ber chung (11a4–12a4)

1-2-2-4. Specifically, the history: how ['Brom ston pa] relied on Atiśa (12a4–13b4)

1-2-3. The circumstances of letting qood qualities descend (13b5–14a5)

1-3. The way of constructing [Rwa sgreng] (14a6–22a8)

1-3-1. The history: where Ston pa rin po che ['Brom ston pa] founded the principal temple by the practice of offering virtues (14a7–18a3)

1-3-1-1. The history: between the passing of Jo bo and the arrival at Rwa sgreng (14a8–15a4)

1-3-1-2. The actual way of founding Rwa sgreng after ['Brom ston pa's] arrival (15a4–17b5)

1-3-1-2-1. How ['Brom ston pa] built the *Dgon pa gong ma* and his own private residence upon investigation (15a5–16a5)

1-3-1-2-2. When ['Brom ston pa] built the *Dbu rtse rin po che* (16a5–17b1)

1-3-1-2-2-1. In the beginning counting the general chronological years since the Teacher's nirvana, and identifying the year of that itself (16a8–16b2)

1-3-1-2-2-2. How to construct the unique style of building by finding the eye of geographical landscape (16b3–17a7)

1-3-1-2-2-3. The circumstances in which he performed the consecration of that (17a7–8)

1-3-1-3. How for many years ['Brom ston pa] cared for his disciples and how he demonstrated nirvana (17b5–18a3)

1–3–2. The history: the one who perfomed and built another principal temples (18a3–22a4)

1–3–2–1. The one who built the *Ka gnyis ma'i khyam smad* (18a6–18b3)

1–3–2–2. The one who built the *Dbu rtse ka ba bcu gsum ma* (18b3–19b2)

1–3–2–2–1. The history of the building of *Ka ba bcu drug ma* (18b4–19a7)

1–3–2–2–2. The situation of how he performed the consecration of that (19a7–19b2)

1–3–2–3. The one who built the *Ka ba nyi shu rtsa bzhi ma* (19b2–20b7)

1–3–2–3–1. When he built [it] (19b3–20a2)

1–3–2–3–2. The one who built [it] (20a2–20b4)

1–3–2–3–3. The one who concentrated [it] (20b4–6)

1–3–2–4. The one who built the *Ka bzhi ma* (20b7–21a2)

1–3–2–5. The history: how and by whom the top of the precious principle temple has decorated with golden crown (21a2–21b2)

1–3–2–6. The history: the one who made the ledge (*spen bar*)[52] [of the building] (21b2–22a4)

Chapter 2. An explanation of the "sacred objects (*rten*)" in (Rwa sgreng) (22a8–31b8)

2–1. An explanation of the external sacred objects (22b1–24b1)

2–2. An explanation of the internal sacred objects (24b1–32a1)

2–2–1. Body sacred objects (24b3–28b5)

2–2–2. Speech sacred objects (28b5–29a4)

2–2–3. Mind sacred objects (29a4–31b2)

2–2–4. Offering substances (31b2–32a1)

[Conclusion verse] (32a1–32a5)

[Colophon] (32a5–32a8)

There are many remarkable original descriptions following section three of chapter one (1–3) and chapter two. Among them we find discussion of the abbatial sucessions, the construction and its sponsors, the relationship with Mi nyag (Xixia), and of the sacred objects (*rten*) of Rwa sgreng monastery.

[52] It assumes that *spen bar* is the same as *spen bad* and *mda' yab*. According to Goldstein (2001: 658), *spen bad* is the same as *spen rgyan*, and it means "red top of the walls of monasteries and temples that are made of Tamarisk stalks."

5. The abbatial succession of Rwa sgreng monastery

The *Rwa sgreng nyi ma'i 'od zer* presents the following succession of abbots:

	Rwa sgreng nyi ma'i 'od zer		*Gsal ba'i sgron me*
1	'Brom ston pa Rgyal ba'i 'byung gnas (1005–1064)	(eight years)	1
2	Rnal 'byor pa chen po (Shes rab rdo rje, 1015–1078)	thirteen years	2
3	Dgon pa ba Dbang phyug rgyal mtshan (1016–1082)[53]	seven years	3
4	Po [/Pu] to ba Rin chen gsal (1027–1105)[54]	one year	4[55]
5	Zhang 'Od 'jo ba (?–1150)	twelve years	5
6	Dge bshes Sgang Thang dkar ba (?–1173)[56]	twenty-nine years	
7	Dgon 'Od 'jo ba (?–1229)[57]	sixteen years	
8	Rgya 'dul ba[58]	one year	
9	Slob dpon Jo gdan Rtsang pa[59]	five years	
10	Slob dpon Ko khyim pa (Ye shes bla ma, b. 11th c./ 12th c.)	three years	
11	Slob dpon Sna ra ba (?–1283)	fourteen years	

53 Dgon pa ba was one of the disciples of Atiśa. *Gsal ba'i sgron me*: 109b6–114a4.

54 Po to ba was a disciple of 'Brom ston pa. *Gsal ba'i sgron me*: 215b4–222b2. In the earlier texts such as *Dge bshes ston pa'i rnam thar* and the manuscript discovered from Khara khoto (e.g. K.K.V.b.021c, K.K.V.b.09.f. For the details of Khara khoto manuscript, see below Chapter 7), Po to ba's name often appears as Pu to ba.

55 *Deb ther sngon po*: ca, 13b4 mentions that Po to ba was an abbot for three years.

56 Dge bshes Sgang Thang dkar ba might be Sgang Thang dkar ba Rdo rje rin chen, who was one of Dge bshes Stabs ka ba's "four principal disciples" (*thugs sras bzhi*). *Gsal ba'i sgron me*: 241a4.

57 There is no information on Dgon 'Od 'jo ba in the *Gsal ba'i sgron me*.

58 If Rgya 'dul ba is Rgya 'dul ba Dbang phyug tshul khrims, he appears in the *Gsal ba'i sgron me*: 338a1 as a teacher of Bya 'dul ba 'dzin pa Brtson 'dus 'bar (1100–?). Also, Rgya 'dul ba's name appears in the *Gsal ba'i sgron me*: 224a6 as a teacher of Dge bshes Dol pa Shes rab rgya mtsho (1059–1131), who was known as a composer of *Be'u bum sngon po*.

59 It is supposed that Jo gdan Rtsang pa is a master from Jo gdan monastery. Chos 'phel (2004: 202–203) says that Jo gdan was a brunch monastery of Rwa sgreng. However, there is no mention about Jo gdan monastery in the *Gsal ba'i sgron me*. Or, the other possibility is, Jo gdan Rtsang pa may be Jo gdan tshogs pa which is the vinaya transmission community from Śākyaśrībhadra (1127/40–1225). If this is the case, he may be a person who is related to Jo gdan tshogs pa. For Jo gdan tshogs pa, see Heimbel (2013).

12	Slob dpon Gur ston	fifteen years	6

The *Rwa sgreng nyi ma'i 'od zer* presents a list of abbots that spans from abbot 'Brom ston pa to abbot Slob dpon Gur ston. A comparison of the *Rwa sgreng nyi ma'i 'od zer* and other texts, such as *Gsal ba'i sgron me* and *Deb ther sngon po*, reveals some differences in terminology and the order of the abbots. The *Gsal ba'i sgron me* does not list any abbot between Zhang 'Od 'jo ba[60] and Slob dpon Gur ston. However, the *Deb ther sngon po* states that Zhang 'Od 'jo ba was an abbot for a short period of time, and that he appointed Slob dpon Gur ston as the next abbot.[61]

Interestingly, the examination of the succession of abbots at Rwa sgreng reveals that the monastery seems to have been on the decline during or after the tenure of the fourth abbot, Po to ba. 'Brom Shes rab me lce states in the *Rwa sgreng nyi ma'i 'od zer* that there was no abbot for sixty-five years after Po to ba.[62]

> *de nas dge bshes pu to bas gdan sa mdzad pa'i skabs su: dpon chos kyi rgyal po la sogs pa'i khams pa ma rungs [rung] pa 'ga' zhig gis bzhugs dbang ma byung bas| lo gcig las ma bzhugs so :*
>
> Then, when Dge bshes Pu to ba became the head, he was not permitted to stay in that position on account of some "coarse Khams pa" (*khams pa ma rungs [rung] pa*), ruler Dpon chos kyi rgyal po, etc. Therefore, he stayed there only one year.
>
> *dang po lo tshigs gang yin pa ni/ ka gnyis ma bzhengs nas lo dgu bcu rtsa gsum lon pa na dge ba'i bshes gnyen zhang 'od 'jo bas rwa sgreng gi gdan sa la byon ste| rwa sgreng dang 'od 'jo gnyis lo bcu gnyis su skyangs| de yan chad la pu to ba bzhud ting [deng] phyin chad der lo drug bcu rtsa lnga'i bar der gdan sa ba la sogs pa gtan phebs pa med|*
>
> Thirteen years after the building of Ka gnyis ma, Dge ba'i bshes gnyen Zhang 'Od 'jo ba

---

[60] There are no details on Zhan 'Od 'jo ba in the *Gsal ba'i sgron me* and other sources. *Gsal ba'i sgron me*: 241a2 says Zhang 'Od 'jo ba's name is Dar ma g.yung drung, but his name appears as Dar ma grags in the *Dge bshed ston pa'i rnam thar*: 198a2.

[61] *Bai ḍūrya gser po*: 183 comments on the abbot of Rwa sgreng monastery as follows, "A mes Byang chub rin chen, Dgon pa ba Dbang phyug rgyal mtshan, Rngog lo, Po to ba, Shar ba, Stabs ka ba, Zhang Dar ma g.yung drung, Sgang Thang dkar ba Rdo rje rin chen, Dol pa Shes rab rgya mtsho, 'Od 'jo Dar ma grags. From this, the monastic seat was separated into upper (*stod*) and lower (*smad*), and Mkhan po Gur ston was appointed. Like that, Rma ston Shes rab rin chen, Mkhan chen Shes rab rdo rje, 'Dul 'dzin 'Jam dbyangs rin chen grags..."

[62] *Rwa sgreng nyi ma'i 'od zer*: 18b6–7 and 19b3–5.

> took over as head of Rwa sgreng monastery, and he led both Rwa sgreng and 'Od 'jo[63] for twelve years. Prior to that, there was no regular leader for sixty-five years after Pu to ba left [Rwa sgreng].

It seems clear that the abbacy was vacant for some time between Po to ba and Zhang 'Od 'jo ba. This episode is also mentioned in the *Deb ther sngon po*, although the details are slightly different:[64]

> *dgon pa ba gshegs rjes gdan sa med pas rwa sgreng ba la chos kyi mu ge yod zer/ phyi nas po to ba gzhan don mdzad pa la zhugs pa zhig spyan drangs te lo gsum gdan sa mdzad/ khams pa sgom chung ba zer ba zhig gis kho de na byed sha dang pher sha che zer ba'i tshig ngan btab pa gsan pas/ nam la bros bas snye'u zur pas pha wong thang du zin/ da slob dpon gyi spyod ba 'di ci yin zhus pas/ slob dpon gyi spyod pa 'di ci yin bya ba de ka ci yin/ nga rug pa'i lha khang gog bor li mo'i bu'i thang du 'gro gsung nas bzhugs ma bzhed par thegs/ de rjes la gdan sa ba 'dra ba 'ga' re byung ba thams cad sku tshes ma zin bar grongs pas/ rwa sgreng gi gdan sar 'gro mi phod pa byung/ 'od 'jo pas rwa sgreng gi gdan sa bzung/...*
>
> After the death of Dgon pa ba there was no abbot [at Rwa sgreng] and it was said that "the people of Rwa sgreng were starving for Dharma".[65] Later, Po to ba, who was working for the benefit of others, was invited, [and] was abbot for three years. He heard that a Khams pa named Sgom chung ba was saying harsh things—"he was a bogus and boastful person"—[and then] he fled during the night, but Sne'u zur pa (Ye shes 'bar, 1042–1118)[66] overtook him at Pha won thang[67] and asked, "What is this behavior of the master (*slob dpon*)?" Po to ba replied, "What sort of manners are these to ask the master about his behavior? I am going to the ruined Rug pa'i lha khang[68] to see the Son of Li mo."[69] Unwilling to stay, he resumed his journey. After that, there

[63] 'Od 'jo monastery was one of three monasteries—'Od 'jo, Stabs ka, and Phra phu—founded by Dge bshes Stabs ka ba. *Gsal ba'i sgron me*: 241a3.

[64] *Deb ther sngon po*: ca, 12b3–6. There are translations for this part, Roerich (1949: 266–267) and Hadano (1954: 96). Hadano (1954: 70–175) is a very detailed Japanese translation of ca: jo bo rje brgyud dang bcas pa'i skabs, *Deb ther sngon po*. Also, there are similar descriptions in the *Gsal ba'i sgron me*: 108b5–109a3.

[65] Roerich (1949: 266) translated "there was religious hunger at Rwa sgreng." *Gsal ba'i sgron me*: 108b5 also mentions "A scarcity of dharma would occur for the people of Rwa sgreng" (*rwa sgreng pa la chos kyi mu ge'i thebs su yong*).

[66] Sne'u zur pa is a disciple of Dgon pa ba. *Gsal ba'i sgron me*: 120a5–122a3.

[67] Pha won thang, or Pha bong thang is a place name near Rwa sgreng monastery. See Gzim sprul Bstan 'dzin ye shes (2012: 125–126).

[68] It must be Rug pa'i mchod khang in Klungs shod, which was founded by Rug pa Ston sgom, a disciple of Stod lung pa Rin chen snying po (1032–1116). *Gsal ba'i sgron me*: 171a6.

[69] Roerich (1949: 267) translated that "Son of Li mo" was Sha ra ba.

> were several nominal abbots who all passed away before their time. Therefore, it happened that no one was able to become abbot of Rwa sgreng. Then 'Od 'jo took over the abbotship of Rwa sgreng...

Then, according to the *Rwa sgreng nyi ma'i 'od zer*: 18b7–19a3, after Po to ba's death, Rwa sgreng monastery fell into a complete decline. It is said that women occupied the monastery as a market (*mo khrom*), and that wild dogs, goats, sheep (*ra lug*) lived there. It is not clear why the monastery declined soon after its founding, despite being the main monastery of the Bka' gdams school. It is rare, compared to other Bka' gdams monasteries of the same period, to find mention of Rwa sgreng in available sources. Available sources contain a great deal of information about Gsang phu ne'u thog, for example, founded in 1072 by Rngog Legs pa'i shes rab, which produced many remarkable scholars and flourished as a monastic college.[70] The *Deb ther sngon po* and *Gsal ba'i sgron me* similarly devote many pages to Lo monastery, founded by Spyan snga pa Tshul khrims 'bar (1038–1103), and to Bya yul monastery, founded by Bya yul ba Gzhon nu 'od (1075–1138).[71] It is also very difficult to find any information regarding relations between Rwa sgreng and other Bka' gdams monasteries in available sources. It seems that Rwa sgreng was only remotely connected to other Bka' gdams monasteries, particularly to the central monasteries, such as Gsang phu, during the Bka' gdams pa period.

[70] Rngog Legs pa'i shes rab was a disciple of Atiśa. *Gsal ba'i sgron me*: 75a2–76a6. Gsang phu sne'u thog is located in present day Chu shur rdzong, Lhasa Prefecture, and it is known as one of the so-called Gdan sa drug (the Great Six Monastries) along with Snye thang bde ba can (Ra stod), Tshal gung thang, Dga' gdong, Skyor mo lung, and Zur phu. Phywa pa Chos kyi seng ge (1109–1169) was an abbot of Gsang phu ne'u thog for eighteen years.

[71] Spyan snga pa was a disciple of 'Brom ston pa, and Bya yul ba was a disciple of Spyan snga pa. The biographyies of the successive abbots of both monasteries, Lo monastery and Bya yul monastery appear in the *Deb ther sngon po*: ca, 20b1–29a3 (Roerich (1949: 284–306), Hadano (1954: 127–155)) and the *Gsal ba'i sgron me*: 164b1–215b4, and these provide far greater detail than the description of Rwa sgreng monastery. For details on the two monasteries, see Iuchi (2010).

6. Constructions and sponsors

Regarding the construction of Rwa sgreng monastery, according to section three of chapter one (1–3), we know that many structures were constructed between 1056 and the end of the thirteenth century. Some of the buildings still exist under the same names, and we can identify them in modern publications, such as Gzim sprul Bstan 'dzin ye shes (2012).[72] Similarly, section three of chapter one (1–3) discusses each structure, and tells us who sponsored the building and who consecrated it. The following table includes the date, founder, sponsor, and consecrator for each structure listed in the *Rwa sgreng nyi ma'i 'od zer*:

Name of Constluction	Date	Founder	Sponsor	Consecrator
Upper hermitage (*dgon pa gong ma*)	1056	'Brom ston pa	–	–
Private residence (*gzim chung*) of Rnal 'byor pa chen po	1056	'Brom ston pa	Dgra bcom (Ber family)	–
Private residence of Dgon pa ba	1056	'Brom ston pa	Lhun po (Ber family)	–
Private residence of Rnal 'byor pa Shes rab rdo rje[73]	1056	'Brom ston pa	Shakya grags (Ber family)	–
Private residence of Rnal 'byor pa Byams pa'i blo gros[74]	1056	'Brom ston pa	Bla ba kha ser (Ber family)[75]	–
Surrounding wall (*lcags ri*) of four private residence [76]	1056	'Brom ston pa	Zhang drung pha bzhi	–
Ka gnyis ma: Principal temple (*dbu rtse rin po che*)	1057	'Brom ston pa	–	–

[72] We can trace some of the construction that appears in the *Rwa sgreng nyi ma'i 'od zer* to the present Rwa sgreng monastery. There is no complete plan of Rwa sgreng monastery in modern publications, so we must investigate them through further research and fieldwork and comparison with texts.

[73] Rnal 'byor pa Shes rab rdo rje is a disciple of Atiśa, and he mainly stayed at Gsang phu. See *Gsal ba'i sgron me*: 83a4–83b2.

[74] Rnal 'byor pa Byams pa'i blo gros is a disciple of Atiśa. He is one of "the disciples of Atiśa from Khams" (*khams pa sku mched lnga*). See *Gsal ba'i sgron me*: 83a2–3.

[75] The name of Bla ba kha ser appears as Bla ma kha ser in the *Dge bshes ston pa'i rnam thar*: 186a5.

[76] Four private residences were private residences of Rnal 'byor pa chen po, Dgon pa ba, Rnal 'byor pa Shes rab rdo rje, and Rnal 'byor pa Byams pa'i blo gros.

Lower courtyard (*khyams smad*), small courtyard (*khyams chung*), *and* stable (*nag tshang*)[77] of Ka gnyis ma	–	Rnal 'byor pa chen po	Dar ma ye shes (Ber family)	–
Dbu rtse ka ba bcu drug ma	1064[78]	Dpon gyad pa and Zir khu Chos kyi grags pa[79]	–	–
Ka ba nyi shu rtsa bzhi ma	1149[80]	Dpon Se bo Gzhon tshul (Ber family)	Dpon Se bo Gzhon tshul (Ber family)	Rin chen sgang pa Sangs rgyas dbon[81]
Ka bzhi ma	Mid. 12th c.[82]	Yon btsun Brtson 'grus rdo rje[83]	–	Dgon 'Od 'jo ba

According to this section, it seems that most of the sponsors were local figures from around Rwa sgreng from the Ber family (*Ber rgyud*). This family seems to be the same family of Zhang 'phrang kha ber chung, who invited 'Brom ston pa to Rwa sgreng and donated the property for the monastery to him. 'Brom ston pa met Zhang 'phrang kha ber chung before he ever met Atiśa,[84] at which time Zhang 'phrang kha ber chung asked 'Brom ston pa to build a monastery and become his preceptor (*bla mchod*). However, 'Brom ston pa was given more priority to staying there than to going to Mnga' ris in order to meet Atiśa. Later, after the death of Atiśa, 'Brom ston pa decided to build a monastery in Rwa sgreng upon the repeated request from the Ber family.[85] The *Rwa sgreng nyi ma'i 'od zer* explains as follows:[86]

---

77 *Bod rgya tshig mdzod chen mo*: 1500.

78 *Rwa sgreng nyi ma'i 'od zer*: 19a8 states that it was in the dragon year, eight years after the building of Dbu rtse ka gnyis ma.

79 Unspecified masters.

80 *Rwa sgreng nyi ma'i 'od zer*: 19b3–4 states that it was ninty-three years after the building of Ka gnyis ma during the fifth abbot, Zhang 'Od 'jo ba.

81 According to the *Gsal ba'i sgron me*: 142b3–4, Rin chen sgang pa maintained it until the age of seventy-three, and he was a proprietor of the Bka' gdams teachings in the northern direction of *dbu ru*.

82 During Dgon 'Od 'jo ba. *Rwa sgreng nyi ma'i 'od zer*: 20b8–21a1.

83 According to the *Rwa sgren nyi ma'i 'od zer*: 21a1, Yon btsun Brtson 'grus rdo rje is a disciple of Zhang 'Od 'jo ba. There is no mention of this in the *Gsal ba'i sgron me*.

84 See 1–2–2–3: How 'Brom ston pa met with 'Phrang kha ber chung (11a4–12a4).

85 At first, 'Brom ston pa was thinking of building a temple in Gnam bye [gyi] ma lung (the present day, near of Yangs pa can), but he could not build it because of the jealousy of a Yogis named Khyi ston byo ye (*Gsal ba'i sgron me*: Khyi ston jo yes). See *Rwa sgren nyi ma'i 'od zer*: 14b8–15a1 and *Gsal ba'i sgron me*: 100a3. Also, for Gnam bye ma lung, see Sørensen, P.K. and Hazod, G. (2007: 404, n.5).

86 *Rwa sgreng nyi ma'i 'od zer*: 15a1–4. There is a similar description in the *Gsal ba'i sgron me*: 100b4–101a2.

nyin gcig [upper inter lineally: sdo] skyo sangs la byon pa'i shul [bshul] lam du| sprang po gcig [upper inter lineally: dang] phrad| gang nas 'ongs dris pas| rlung [klung] shod rong nas 'ong zer| de phyogs na kha skad ci 'dug dris pas| gzhan ji mi 'dug zhang 'phrang ka ber chung gi bu jo sras chos tog [grags?] ces bya ba'i chos pa cig yod pa| dge bshes ston pa'am cig yod pa gdan 'dren du phyin pas 'phan yul ngan chus khyer nas shi zer skad| kha skad che'o gsung| de nas thugs la rtse lhangs kyis gyur nas tshur byon par dgongs pa'i dus su| zhang 'phrang ka ber chung gi bu lhun po bya bas spyan drangs ste| rwa sgreng du lug gi lo la byon nas phyags [phyag] phab bo ⁝

One day, along the road that leads to Sdo skyo snags,[87] he ['Brom] met a beggar.
"Where are you from?" he asked.
"From Rlung (*Klung*) shod rong," [the beggar] replied.
"What is the news there?"
"Nothing much. There is a religious person there by the name of Jo sras chos tog (*grags*?), who was a son of Zhang 'phrang ka ber chung. While on his way to invite a Dge bshes ston pa or someone, he was swept away by the Ngan chu River of 'Phan yul and died."[88]
"That is big news!"
Then, when, having been deeply moved, he had made up his mind to go back, Lhun po, the son of Zhang 'phrang kha ber chung, invited him. He arrived at Rwa sgreng in the sheep year (1055), and settled there.

This episode has been generally well known due to its appearance in the *Ggsal ba'i sgron me*.[89] However, it has been hitherto unknown that the Ber family was the principal sponsor to Rwa sgreng following 'Brom ston pa. Other texts, with the exception of *Dge bshes ston pa'i rnam thar* do not mention the Ber family, in addition to 'Brom ston pa, as sponsors to the constrution of the early structures at Rwa sgreng.[90] Interestingly, the third section of chapter one (1–3) in the *Rwa sgreng nyi ma'i 'od zer* provides detailed information on the five generations after Zhang 'phrang kha ber chung. The pedigree of the Ber family, as it appears in the *Rwa sgreng nyi ma'i 'od zer*, is as follows:

---

87 There is no description of this place in the *Gsal ba'i sgron me*.
88 For the Ngan chu river, see Sørensen, P.K. and Hazod, G. (2007: 605–606, 608, Fig. 35).
89 See *Gsal ba'i sgron me*: 100b4–101a2.
90 The Ber family also appear as a sponsor in the *Dge bshes ston pa'i rnam thar*: 186a2–5, 198a2.

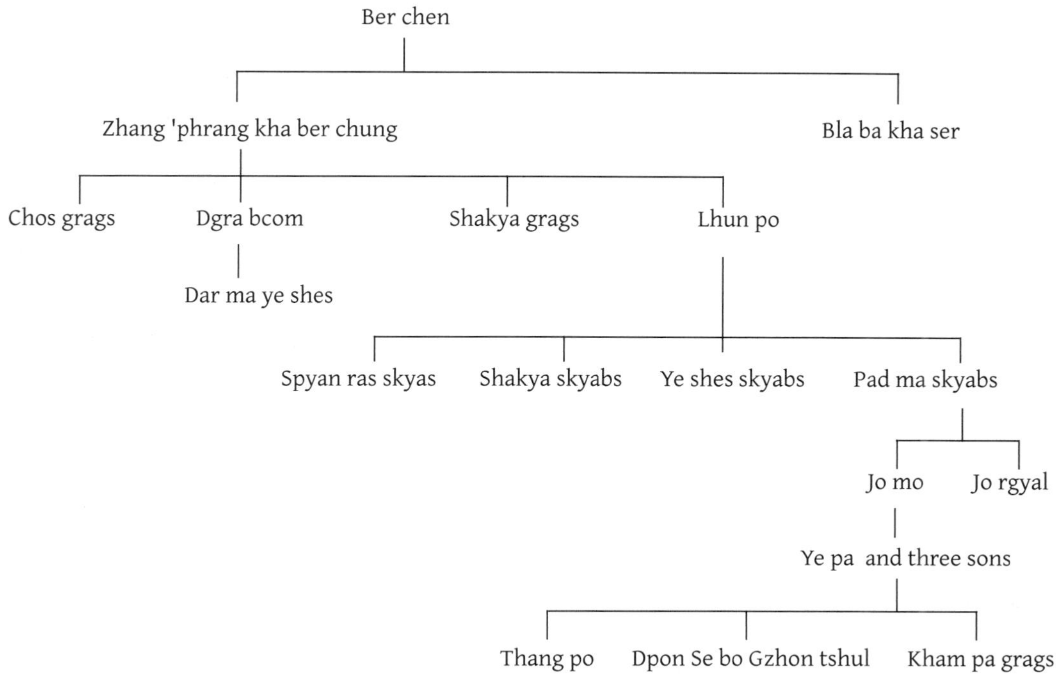

This information is of particular interest, as very little has been preserved regarding the social surroundings of Rwa sgreng and the activities of local lay people during that time.

7. Relationship with the Xixia Court

Interestingly enough, the third section of chapter one (1–3) also contains a brief description of the relationship between Rwa sgreng and the king of Mi nyag.[91] Mi nyag, known in Chinese as Xixia (西夏), was a kingdom created by a group of people known as the Tangut. The kingdom existed as an independent state from 1032 to 1227,[92] a period that coincides with the period in which the Bka' gdams school flourished in central Tibet. The description that indicates the relationship between Rwa sgreng monastery and the Xixia court appears only in the *Rwa sgreng nyi ma'i 'od zer.*[93]

According to the *Rwa sgreng nyi ma'i 'od zer*, during the tenure of Zhang 'Od 'jo ba, the fifth abbot of Rwa sgreng, his disciples enjoyed a monk-patron relationship (*mchod yon*) with the king of Xixia. It is supposed that the period of Zhang 'Od 'jo pa was of the same duration as the reign of King Weiming Renzong (嵬名仁宗, reign: 1139-1193). The *Rwa sgreng nyi ma'i 'od zer* states as follows:[94]

> *de nas zhang 'od 'jo ba bzhugs pa'i dus de na| me [mi] nyag gi [under inter lineally: rgyal po mnga' dar ba'i dus de legs par gda' bas] rgyal po'i bla mchod la zhang 'od 'jo ba'i slob ma dge bshes gdugs phub pa rang la nyi shu rtsa lnga tsam yod par gda'| de'i dus na me [mi] nyag rgyal pos dbus byas pa mdo smad| tsang [gtsang] dbus thams cad kyi chos kyi 'bul pa| nor kyi [gyi] 'bul pa| slob gnyer kyi [gyi] byed pa: yang dag pa gcig byung| kun kyis bskur [bkur] ba'i gnas gcig byung: tha na gnas der tshong du yang dag pa gcig [under inter lineally: yang] byung| de'i dus na dge 'dun la longs spyod mnga' thang bsam gyis mi khyab pa yod skad| zhang 'od 'jo ba gdan sar byon ste [te] lo [illegible: drug] bcu tham pa lon| [upper inter lineally: ka gnyis ma bzhengs nas lo skor bcu gnyis song nas rta lor] sa pho 'brug gi lo la rmang brtsal [brtsam] par gda': de ni lo tshigs gang yin pa'o :*
>
> Then, during Zhang 'Od 'jo ba's tenure, [under inter lineally: as the dominion of the king had spread at the time], at least twenty-five of Zhang 'Od 'jo ba' disciples who were scholars (*dge bshes*) with parasol carriers (*gdugs phub pa*) were among the court chaplains (*bla mchod*) of the Mi nyag King. During that period, all the offerings of Dharma, offerings of wealth, and work of scholars from Mdo smad, Tsang, and Dbus

[91] This topic was already discussed by me at the 13th IATS (Ulaanbaatar, Mongolia 2013), in a paper titled "A Study on Rwa sgreng monastery in the Early Period of the Bka' gdams School" and in Iuchi (2013).

[92] The Tangut script was "created" by King Li Yuan hao (李元昊, 1003–1048) in 1038 and a number of Chinese and Tibetan scriptures were translated into Tangut. In 1227, Khara-khoto was conquered by Genghis Khan (1206–1227).

[93] It is thought that Lhun grub chos 'phel (1994: 88) is a quotation from the *Rwa sgreng nyi ma'i 'od zer.* This episode does not appear in the *Dge bshes ston pa'i rnam thar.*

[94] *Rwa sgreng nyi ma'i 'od zer*: 19b6–20a2.

> were centered on the Mi nyag King. He was a righteous person, a person that everyone served, and even became an upright person to do business with. It is said that the sangha at that time possessed inconceivable wealth and power. Zhang 'Od 'jo ba arrived at the see [of Rwa sgreng], and sixteen (?) years passed. [upper inter lineally: When a cycle of twelve years had passed following the construction of Ka gnyis ma (the principal temple with twenty-four pillars), in the horse year] the earth-male-dragon-year (1148) the foundation was strong. This is what [happened] in the intervening years.

We find evidence of the relationship between Bka' gdams masters and the Xixia court in a manuscript discovered at the Khara-khoto site.[95] The texts discovered at Khara-khoto are written in Tangut, Tibetan, Chinese, and Mongolian, and cover a wide range of genres including Buddhist scriptures, ritual texts, letters, and calendars. The majority of Khara-khoto texts are now housed in the Stein Collection at the British Library and the Kozlov Collection at the Institute of Oriental Studies, St. Petersburg Branch of the Russian Academy of Science.[96] Khara-khoto is located in present-day A la shan meng E ji na zhi (阿拉善盟額済納旗) in Inner Mongolia, PRC. The fortress of Khara-khoto flourished as an important transportation and commercial hub during the time of the Xixia kingdom.

Among the texts in the Stein Collection, there are two sets of fragmentary manuscripts related to the Bka' gdams school. One consists of five-fragmentary manuscripts (K.K.V.b.021.c, K.K.V.b.011.c, K.K.V.b.034.b, K.K.V.b.09.f, and K.K.V.b.09.i) that are similar to the *gsung thor bu* (a collection of writings) of the Bka' gdams masters.[97] Another fragmentary manuscript (K.K.V.b.035.b) found in the Stein Collection was discovered in the same stūpa as the five-frangmentary manuscripts. It can be identified by its colophon as *Rgyud bla ma'i bsdus don*, a summary of the *Uttaratantra* written by Rngog Lo tsā ba Blo ldan shes rab (1059–1109).[98] Because these fragmentary manuscripts were discovered

---

[95] Prof. Kirill Solonin, Renmin University (Beijing, PRC) discusses on the Atiśa's work of Tangut version from Khara-khoto in his forthcoming article, "Dīpaṃkara in Tangut Context: An Inquiry into Systematic Nature of Tibetan Buddhism in Xixia."

[96] The Stein Collection, which was brought by A. Stein (1862–1943) includes one thousand fifty-six texts and text fragments in Tibetan. These texts are preserved in twelve boxes which are filed under the requisition numbers IOL Tib. M 1 to 12 in the British Library. The catalogue of Khara-khoto texts in the Stein Colletion will be published by Prof. Tsuguhito Takeuchi, Kobe City University of Foreign Studies (Kobe, Japan) and me in 2016. The Kozlov Collection, which was brought by P. K. Kozlov (1863–1935) has more than one hundred Tibetan texts and text fragments. The Tibetan text from Khara-khoto in the Kozlov Collection is assigned the number XT. See Takeuchi (1995: 49).

[97] The manuscript is in *pothi* style and hand written in *dbu med* script. It is thought that the contents are very similar to the so-called *gsung thor bu* genre, because the names of Bka' gdams pa masters such as Dge bshes Ston pa, Pu to ba, Bya yul ba, and Sne'u zur pa appears frequently in the text and it contains many quotations of Bka' gdams pa masters.

[98] For the transcription and translation of this manuscript, see Kano (2008).

together with manuscripts in Tangut script[99] in a stūpa located to the northwest of the fortress (site number: K.K.V.b.),[100] they are presumed to be from the period of the kingdom or shortly after its Mongol conquest in 1227.[101]

The passage from the *Rwa sgreng nyi ma'i 'od zer* translated above may now explain why the manuscripts belonging to the Bka' gdams school's literary legacy were discovered at Khara-khoto. It also provides evidence of a substantial and very early monk-patron relationship between the Bka' gdams school and the Xixia royal court.[102] In addition, the tenure of Zhang 'Od 'jo ba was a stable period for Rwa sgreng monastery, as mentioned in above Chapter 5. Following Po to ba, there was a sixty-five year hiatus. As proof of this, the tenures of Zhang 'Od 'jo ba, of Dge bshes Sgang Thang dkar ba (the sixth abbot), and of Dgon 'Od 'jo ba (the seventh abbot) were comparatively long, though the other abbots' tenures lasted for only short periods. Because Dgon 'Od 'jo ba passed away in the earth-female-ox-year (1229),[103] the period of Xixia completely coincides with the tenures of these three abbots. Therefore, we can assume that Rwa sgreng monastery had a relationship with the Xixia court from the time of Zhang 'Od 'jo ba's tenure, and that it flourished with some sort of backing from the court.

---

[99] e.g. K.K.V.b.013.n. See Iuchi (2011: 29, n.18).

[100] Stein, himself, assigned a site number to each text. The texts discovered from the ruins of Khara-khoto were given designations beginning with "K.K.."

[101] According to Vorobyova-Desyatovskaya (1995: 46), the Tangut script was used after the Xixia kingdom until about the sixteenth century.

[102] As van der Kuijp (1993) explains, 'Gar dam pa Gzhon nu rdo rje (1180–?1240), who was an uncle of U rgyan pa visited the Xixia court in the beginning of the thirteenth century. Also a Kashmirian monk, Jayānanda (12th–13th c.) visited the Xixia court via Tibet. Because the tenure of Zhang 'Od 'jo ba occurred by 1150, the relationship between Rwa sgreng monastery and the Xixia court would date back to much earlier than them.

[103] See *Rwa sgreng nyi ma'i 'od zer*: 21b3.

Appendix

The Sacred Objects (*rten*) of Rwa sgreng monastery

Chapter two of the *Rwa sgreng nyi ma'i 'od zer* describes in detail the sacred objects (*rten*) of body (*sku*), speech (*gsung*), and mind (*yid*) that were external to and internal to Rwa sgreng monastery. It is the most detailed source that we have on the kinds of sacred objects that Rwa sgreg monastery had during the Bka' gdams period. Originally, most of the sacred objects of the monastery were the remains of Atiśa, which were divided by 'Brom ston pa. The *Rwa sgreng nyi ma'i 'od zer* states as follows:[104]

> *jo bo gnye [snye] thang na sku gshegs kha'i rjes su/ dge bshes ston pa'i thugs gongs [dgongs] la¦ jo bos [bo'i] thugs gongs [dgongs] bskang ba'i phyir gtsug lag khang gcig gnye [snye] thang na bzhengs sam dgongs pa la¦ sangs ston la stad [gtad] pa ched po mi 'dug/ jo bo'i phyag dpe' dang rten gsum rnas [rnams] dge 'dun rma tsho kun khong dbang zer yin 'dug pas skabs der shin tu thugs ma bde nas¦ jo bos kyang kho bos mi 'grub pa'i bya ba la gtad¦ bong thor la tshal [tshwa] skal snyam du dgongs pa'i dus su¦ rje btsun ma sgrol ma'i zhal nas¦ khyod de tsam du thugs mi bde mi dgos¦ khyed kyi bya ba thams cad ngas sgrubs [bsgrub] pa yin gyi gsung¦ des thugs bde 'bol kyis [gyis] song ba'i skabs su¦ dge bshes ka [ska] bas byon te¦ thams cad kyi bgo bsha' dang¦ bskye [skyes] god ['god or bgos] mdzad de¦ ka [ska] ba de khu rngog gsum la sogs pa kun kyi [gyi] thugs gtod pa yin par 'dug¦ dge bshes khu ston la jo bo shakya'i gser sku gcig phul¦ rngog la mchod rten brgyad pa gcig dang¦ sgrol ma'i sku gcig phul¦ 'khar bsil dang¦ lugs [blugs] sku chung chung kha yar dang¦ chos sgrol mdzad gcig rnams gnye [snye] thang du bzhugs¦ de nas dge bshes ston pa la pha'i rus pa bu la dgos pa yin pas¦ jo bo'i gdung 'di rnams khyod tshags gyis [kyis] ¦ rgya dpe' lo tshtsa ba la dgos pas¦ phyag dpe' 'di rnams kyang khyod tshags gyis [kyis] gsung¦ jo bo'i thugs dam rtsis [rtsa] che shos bla ma gser gling pa'i gdung khang dngul gdugs can chung ba 'di yin pas 'di yang khyod gyis [kyis] gsung nas¦ dge bshes ston pa nyid ji ltar bzhed pa rnams phul¦*
>
> After the Lord (Atiśa) passed away in Gnye thang (*Snye thang*),[105] Dge bshes Ston pa wondered "Should I establish a temple at Gnye thang in order to fulfill the Lord's wishes?" He thought it wouldn't be too big a burden to lay on Sangs ston. ['Brom ston pa] was not very satisfied when Dge 'dun Rma tsho (Byang chub rdo rje, b. 11th c.) said that all the scriptures and the three sacred objects were [under] his control. Jo bo also

[104] *Rwa sgreng nyi ma'i 'od zer*: 14a8–14b6. There is a similar description in the *Gsal ba'i sgron me*: 64a2–3.
[105] The spelling of Snye thang appears *gnye thang* or *gnye' thang* in the *Rwa sgreng nyi ma'i 'od zer*.

gave me the unwilling thing. When he was thinking that [it was like] sharing a salt (?) to a two-year-old donkey, Rje btsun sgrol ma (Tārā) said, "You, don't need to anxious like that. I settled all of your matters". When ['Brom ston pa] was comforted by that, Dge bshes Ka (Ska) ba (Shākya dbang phyug, b. 10th c.)[106] arrived [there] and apportioned and shared the merit. As for Ka ba, he trusted Khu Rngog 'Brom gsum and others. [Ka ba] gave the golden statue of Jo bo Shākya to Dge bshes Khu ston; the "*mchod rten brgyad pa*" (the eighth stūpa) and a statue of *Sgrol ma* to Rngog (Legs pa'i shes rab); and *'khar bsil* (?), some indivisible (*chang chung kha yar*) metal statues, and *chos sgrol mzhad* (?) were left at Gnye thang. Then, [Ka ba] said to Dge bshes Ston pa, "You, keep these remains and others because the son needs the father's bone. You keep these scriptures, because the translator needs Sanskrit texts. You also keep this small memorial stūpa of Gser gling pa (Chos kyi grags pa, 10th c.)[107] with a silver parasol (*bla ma gser gling pa'i gdung khang dngul gdugs can chung ba*) because it is the most precious spiritual object (*thugs dam*) of Jo bo. [Ka ba] gave whatever Dge bshes Ston pa wanted.

Hereafter we will briefly examine accounts of the sacred objects of body, speech, and mind internal to Rwa sgreng monastery, comparing descriptions of them given in the *Dge bshes ston pa'i rnam thar* and by Lhun grub chos 'phel (1994).

Firstly, concerning the sacred bodily objects, the *Rwa sgreng nyi ma'i 'od zer* mentions that Rwa sgreng monastery has two types of sacred bodily objects: statues made of metal and paintings on fabric.[108] There are more than thirty-six hundred thangkha paintings and more than three hundred metal statues in the collection.[109] Among them, the principal and oldest sacred bodily object is the statue of 'Jam dpal rdo rje (Mañjuśrīvajra). This principal sacred object still remains in Rwa sgreng monastery, and a photograph of it provided in Gzim sprul bstan 'dzin ye shes (2012: 55).[110] The *Rwa sgreng nyi ma'i 'od zer* describes the history of the statue of 'Jam dpal rdo rje as follows:[111]

---

[106] Dge bshes Ka ba, or Ska ba was a disciple of Atiśa. He was one of the people who went to Mang yul to invite Atiśa to Dbu gtsang. *Gsal ba'i sgron me*: 83b3–6.

[107] Gser gling pa was one of Atiśa's teachers in India.

[108] *Rwa sgreng nyi ma'i 'od zer*: 24b2.

[109] *Rwa sgreng nyi ma'i 'od zer*: 25b2, 28b4.

[110] Lhun grub chos 'phel (1994: 10) mentions that the statue of 'Jam dpal rdo rje was lost for a long time in Rwa sgreng, and was found again owing to the Tenth Paṇ chen (Chos kyi rgyal mtshan, 1938–1989). The detail of its return are unknown, but according to Dpal brtsegs bod yig dpe rnying zhib 'jug khang (2004: 12), a lot of rare texts were brought from Tibet to the Cultural Palace of Nationalities (民族文化宫), Beijing in 1962. Then, it was returned to Tibet again by the Tenth Paṇ chen Lama. The rare texts in 'Bras spung monastery faced the same situation. Therefore, it is assumed that the statue of 'Jam dpal rdo je was one of them. Also see Iuchi (2006: 22–23).

[111] *Rwa sgreng nyi ma'i 'od zer*: 24b3–5.

jo bo 'jam dpal rdo rje lugs ma zhal gsum phyag drug pa padma'i gdan la bzhugs pa/ khru gang tsam gcig bzhugs pa de'i lo rgyus ni/ dang po lī [li'i] [illegible: rgyal] po gcig gi thugs dam/ de nas gcig nas gnyis su rgyud [brgyud] pas jo bo'i phyag du [tu] byon jo bos bshes gnyen ston pa [par] gnang/ slob ma gzhan rnams kyis phrag dog byas kyi dogs nas nu [na] bza' mang pos gril [dril] nas ra phags du bzhugs yin gdan 'dren/ phyis bsam yas nas rwa sgreng du byon te snang ba dag pa la chos gsungs pa yin skad/ rwa sgreng du byon pa'i rten kyi [gyi] snga shos lags/

The history of the cast image of the three faced, six armed Jo bo 'Jam dpal rdo rje seated on a lotus throne is as follows: it was originally a spiritual object of a king of Li (*Li yul*, Khotan). It was passed from hand to hand until it came into the hands of the Lord (Atiśa). The Lord gave it to Bshes gnyen Ston pa ('Brom ston pa). Out of concerns about the jealousy of other disciples, it was kept wrapped up in many vestments. Later, it came from Bsam yas to Rwa sgreng, and it is said that it taught Dharma [to those of] pure perception. This is the oldest sacred object to have come to Rwa sgreng.

Secondly, as for the sacred objects of the speech, the *Rwa sgreng nyi ma'i 'od zer* mentions that Rwa sgreng monastery held ten million sets of scriptures as sacred objects of the speech.[112] Among them were texts such as fifty volumes (*pothi*) that were the "books of the Lord (Atiśa)," thirty volumes of 'Brom ston pa's original texts,[113] three hundred tantric texts, and three thousand and thirty commentarial texts.[114] The *Rwa sgreng nyi ma'i 'od zer* only mentions the books of the Lord in a very general way, but *Dge bshes ston pa'i rnam thar* mentions that there were "Sanskrit texts" (*rgya dpe*) among them.[115] As mentioned above, these texts were given to 'Brom ston pa.[116] The *Rwa sgreng nyi ma'i 'od zer* does not provide details regarding these texts, but Lhun grub chos 'phel (1994) does.[117]

---

112 *Rwa sgreng nyi ma'i 'od zer*: 29a3.

113 "*thugs dam phyi ma*" *Rwa sgreng nyi ma'i 'od zer*: 28b5.

114 *Rwa sgreng nyi ma'i 'od zer*: 28b5–29a4.

115 See *Dge bshes ston pa'i rnam thar*: 200a6. The *Rwa sgreng nyi ma'i 'od zer*: 14b5 states "*rgya dpe*" only once.

116 *Rwa sgreng nyi ma'i 'od zer*: 14b5. According to the *Rnam thar rgyas pa yongs grags* and *Gsal ba'i sgron me*, some of Sanskrit texts were returned to India by Lho brag pa Phyag khri mchog (b. 11th c.), who was a disciple of of Atiśa. *Rnam thar rgyas pa yongs grags* (1979: 362), *Gsal ba'i sgron me*: 71b6.

117 Lhun grub chos 'phel (1994: 138) lists the Sanskrit manuscripts in Rwa sgreng as follows: as the Sanskrit text of Atiśa, 1) *gser gyi snye ma*, 2) *dgra nag gi rgyud*, 3) *kyee rdo rje'i sgrub thabs gnyis*, 4) *bstod pa le'u bcu gsum pa*, 5) *thugs dga' ba'i brjed byang*, 6) *rdo rje theg pa'i 'grel pa*, 7) *rdo rje gur gyi rgyud*, 8) *brgyad ston pa dang de'i 'grel pa*, 9) *'grel pa dag ldan*, 10) *tshad ma de kho na nyid kyi 'grel pa*, 11) *dgra nag dka' 'grel*, 12) *'grel bshad chen mo*, 13) *chos mngon pa mdzod*, 14) *shes rab snying po'i 'grel pa*, 15) *dmyal ba nas 'don pa'i mdo*, 16) *dpal gsang ba 'dus pa'i bde gnyis rtsa 'grel*, 17) *ma hā ma ya'i 'grel pa*, as the Sanskrit text of translator ('Brom ston pa?), 1) *slob dpon dpa' bos mdzad pa'i skyes rabs*, 2) *sprin chen gyi mdo*, 3) *'dod 'jo*, 4) *chos yang dag par gsungs pa'i dpe chen drug*, 5) *dpal chen gyis zhus pa'i mdo*, 6) *chos yang dag par brjod pa'i mdo*, 7) *tshad ma kun btus kyi rtsa 'grel*, 8) *sbyin pa la 'jug pa'i gtam*, 9) *sgom rim*, 10) *bsod nams kyi stobs brjod pa'i mdo*, 11) *theg chen gyi mdo bdun*, 12) *kyee rdo rje'i 'grel pa*. Also, for the details of Sanskrit

According to him, they included Sanskrit texts, such as *Prajñāpāramitā* and its commentary, which Atiśa brought with him to Tibet from Bodhgayā (*Rdo rje gdan*). This fact is also mentioned in the colophon to its translation in the Tibetan canon.[118] Dge 'dun chos 'phel (1903–1951) records in his *Gser gyi thang ma* that he went with Rāhula Sāṅkrityāyana (1893–1963) in order to look for Sanskrit manuscripts at Rwa sgreng monastery, but recalls that the monks of Rwa sgreng did not allow them to see the manuscripts at that time.[119] Dge 'dun chos 'phel supposed that the Sanskrit texts would have been very few in number. In any case, information regarding these Sanskrit manuscripts at Rwa sgreng monastery may come to light through further research.[120]

Thirdly, regarding sacred objects of the mind, the *Rwa sgreng nyi ma'i 'od zer* mentions that the monastery holds seven hundred thirty-five memorial stūpas (*gdung khang*),[121] both small and large, as sacred objects of the mind.[122] Among them, the main sacred objects of the mind are the "*Dngul gdugs can*" (silver parasol) in Gser gling pa's memorial *stūpa*. This is said to be the most important remainder of Atiśa, which was distributed to 'Brom ston pa along with the Lord's above mentioned scriptures.[123] The *Rwa sgreng nyi ma'i 'od zer* describes Dngul gdugs can as follows:[124]

> *dngul gdugs can chung ba 'di'i dbang du byas na jo bo rje lha cig gi bla ma gser gling pa'i gdung khang du bzhugs| che chung gi tshad ni spyir khru gang yod pa| dngos [ngos] bzhi la mtho gang yod pa| de la dngul kyi [gyi] gdugs nyis rtsegs yod pa| steng la bya khyung la sogs pa'i bzo phra mo bsam gyis mi khyab pa yod pa| nang sdzongs [rdzongs] su| de bzhin gshegs pa'i ring srel brgya tsa brgyad| bla ma gser gling pa la sogs pa'i bla ma brgya lnga bcu'i gdung ring srel sogs pa mang po bzhugs| rab gnas jo bo nyid kyi bzhugs/ bya[illegible] 'di dang shing gi mchod rten dang| 'ben tshad re las ring bar mi 'bral bar bzhugs pa lags skad// [/] mchod rten chung chung gcig la byin brlabs [rlabs] kyang 'di las che med/ grags pa yang 'di las che ba med//*

manuscripts in Rwa sgreng, see Kano (2012).

118 The colophon of the *Prajñāpāramitā* (D.12: 286a2–4) states: "*...yang slad kyis skyid smad mnye thang na mo cher paṇḍi ta chen po dī paṃ ka ra shrī dznyā na dang/ lo tsā ba 'brom rgyal ba'i 'byung gnas gnyis kyis brgyad stong pa bshad pa'i dus su che long zhig gtan la phebs/ phyis rwa sgreng gi gtsug la khang du lo tsā ba 'brom rgyal ba'i 'byung gnas kyis rgya gar gyi mdo gsum la gtugs nas lan gnyis gtan la phabs/ slad kyis yang lo tsā ba de nyid kyis bshad pa mdzad cing phran tshegs kyang gtan la phabs/* ". Also see Kano (2012: 141–142).

119 *Gser gyi thang ma*: 12–13 [For English translation, see Thupten Jinpa and Lopez (2014: 41) and for Japanese translation, see Kano (2010: 14–15)]. This was in 1934. On the details of the journey of Dge 'dun chos 'phel with Rāhula, see Kano (2010) and (2012). Before Dge 'dun chos 'phel and Rāhula, Ekai Kawaguchi (河口慧海, 1866–1945) visited Rwa sgreng, and he tried to see the Sanskrit manuscript. But he could not see them. Kano (2012: 135–136).

120 For details on the present condition of these manuscripts, see Kano (2012: 149–153).

121 In this case "*gdung khang*" would have a similar meaning with "*gdung rten.*"

122 *Rwa sgreng nyi ma'i 'od zer*: 29a4–31b2.

123 *Rwa sgreng nyi ma'i 'od zer*: 14b5–6.

124 *Rwa sgreng nyi ma'i 'od zer*: 29a4–7

In the case of this "dngul gdugs can chung ba" (small silver parasol), [it was] kept in the memorial stūpa of Gser gling pa who was a Lama of Jo bo rje lha cig (Atiśa). The size is, generally, one *khru* (cubit), [and it is] one *mtho*[125] at the four sides, with a double silver parasol on it, with inconceivable small drawings such as garuḍa on the upper part. As an inside spiritual charm (*nang gzungs*), there are many [relics] such as one hundred eight relics of the Tathāgata, and the remains and relics of one hundred fifty lamas such as Gser gling pa. Jo bo himself consecrated it. It is said that [*dngul gdugs can chung ba*] was not set away from longer than one *'ben tshad* (target's length) with [illegible] and a wooden stūpa. There is also no [other] bigger blessing than this as a small stūpa. There is also no [other] that is bigger than this in terms of its fame.

Here is a detailed list of the sacred objects that were kept at Rwa sgreng monastery by the time of the thirteenth century, based on the *Rwa sgreng nyi ma'i 'od zer*, supported by the descriptions of Lhun grub chos 'phel (1994) (=A) and the *Dge bshes ston pa'i rnam thar* (=B).[126]

1) Sacred objects of body

Sacred objects of body	folio no.	*Rwa sgreng nyi ma'i 'od zer*	A, B
Mañjuśrīvajra	24b3–5	'jam dpal rdo rje	A: (95), B: (199b4)
Master of the teachings	24b5–6	bstan pa'i bdag po	A: khri can mtho gang ma (104)?
About 34 Khasarpaṇa	24b6–7	kha sarpa ṇi sor bzhi tsam	
Khasarpaṇa slightly higher throne with back curtain	24b7–8	jo bo kha sarpa ṇi gdan khri bag tsam mtho ba rgyab yol can	
Jina Amitāba of size one *mkhyid*	25a1–2	rgyal ba 'od dpag med khyud[127] gang cig	

[125] The length between thumb and middle finger. *Bod rgya tshig mdzod chen mo*: 1217.

[126] *Dge bshes ston pa'i rnam thar*: 198a4–201a6 describes the supports, but only briefly. Also, Lhun grub chos 'phel (1994) devotes many pages to the supports, although it includes supports from after the period of Tsong kha pa. e.g., one complete set of paṇḍita hat (*dbu paṇ*) of Tsong kha pa, pieces of the monk's skirt (*sku sham*) and the hair of Rgyal tshab Dar ma rin chen (1364–1432). Lhun grub chos 'phel (1994: 119).

[127] *Khyud* might be *mkhyud* or *mkhyid*. The breadth between the thumb and little finger.

Standing Maitreya on the throne with back curtain of more than a full *mtho* size	25a2	byams pa bzhengs kha ma gdan khri rgyab yol dang bcas pa mtho gang lhag pa gcig	A: byams pa zhing khams ma (104)
Ṣaḍakṣarī [lokeśvara] of about a full *mtho* size	25a2–3	[yi ge?] drug ma mtho gang tsam gcig	
Vākutpādakā of Sgom pa dmar sgom[128]	25a3	sgom pa dmar sgom gyi gsung 'byin ma	
Eight-arms Tārā	25a4	sgrol ma phyag brgyad ma	
Relic of Kailash of size *bhe lu*[129] (inside of the Eight-arms Tārā)	25a4	te si'i ring srel bhe lu gang tsam	
Ten million stūpa (spiritual object of Rnal 'byor pa chen po)	25a4–5	mchod rten bye ba (*alias*: mthong ba don yod, zangs kyi mi bo che)	
Glid Muni in Saṃbhogakāya of size ten years child	25a5–6	thub [pa] longs spyod rdzogs sku tsha gser ma byis pa lo bcu ba tsam cig	
Eleven-faced Mahākaruṇā	25a6–7	jo bo thugs rje chen po zhal bcu gcig pa	A: thugs rje chen po bcu gcig zhal (105)[130]
Standing statue of Tārā (spiritual object of Nāgārjuna)	25a7	sgrol ma bzhengs sku (gsung 'byon ma)	A: gsung 'byong sgrol ma (103–104)
Ṣaḍakṣarī [lokeśvara] (spiritual object of Dpon dbang seng[131])	25a7–8	yi ge drug ma gtso 'khor gsum bzhugs pa	A: thugs rje chen po yi ge drug ma gtso 'khor gsum pa (136)
One *mtho* size image	25a8	sku 'bag mtho gang tsam gcig bzhugs pa	
Representation image of Atiśa (in the *Dbu rtse ka ba bcu drug ma*)	25b1	jo bo'i sku tshab gcig	

128 Unspecified master. The name, Mar sgom appears in the *Gsal ba'i sgrom me*: 118a3. Kha rag sgom chung (dbang phyug blo gros, b. 11th c.) took an ordination under Mkhan po Mar sgom in the site, Lam po (*lam po gnas su*).

129 *Bhe lu* might be a measure of the size.

130 Lhun grub chos 'phel (1994: 105) mentions that it is a spiritual object of Lha lung dpal gyi rdo rje.

131 Unspecified master.

Eleven-faced [statue?] (in the *Dbu rtse ka ba bcu drug ma*)	25b1	bcu gcig zhal	
Five Buddhas of Vajradhātu (in the *Dbu rtse ka ba bcu drug ma*)	25b1	rgyal ba rigs lnga	
Mantrakāyakalaśa? (Kalaśa of mantramūrti?)	25b2	sngags kyi bum sku	
Clay image	25b2	tsha tsha'i brkos phor	
?	25b2	blo rdebs	
Ṣaḍakṣarī [lokeśvara] (one of four spritual objects of Atiśa)	25b3–5	yi ge drug ma	A: (125–126), B: yi ge drug pa mtho drug pa (199a3)
Mahābodhi (one of four spiritual objects of Atiśa)	25b5–6	jo bo byang chub chen po	
Khadiravanika Tārā (one of four spiritual objects of Atiśa)	25b5–6	seng ldeng nags kyi sgrol ma	A: thub pa and seng ldeng nags sgrol gnyis (125, 134), B: sgrol ma seng ldeng ma (199a2)
Trāṇāṣṭaghorāraṇī? (Tārā of Atiśa, one of four spritual objects of Atiśa)	25b6–26a1	jo bos ['jigs] pa brgyad skyob	A: sgrol ma 'jigs pa brgyad skyob ma (130–131)
Golden [illegible] ? (one of fifteen spiritual objects of 'Brom ston pa)	26a1–2	gser [illegible] po	
Śākyamuni (one of fifteen spiritual objects of 'Brom ston pa)	26a2	bcom ldan 'das shākya thub pa	
Vairocana, *Gangs chen mtsho*? (one of fifteen spiritual objects of 'Brom ston pa)	26a2	rnam par snang mdzad gang[s?] chen [/can?] mtsho	

Amitābha (one of fifteen spiritual objects of 'Brom ston pa)	26a2	snang ba mtha' yas	
Maitreyābhisaṃbodhi (one of fifteen spiritual objects of 'Brom ston pa)[132]	26a2	byams pa mngon par byang chub pa	
Buddha bhaiṣajya maharāja (one of fifteen spiritual objects of 'Brom ston pa)	26a2	sangs rgyas sman pa'i rgyal po	
Image of Atiśa, *U yon ma* (one of fifteen spiritual objects of 'Brom ston pa)	26a4–5	jo bo'i sku 'bag u yon ma	A: jo bo'i sku 'dra dbu yon ma che ba (121–123), jo bo'i sku thang dbu yon ma chung ba (123–125)
Mañjuśrīdeśanācakra (one of fifteen spiritual objects of 'Brom ston pa)	26a5–6	'jam dpal brtan pa'i 'khor lo	
Mañjuśrīcalacakra (one of fifteen spiritual objects of 'Brom ston pa)	26a6–7	'jam dpal g.yo ba'i 'khor lo	
Śvetacandanā (one of fifteen spiritual objects of 'Brom ston pa, spiritual object of Se btsun Dbang phyug gzhon nu)	26a7–8	jo mo tsun dhe dkar mo	A: jo mo btsun (137)
White Tārā and green Tārā (one of fifteen spiritual objects of 'Brom ston pa)	26a8–26b5	sgrol ma dkar sngon gnyis	A: (127–128)
Aṣṭacaitya (one of fifteen spiritual objects of 'Brom ston pa)	26b5–7	mchod rten brgyad pa	

132 According to the *Rwa sgreng nyi ma'i 'od zer*: 26a3, the above five spiritual objects of 'Brom ston pa are made by gold, and the sze is about twelve *mtho* size.

Small golden statue of Mañjuśrīvajra (one of fifteen spiritual objects of 'Brom ston pa)	26b7–9	'jam dpal rdo rje gser lha chung chung	A: gshin rje gshed kyi sku (125)
[Statue of] Śrīgaṇapati (one of fifteen spiritual objects of 'Brom ston pa)	26b9–27a1	dpal tshogs kyi bdag po	
Trisamayavyūharāja (one of four spiritual objects of Rnal 'byor pa[133])	27a1–2	jo bo dam tshig gsum bkod pa'i [rgyal po] gtso 'khor lnga po	A: dam tshig gsum bkod pa'i rgyal po (135)
Ṣaḍaksarā [lokeśvara] (one of four spiritual objects of Rnal 'byor pa)	27a2	yi ge drug ma gtso 'khor gsum po	
108 rosaries of Bodhicitta	27a3	bo dhi tsi ta'i phreng ba brgya rtsa brgyad pa	
Monk's robe from India	27a3	chos gos rgya gar ma	
Pakṣitarunī (/rātrīvasudharā) (one of four spiritual objects of Rnal 'byor pa)	27a4	bya 'dab 'og ma'i dbyang rta	A: bya 'dab shar ma (132–133), bya 'dab nub ma (133, spiritual object of Jo legs[134])
Acala, *Me ri ser po can* (one of four spiritual objects of Rnal 'byor pa)	27a4–5	jo bo mi g.yo ba, me ri ser po can	A: rje btsun mi g.yo ba, rwa sgreng gi mi g.yo ba me ris ser po can (131), B: mi g.yo ba (199a5)
Akṣobhya of Dgon pa ba	27a6–7	dgon pa ba'i 'od mi 'khrugs pa	
Eleven-faced Mahākaruṇā (spiritual object of King Udayibhadra)	27a7–b2	jo bo thugs rje chen po bcu gcig zhal	A: bcu gcig zhal (130)

[133] I assume him to be Rnal 'byor pa, or Rnal 'byor pa chen po in the text means as Rnal 'byor pa Shes rab rdo rje who was the second abbot of Rwa sgreng.

[134] Jo legs is Jo bo legs (b. 11th c.), who was a disciple of 'Brom ston pa. See *Gsal ba'i sgrom me:* 106a4–106b1.

Goddess, *dkar chung ma* (spiritual object of Nāropa)	27b2	jo mo dkar chung ma	
Raktayamāri (spiritual object of teacher of Atiśa)	27b3–6	gshed dmar ma he la bcibs pa	
Statue of Śākyamuni	27b6	bcom ldan 'das shākya thub pa'i sku	
Small (khadiravanika) Tārā bodhisattva	27b6–7	jo bo seng ldeng nags kyi sgrol ma chung chung	A: seng ldeng nags sgrol (134–135, spiritual object of Smyug rum pa[135])
Master of the teachings	27b7	bstan pa'i bdag po	
Two Tārās	27b7	jo mo sgrol ma gnyis	
Two blue Tārās?	27b7	jo mo sngon po gnyis	
Godess, *'Od zer can* (spiritual object of Spyan snga rin po che[136])	27b7–8	lha mo 'od zer can	A: 'od zer can ma (131, 134, spiritual object of Spyan snga ba)
Tārā (spiritual object of Rong po rdo rje[137])	27b8	jo bo sgrol ma	
Eleven-faced Ṣaḍakṣarī (spiritual object of Khri srong lde btsan[138])	27b8–9	jo bo yi ge drug pa bcu gcig [zhal]	A: spyan ras gzigs bcu gcig zhal (132)
Ṣaḍakṣarī [lokeśvara] (spiritual object of Nag tsho Tshul khrims rgyal ba, 1011–1064)	27b9	yi ge drug pa gtso 'khor gsum bo	

135 Smyug rum pa chen po (b. 11th c.), who is a disciple of Spyan snga pa Tshul khrims 'bar. See *Gsal ba'i sgrom me:* 171a4–6.

136 Spyan snga pa Tshul khrims 'bar?

137 Unspecified master.

138 Khri srong lde btsan (742–c. 800).

Master of the teachings (spiritual object of Mtha' bzhi[139])	28a1	bstan pa'i bdag po	
Two Acalas (spiritual object of Mtha' bzhi)	28a1	jo bo mi g.yo	
Avalokīteśvara practitioner in meditateon (spiritual object of Mkha' ru ba)	28a1–2	spyan ras gzigs gar gyi dbang po	
Kurukullā (spiritual object of Mtha' bzhi)	28a2	jo mo ku ru ku le	
Mahākaruṇā (spiritual object of Dge bshes phyag dar)	28a2	thugs rje chen po	
Acala (spiritual object of Bya yul ba)	28a2	mi g.yo ba	
Vajrapāṇi	28a2–3	phyag na rdo rje	A: (130)
Fifteen pathas	28a3	thang sku bcwo lnga	
Image of Dge bshes ston pa (spiritual object of Snubs Gzhon nu dbang phyug 'od?)	28a3–4	dge bshes ston pa'i sku 'bag	
Vision of Vajratārā (spiritual object of Rnal 'byor pa Phyag khri mchog[140])	28a4	jo mo rdo rje sgrol ma zhal gzigs	
Vision of Acala (spiritual object of Dge bshes Ko khyim pa[141])	28a4	mi g.yo ba zhal gzigs	
Ṣaḍakṣarī [lokeśvara] (spiritual object of Ka ma ba[142])	28a4	jo bo yi ge drug pa	

139 Mtha' bzhi is supposed to be Mtha' bzhi sgom pa (b. 11th c.). According to the *Rwa sgreng nyi ma'i 'od zer*: 18b8–19a7, he studied under both of 'Brom ston pa and *Sku mched gsum* (Po to ba, Phu chung ba Gzhon nu rgyal mtshan, 1031–1106, and Spyan snga pa). He visited Rwa sgreng and contributed the monastery after Po to ba's decline.

140 See note 116.

141 Ko kyim pa Ye shes bla ma, the tenth abbot of Rwa sgreng. See 5. The abbatial succession of Rwa sgreng monastery.

142 Ka ma ba Shes rab 'od (1057–1131), who was a disciple of Dgon pa ba. See *Gsal ba'i sgron me*: 114a6–114b4.

Vison of Mahākāla (spiritual object of Ka ma ba)	28a4	chos skyong mgon po zhal gzigs
Image of 'Brom ston pa (spiritual object of Btsun pa rdo rje 'od[143])	28a5	ston pa'i sku 'bag
Khasarpaṇa (spiritual object of Shar ba)	28a5	jo bo kha sarpa ṇi
Atiśa's Robe (spiritual object of head of sangha)	28a5	jo bo'i chos gos
Image of Khams pa lung pa	28a5	khams pa lung pa'i sku 'bag
Image of Ka ma ba	28a5–6	ka ma ba'i sku 'bag gser
Statue of Sding pa, Mañjuśrīvīra	28a6	sding pa'i sku [']bag 'jam dpal dpa' bo
Image of Rin chen sgang pa (spiritual object of Dol pa Yon tan seng ge[144])	28a6	rin chen sgang pa'i sku 'bag
Vairocana, *Gangs can mtsho* (spiritual object of Stod lungs pa)	28a6–7	rnam par snang mdzad gangs can mtsho
Buddha, *Chags pad ma'i spyang*	28a7	sangs rgyas ma chags pad ma'i spyang
Amalākāśaśrī	28a7–8	dri med nam mkha' dpal
Śrīhṛdayakūṭamantrarāja?	28a8	dpal gyi snying rnam par brtsegs pa sgrags pa'i [grags pa'i ?] rgyal po
Abhisaṃbodhimaitreya	28a8	byams pa mngon par byang chub pa
Buddhabhaiṣajyarāja	28a8	sangs rgyas sman pa'i rgyal po

143 Zhang btsun Rdo rje 'od (1122–1194) is the third abbot of Snar thang monastery. See *Gsal ba'i sgron me*: 251a1–3.

144 Unspecified master.

Jina Śākyamuni	28a8	rgyal ba shākya thub pa	
Ten [statues?] superintended by the assembly of Atiśa (spiritual object of Zhang 'od 'jo ba[145])	28a9	jo bo'i chos gras dbu mdzad pa bcu tham pa	A: jo bo chos grwa che ba (132)
Mahābodhi (spiritual object of Stabs kha [ka] ba)	28a9	byang chub chen po	
Eleven-faced jo bo (spiritual object of Stabs kha [ka] ba)	28a9	jo bo bcu gcig zhal	A: bcu gcig zhal (133)
Eleven spiritual object of Dgon 'Od 'jo ba[146]	28b1	dgon 'od 'jo ba'i thugs dam bcu gcig	
Ten spiritual objects of Lha rje Zir [Zur?] sman[147]	28b1	lha rje zir [zur?] sman gyi thugs dam bcu	
Large image (spiritual object of Sum pa Sked nyag pa[148])	28b1	sum pa sked nyag pa'i thugs dam sku 'bag chen po	
Spiritual object of Jo gdan dbon po[149]	28b1	jo gdan dbon po'i thugs dam	
Great statue of Dgon 'Od 'jo ba	28b1	dgon 'od 'jo ba'i sku [chen po]	
Maitreya (spiritual object of Dar ma ye shes of Ber Family[150])	28b2	ber rgyud dar ma ye shes kyi thugs [dam] mi g.yo ba	
Tārā, *Lha sa ma* (spiritual object of Jo bo yab sras and Slob dpon Sna ra ba)	28b2	jo bo lha sa ma	A: jo bo lha sa ma (135, 137)

[145] The 5th abbot of Rwa sgreng. See Chapter 5.
[146] The 7th abbot of Rwa sgreng. See Chapter 5.
[147] Unspecified master.
[148] Unspecified master.
[149] Unspecified master. But it is supposed that the person, who are related to Jo gdan monastery. See note 59.
[150] See 6. Constructions and its sponsors.

Two sets of thousand Buddha (dvisahasra)	28b2	sangs rgyas stong rtsa gnyis
Seven (buddha) Bhaiṣajyaguru	28b3	jo btsun mar yug gi sman bla bdun
Twelve sacred object made by Spro [Spra?] ston[151]	28b3	spro [spra?] ston gyi [gyis?] mdzad pa bcu gnyis
Seven? (Three?) Mahādevī	28b3	byang chub grags kyi la mo che bdun [gsum]
Five goddesses?	28b3	rigs lnga ser 'jam gyi lha mo lnga
Nine spiritual objects of Slob dpon Gur ston[152]	28b3	slob dpon gur ston gyi thugs dam dgu

2) Sacred objects of speech

Sacred objects of speech	folio no.	*Rwa sgreng nyi ma'i 'od zer*	A, B
Sanskrit texts of Atiśa about more than fifty volumes	28b5	jo bo'i phyag dpe' po ti lnga bcu lhag tsam	A: rgya dpe (138), B: jo bo'i rgya dpe lnga bcu lhag (200a6)
Primal texts of 'Brom ston pa about thirty volumes and more	28b5	dge bshes ston pa'i thugs dam phyi mo [po ti gsum bcu rtsa lhag]	A: bod dpe (139), B: (200b1)
Scriptures with gold ink	28b5	gser gyi glegs bam	
"*spar khabs [khab] can*" (spiritual object of Rnal 'byor pa chen po)	28b5	spar khabs [khab] can	A: (139)
"*spar khabs [khab] can*" (spiritual object of 'Brom ston pa)	28b5–6	spar khabs [khab] can	A: dngul gyi spar gab can (139)

151 Wrong spelling? Unspecified master.
152 The twelfth abbot of Rwa sgreng. See Chapter 5.

Many scriptures ? (spiritual object of Mkhan po Gu shrī)	28b6	mkhan po gug [/gu] shri'i thugs dam mtshan mangs	A: mkhan po gug shri'i mtshan mangs (139)
Scriptures written with silver ink, and scriptures on navy blue paper with gold ink[153]	28b7	po ti skya bo dang sngon po	
Eight sets of scriptures written with gold ink	28b7–8	gser gyi mdo mangs tshar brgyad	B: mdo mangs tshar bdun (200a4)
Twelve sets of scriptures written with silver ink	28b8	mdo mangs dkar po tshar bcu gnyis	
Sixty-two sets of *Śatasāhasrikā Prajñāpāramitā* writing with gold ink	28b8	gser 'bum tshar drug bcu rtsa gnyis	B: gser 'bum lnga bcu rtsa drug (200a1)
[illegible] (1300)	28b8	[illegible]s pa dkar po stong sum brgya	
Pañcaviṃśatisāhasrikā Prajñāpāramitā (90 or 108 sets)	28b8	rin po che'i yum bar ma[154] tshar dgu bcu [brgya rtsa brgyad yang zer]	
120 sets of *Pañcaviṃśatisāhasrikā Prajñāpāramitā* writing with silver ink (120 sets)	28b8	*nyi khri* dkar po tshar brgya nyi shu	A: *nyi khri* tshar drug (120), B: *nyi khri* brgyad bcu rtsa bdun (200a1–2)
Scriptures (380 sets?)	28b8–29a1	rin po che'i glegs? bam gsum rgya [illegible] brgyad bcu?	
Aṣṭasāhasrikā Prajñāpāramitā writing with silver ink about more than 275 sets	29a1	*brgyad stong pa* skya bo nyis stong dang bdun bcu rtsa lnga lhag pa	B: *brgyad stong pa* bzhi brgya nyi shu rtsa brgyad (200a2)
Buddhāvataṃsaka Sūtra	29a1	*sangs rgyas phal po che*	
Ratnakūṭa Mahāyāna Sūtra	29a1	*dkon brtsegs*	B: *dkon brtsegs* (200a3)

[153] It might be also *po ti skya bo* means scripture covered with a grey book cover (*dpe ras*), and *po ti sngon po* means scripture covered with a blue book cover.

[154] *Yum bar ma* might be same as *yum 'bring ba.*

Daśasāhasrikā Prajñāpāramitā[155]	29a1	*shes rab khri pa*	
Aṣṭasāhasrikā Prajñāpāramitā	29a1	*khri brgyad stong pa*	B: *khri brgyad stong pa* bzhi (200a2)
Prajñāpāramitā [ratnaguṇa] Sañcayagāthā [156]	29a1	*shes rab sna tshogs*	
? (200 sets)	29a2	dkar po [thu bas spyan?] tshar nyis brgya	
? (450 sets)	29a2	gser bsdud [mdo sdud][157] phyed dang lnga brgya	
Tantras such as *Guhyasamāja* (300 volumes)	29a2	*dpal gsang ba 'dus pa* la sogs pa rgyud kyi po ti sum brgya	
Śāstra (3030 volumes)	29a2–3	bstan chos kyi po ti sum stong sum bcu tham pa	

3) Sacred objects of mind

Sacred objects of mind	folio no.	*Rwa sgreng nyi ma'i 'od zer*	A, B
[Stūpa with] a small silver parasol (Gser gling pa's memorial stūpa)	29a4–6	dngul gdugs can chung ba	A: (106)
108 relics of Buddha (inside of [Stūpa with] a small silver parasol)	29a6	de bzhin gshegs pa'i ring srel brgya rtsa brgyad	
Relics of 150 Lamas such as Gser gling pa (inside of [Stūpa with] a small silver parasol)	29a6	bla ma gser gling pa la sogs pa'i bla ma brgya lnga bcu gdung ring srel	
? and Wooden stūpa	29a6–7	[illegible] 'di dang shing gi mchod rten	

155 D. 11.

156 D. 13.

157 mdo sdud pa gser bris ma?

One finger span (*mtho*) size of moon mirror with hundred drapes (spiritual object of Nāropa)	29a7–9	zla ba me long gi rgya yol can mtho gang lhag pa gcig	
[Stūpa with] a large silver parasol of Atiśa	29a8–30a2	jo bo dngul gdugs can che ba	A: (113–116)[158]
Memorial stūpa of Dge bshes ston pa	30a2–3	dge bshes ston pa'i gdung khang	
Memorial stūpa of Rnal 'byor pa chen po	30a3, 30b1	rnal 'byor pa chen po'i gdung khang	B: (200b5)
Memorial stūpa of Dgon pa ba	30a3–4	dgon [pa] chen po'i gdung khang	B: (200b5)
Memorial stūpa of Ka ma ba	30a4–5	dge bshes ka ma ba'i gdung khang	
Memorial stūpa of Sdings po[159]	30a5	dge bshes sging [sdings] po'i gdung khang	
General memorial stūpa of Dge bshes Mtha' bzhi, Rgya'u ra ba[160], and Ko khyim pa	30a5–6	dge bshes mtha' bzhi, rgya'u ra ba, ko khyim pa gsum gyi spyi'i gdung khang	
Relic of Buddha	30a6	de bzhin gshegs pa'i ring srel	A: (143)?
Head image of Brāhman's kapāla	30a6–7	bram ze'i thod sku	
Begging bowl of skull	30a7	sha ri'i bu'i lhung bzed	
Hevajra thangka	30a7	dpal dgyes pa rdo rje'i thang sku	
108-crystal rosary (spiritual object of Atiśa)	30a7	shel gyi phreng ba brgya rtsa brgyad pa gcig	
Rosary made from fruit of Bodhi-tree	30a8	bo do rtse'i [bo de tse'i] [161] phreng ba	

158 Additionally, Lhun grub chos 'phel (1994: 116–117) mentions on the existence of *dngul gdugs can 'bring ba*.

159 It is assumed that Sdings po pa is Rtog ldan sding po ba Snubs chos 'bar (1053?/ 1065?–?). According to the *Gsal ba'i gsal ba'i sgron me*: 178b4–5, he was the third abbot of Lo monastery.

160 Unspecified master.

161 See *Bod rgya tshig mdzod chen mo*: 1842 and Goldstein (2001: 725).

Monk robe	30a8	chos gos
Ladle	30a8	blug gzar
Memorial stūpa of Dpon chos kyi rgyal po[162]	30a9	dpon chos kyi rgyal po'i gdung khang
[Stūpa?] appeared by the precious mind of Pu to ba	30a9–30b1	pu to ba'i thugs gsum byon pa'i gcig
Self-created statue of 'Brom ston pa	30b1, 30b5–6	dge bshes ston pa'i sku rang byon
Memorial stūpa of Stabs ka ba	30b1, 31a8–31b1	stabs kha [ka] ba'i gdung khang
Memorial stūpa of Rnal 'byor pa chen po	30b2–3	rnal 'byor chen po'i gdung khang
Memorial stūpa of Khams pa lung pa[163]	30b3	kham [khams] pa lung pa'i gdung khang
Memorial stūpa of Mtha' bzhi pa	30b3	dge bshes mtha' bzhi'i gdung khang
Memorial stūpa of Shar ba	30b4	shar ba'i gdung khang
General memorial stūpa of Stabs ka ba and Dgon pa ba sum sgom[164]	30b4	stabs kha [ka] ba dang dgon pa ba sum sgom gnyis kyi spyi'i gdung khang
Memorial stūpa of Zhang 'Od 'jo ba	30b4–5, 30b7–8	zhang 'od 'jo ba'i gdung khang
Memorial stūpa of Sgang thang dkar po[165]	30b5	sgang thang dkar po'i gdung khang
Memorial stūpa of Dgon 'Od 'jo ba	30b5–6	dgon 'od 'jo ba'i gdung khang
Memorial stūpa of Bla chungs shrī [166]	30b6	bla chungs shri'i gdung khang

[162] Unspecified master.
[163] Khams pa lung pa Shākya yon tan (1025–1115). See *Gsal ba'i sgron me*: 106b5–107b1.
[164] Unspecified master.
[165] Sgang Thang dkar ba Rdo rje rin chen. See note 56.
[166] Unspecified master.

Memorial stūpa of Mnga' ris pa cham cho med[167]	30b6–7	mnga' ris pa cham cho med kyi gdung khang	
Memorial stūpa of 'Phrang sa jo gdan[168]	30b7	'phrang sa jo gdan kyi [gyi] gdung khang	
Memorial stūpa of Dge bshes Srang sgo ba[169]	30b7	dge bshes srang sgo ba'i gdung khang	
Silver parasol in the memorial stūpa of Atiśa and 'Brom ston pa	30b8–9	dngul las byas pa dngul kyi [gyi] gdugs	B: (200b5)
Blessing stūpa?, called Amitābha	30b9–31a1	a mi de ba can bya ba byin brlabs [rlabs] can	
Bkra shis sgo mangs stūpa with wavy line, *stag ra*	31a1–2	[ser chab can] stag ra dang dbang gi bkra shis sgo mangs	A: mchod rten bkra shis sgo mang (149)
Pad ma kha sbyor (the union of lotuses?) of Stong brtsan na mgo ba	31a2–3	stong brtsan na mgo ba'i pad ma kha sbyor	
Memorial stūpa of Spyan snga rin po che[170]	31a3	spyan snga rin po che'i gdung khang	B: (200b5)
Memorial stūpa of Sne'u zur ba	31a4	sne [sne'u] zur ba'i gdung khang	
Eyes and tongue	31a4	spyan ya gcig dang ljags	
Silver memorial stūpa	31a4	dngul gyi gdung khang	
Memorial (silver) stūpa of Bya yul ba Sangs rgyas sgom pa[171]	31a4–5	bya yul pa [ba] sangs rgyas sgom pa'i gdung [khang?]	
Memorial stūpa of Bya yul ba	31a5, 31a7	bya yul ba'i gdung khang	
Memorial stūpa of 'Od 'jo ba	31a5	'od 'jo ba'i gdung khang	
Memorial stūpa of Rin chen sgang pa dgyed tsho[172]	31a5	rin chen sgang pa dgyed tsho de'i gdung khang	

[167] Unspecified master.
[168] Unspecified master.
[169] Unspecified master.
[170] It is assumed to be Spyan snga pa Tshul khrims 'bar.
[171] Unspecified master. The name, Bya yul ba Sangs rgyas sgom pa and Bya yul ba Sangs rgyas sgom pa phyi ma appears in the *Gsal ba'i sgron me*. According to the *Gsal ba'i sgron me:* 149a5, Bya yul ba Sangs rgyas sgom pa is a contemporary master with Khrom gzher rin chen seng ge (*shing mo sbrul*: 1185?– *chu mo yos*: 1243?) of Bya yul monastery. According to the *Gsal ba'i sgron me:* 210b2, Bya yul ba Sangs rgyas sgom pa phyi ma is a disciple of Rtogs ldan bzang mo ba (*sa pho stag*: 1218 or 1278?–?).
[172] Unspecified master. It is assumed to be a master from Rin chen sgang pa monastery.

Stūpa with throne of bouquet lotus (Memorial stūpa of Atiśa and 'Brom ston pa)	31a5–6	pad spungs gdan khri can gnyis po, jo bo yab sras kyi gdung khang
Memorial stūpa of 'Chad kha pa[173]	31a6	'chad kha pa'i gdung khang
Self-created statue of Yoginī	31a6–7	rnal 'byor ma'i sku rang byon
Memorial stūpa of Brag dkar ba[174]	31a7–8	brag dkar ba sngan [sngon] ma'i gdung khang
Memorial stūpa of Dge bshes Don mo ri pa[175]	31a8	dge bshes don mo ri pa'i gdung khang
Memorial stūpa of Rin chen Sgang pa Sangs rgyas dbon[176]	31a8	rin chen sgang pa sangs rgyas dbon gyi gdung khang

173 'Chad kha ba Ye shes rdo rje (1101–1170). See *Gsal ba'i sgron me*: 241b3–245b3.

174 Brag dkar ba (1032–1111) is a disciple of Po to ba . See *Gsal ba'i sgron me*: 223a5–223b4.

175 Unspecified master.

176 It is assumed that Rin chen sgang pa Sangs rgyas dbon (?–1238?) is Sangs rgyas dbon, who was a disciple of Sangs rgyas ston pa (?–1193?) in the lineage of in the the *Gsal ba'i sgron me*: 156b5–6.

Bibliography and Abbreviations

Tibetan sources

Bai ḍūrya ser po = Sde srid Sangs rgyas rgya mtsho (1653–1705), *Dpal mnyam med ri bo dga' ldan pa'i bstan pa zhwa ser cod pan 'chang ba'i ring lugs chos thams cad kyi rtsa ba gsal bar byed pa bai ḍūrya ser po'i me long*, Xining: Krung go bod kyi shes rig dpe skrun khang, 1989.

Bu ston chos 'byung = Bu ston Rin chen grub (1290–1364), *Bde bar gshegs pa'i bstan pa'i gsal byed chos kyi 'byung gnas gsung rab rin po che'i mdzod*, Beijing: Krung go bod kyi shes rig dpe skrun khang, 1988.

Deb ther sngon po = 'Gos Lo tsā ba Gzhon nu dpal (1392–1481), *Deb ther sngon po: The Blue Annals*, Śata–Piṭaka Series 212, New Delhi: International Academy of Indian Culture, 1974.

Dge bshes ston pa'i rnam thar = Mchims Nam mkha' grags (1210–1285), *Dge bshes ston pa'i rnam thar* [*dbu can* manuscript], TBRC W2CZ7888.

Gsal ba'i sgron me = Las chen Kun dga' rgyal mtshan (1432–1506), *Bka' gdams kyi rnam par thar pa chos 'byung gsal ba'i sgron me*, *Bod kyi lo rgyus rnam thar phyogs bsgrigs* [block print, 17th c., ordered by the Fifth Dalai Lama], set 1, vol.3, Xining: Mtsho sngon mi rigs dpe skrun khang, 2010.

Gser gyi thang ma = Dge 'dun chos 'phel (1903–1951), *Rgyal khams rig pas bskor ba'i gtam rgyud gser gyi thang ma*, In Hor khang Bsod nams dpal 'bar (ed.), *Dge 'dun chos 'phel gyi gsung rtsom*, 2, (*Gangs can rig mdzod*, 11), Lhasa: Bod ljongs bod yig dpe rnying dpe skrun khang, 1994, 3–188.

Mdo smad chos 'byung = Brag dgon Zhabs drung Dkon mchog bstan pa rab rgyas (1801–after 1866), *Yul mdo smad kyi ljongs su thub bstan rin po che ji ltar dar ba'i tshul gsal bar brjod pa deb ther rgya mtsho*, Smon lam rgya mtsho (ed.), Lanzhou: Kan su'u mi rigs dpe skrun khang, 1982.

MHTL = A khu ching Shes rab rgya mtsho (1803–1875), *Dpe rgyun dkon pa 'ga' zhig gi tho yig: Materials for a History of Tibetan Literature*, part 3, Śata-Piṭaka Series 30, New Delhi: International Academy of Indian Culture, 1963, 503–601 (Reprint Kyoto: Rinsen, 1981).

Rnam thar rgyas pa yongs grags = Mchims Nam mkha' grags (1210–1285), *Jo bo rin po che rje dpal ldan a ti sha'i rnam thar rgyas pa yongs grags*, In Mkha' 'gro tshe ring (ed.), *Jo bo rje dpal ldan a ti sha'i rnam thar bka' gdams pha chos*, Xining: Mtsho sngon mi rigs dpe skrun khang, 1994, 44–228.

Rwa sgreng nyi ma'i 'od 'zer = 'Brom Shes rab me lce (13th–14th c.), *Rgyal ba'i dben gnas rwa sgreng gi bshad pa nyi ma'i 'od zer*, In Dpal brtsegs bod yig dpe rnying zhib 'jug khang (ed.), *Bod kyi lo rgyus rnam thar phyogs bsgrigs*, set 1, vol.11, Xining: Mtsho sngon mi rigs dpe skrun khang, 2010.

Tshad ma shes rab sgron ma = Mtshur ston Gzhon nu seng ge (ca. 1150–1210), In Dpal brtsegs bod yig dpe rnying zhib 'jug khang (ed.), *Bka' gdams gsung 'bum phyogs sgrigs*, set 3, vol.87, Chengdu: Si khron mi rigs dpe skrun khang, 2009.

Secondary literature

Bod rgya tshig mdzod chen mo = Zhang, Y. 张怡荪 et al. (eds.) (1993), *Bod rgya tshig mdzod chen mo*, Beijing: Mi rigs dpe skrun khang.

Chos 'phel (2004), *Gangs can bod kyi gnas bshad lam yig gsar ma, 2: lha sa khul gyi gnas yig*, Beijing: Mi rigs dpe skrun khang.

D. = Ui, H. 宇井白寿 et al. (eds.) (1934), *Chibetto daizōkyō sōmokuroku* (西藏大蔵経総目録) [*Complete Catalogue of the Tibetan Buddhist Canons*], Tokyo: Tohoku teikoku daigaku bungakubu (東北帝国大学法文学部) [The Department of Law and Letters, Tohoku Imperial University].

Dpal brtsegs bod yig dpe rnying zhib 'jug khang (2004), *'Bras spungs dgon du bzhugs su gsol ba'i dpe rnying dkar chag*, Beijing: Mi rigs dpe skrun khang.

Dpal brtsegs bod yig dpe rnying zhib 'jug khang (2010), *Bod kyi lo rgyus rnam thar phyogs bsgrigs kyi dkar chag*, Xining: Mtsho sngon mi rigs dpe skrun khang.

Dung dkar Blo bzang 'phrin las (2002), *Dung dkar tshig mdzod chen mo*, Beijing: Krung go bod rig pa dpe skrun khang.

Eimer, H. (1979), *Materialien zu einer Biographie des Atiśa (Dīpaṃkaraśrījñāna)*, 1 Teil: Einführung, Inhaltsverzeichnis, Namensglossar, 2 Teil: Textmaterialien, Asiatische Forschungen, 67, 68, Wiesbaden: Otto Harrassowitz.

Eimer, H. (2008), "Sources for the vita of 'Brom ston rgyal ba'i 'byung gnas," In O. Almogi (ed.), *Contributions to Tibetan Buddhist Literature, PIATS 2006: Tibetan Studies: Proceedings of the Eleventh Seminar of the International Association for Tibetan Studies, Königswinter 2006*, Halle: International Institute for Tibetan and Buddhist Studies GmbH, 377–392.

Goldstein, M.C. (ed.) (2001), *The New Tibetan-English Dictionary of Modern Tibetan*, Berkeley: University of California Press.

Gzigs pa sprul sku Blo bzang bzod pa and Phun tshogs rab rgyas (2006), *Dpal gyi chos sde chen po rwa sgreng rgyal ba'i dben gnas kyi zab gsang cho ga'i rim pa la 'jug tshul rgya cher bshad pa mtshungs med bshes gnyen dam pa'i bka' khrid lan mang thob pa'i brjed byang blo gsal padmo bzhad pa'i nyin byed*, Lhasa: Bod ljongs mi dmangs dpe skrun khang.

Gzim sprul Bstan 'dzin ye shes (2012), *Rwa sgreng chos sde chen po'i gnas yig*, Lhasa: Bod ljongs mi dmangs dpe skrun khang.

Hadano, H. 羽田野伯猷 (1954), "Kadamuhashi: shiryōhen" (カーダム派史資料篇) [The History of Bka' gdams pa: Materials], In *Chibetto indogaku shūsei* (チベット・インド学集成) [*Collected works on Indo-Tibetan Studies*], 1–1, Kyoto: Hōzōkan, 46– 191.

Hadano, H. 羽田野伯猷 (1965), "Chibetto ni okeru bukkyōkan no keisei ni tsuite: Bodaidoutou, Sanpu Bukkyōgaku, Kadamuhōsatsu tōwo megutte" (チベットにおける仏教観の形成について ー菩提道灯・サンプ仏教学・カ-ダム宝冊等をめぐってー) [The Formation of Buddhism in Tibet: On *Lam rim*, Buddhism in Gsang phu, and the *Bka' gdams glegs bam*], In *Chibetto indogaku shūsei* (チベット・インド学集成) [*Collected works on Indo-Tibetan Studies*], 1–1, Kyoto: Hōzōkan, 277–303.

Harter, P-J. (2008), "Mtshur ston Gzhon nu seng ge: *Tshad ma shes rab sgron ma* by Pascale Hugon, Review by: Pierre-Julien Harter," *Journal of the American Oriental Society*, 128–4, 783–784.

Heimbel, J. (2013), "The Jo gdan tshogs sde bzhi: An Investigation into the History of the Four Monastic Communities in Śākyaśrībhadra's Vinaya Tradition," In F. Ehrhard and P. Maurer (eds.), *Nepalica-Tibetica: Festgabe for Christoph Cüppers*, 1, (Beiträge zur Zentralasienforschung, 28–1), Andiast: International Institute for Tibetan and Buddhist Studies GmbH, 187–242.

Hugon, P. (ed.) (2004), *Mtshur ston gzhon nu seng ge: Tshad ma shes rab sgron ma*, Wiener Studien zur Tibetologie und Buddhismuskunde 60, Wien: Arbeitskreis für Tibetische und Buddhistische Studien.

Iuchi, M. 井内真帆 (2006), "Perutseku chiibettobun koseki kenkyūshitsu hensan depun ji shozō koseki mokuroku: shinkan shōkai" (ペルツェク・チベット文古籍研究室編纂『デプン寺所蔵古籍目録』新刊紹介) [Review: The Catalogue of Tibetan works Kept in 'Bras spungs monastery by Dpal brtsegs bod yig dpe rnying zhib 'jug khang], *Bukkyōgaku seminā* (佛教学セミナー) [*Buddhist Seminar*], 83, 16–24.

Iuchi, M. 井内真帆 (2010), "Lo ji: shyoki kadamuha ji'in no hensen" (ロ寺ー初期カダム派寺院の変遷) [The History of Lo dgon pa: the Vicissitudes of an Early Bka' gdams pa monastery], *Otani daigaku kenkyū nenpō* (大谷大学研究年報) [*Annual Report of Researchers of Otani University*], 62, 37–77.

Iuchi, M. 井内真帆 (2011), "Karahoto shutsudo no kadamuha kankei monjo" (カラホト出土のカダム派関係文書) [Bka' gdams pa Manuscripts Discovered at Khara-khoto], *Bukkyōgaku seminā* (佛教学セミナー) [*Buddhist Seminar*], 92, 26–38.

Iuchi, M. (2012), "A Note on the Relationship between the Bka' gdams pa School and Mi nyag/Xixia," *Zangxue xuekan* (藏学学刊) [*Journal of Tibetology*], 8, 58–62.

Iuchi, M. (2013), "Early Bka' gdams pa Masters and Khams 'Dan ma: A Preliminary Study of Monasteries Related to Smṛtijñānakīrti," In C. Cüppers, R. Mayer, M. Walter (eds.), *Tibet after Empire: Culture, Society and Religion between 850-1000: Proceedings of the Seminar Held in Lumbini, Nepal, March 2011*, Lumbini: Lumbini International Research Institute, 215–227.

Iuchi, M. 井内真帆 and Yoshimizu, C. 吉水千鶴子 (2011), *Chibetto bukkyō shūgi kenkyū 9: Tukan issaishūgi kadamuha no shō* (西蔵仏教宗義研究第 9 巻－トゥカン『一切宗義』「カダム派の章」) *[A Study of the Grub mtha' of Tibetan Buddhism vol.9: The Chapter of Bka' gdams pa]*, Studia Tibetica, 44, Tokyo: Toyo Bunko.

van der Kuijp, L. W. J. (1993), "Jayānanda. A Twelfth Century Guoshi from Kashmir Among the Tangut," *Central Asiatic Journal*, 37/ 3–4, 188–197.

Kano, K. 加納和雄 (2008), "Rngog blo ldan shes rab's Topical Outline of the Ratnagotravibhāga Discovered at Khara khoto," In O. Almogi (ed.), *Contributions to Tibetan Literature. Proceedings of the Eleventh Seminar of the International Association for Tibetan Studies, Königswinter 2006*, Halle: International Institute for Tibetan and Buddhist Studies GmbH, 127–194.

Kano, K. 加納和雄 (2010), "Gendun chunpē cho sekai chishikikō dai'isshō wayaku (1)" (ゲンドゥンチュンペー著『世界知識行』第 1 章和訳－1930 年代のチベットにおける梵文写本調査記録) [Japanese Translation of the First Chapter of Dge 'dun chos 'phel's *Gtam rgyud gser gyi thang ma*], *Mikkyōbunka kenkyūjo kiyō* (密教文化研究所紀要) [*Bulletin of the Research Institute of Esoteric Buddhist Culture*], 23, 146–106.

Kano, K. 加納和雄 (2012), "Atisha ni yuraisuru Retin ji kyūzō no bonbun shyahon: 1943 nen no chibetto ni okeru bonpon chyōsa wo kiten toshite" (アティシャに由来するレティン寺旧蔵の梵文写本－1934 年のチベットにおける梵本調査を起点として) [Rāhula Sāṅkṛtyāyana's Visit to Rwa sgreng Monastery and a Sanskrit Manuscript Collection in Possession of Atiśa Once Preserved at Rwa sgreng], *Indo ronrigaku kenkyū* (インド論理学研究) [*Indian Logic*], 4, 123–161.

Lhun grub chos 'phel (1994), *Rwa sgreng dgon pa'i dkar chag*, Chengdu: Si khron mi rigs dpe skrun khang.

Nishida, T. 西田龍雄 (1987), "Chibettogo no hensen to moji" (チベット語の変遷と文字) [Transition and script of Tibetan Language], In Y. Nagano and M. Tachikawa (eds.), *Chibetto no gengo to bunka* (チベットの言語と文化) [*Language and Culture of Tibet*], Tokyo: Tōjusha, 108–169.

Roerich, G.N. (1949), *The Blue Annals*, Delhi: Motilal Banarsidass Publication (reprint 1996).

Roesler, U. and H.U. (2004), *Kadampa Sites of Phempo: A Guide to Some Early Buddhist Monasteries in Central Tibet*, Kathmandu: Vajra Publications.

Roesler, U. (2007), "A Palace for Those Who Have Eyes to See: Preliminary remarks on the symbolic geography of Reting (Rwa-sgreng)," *Acta Orientalia Vilnensia*, 8–1, 123–144.

Roesler, U. (2008), "On the History of Histories: The Case of the Bka' gdams pa-s," In O. Almogi (ed.), *Contributions to Tibetan Buddhist Literature, PIATS 2006: Tibetan Studies: Proceedings of the Eleventh Seminar of the International Association for Tibetan Studies, Königswinter 2006*, International Institute for Tibetan and Buddhist Studies GmbH, Halle: 398–413.

Scherrer-Schaub, C. A. (2002), "Enacting Words. A Diplomatic Analysis of the Imperial Decrees (bkas bcad) and their Application in the *Sgra sbyor bam po gnyis pa* Tradition," *Journal of the International Association of Buddhist Studies*, 25, 1–2, 263–340.

Sørensen, P.K. and Hazod, G. (in Cooperation with Tsering Gyalbo) (2007), *Rulers on the Celestial Plain: Ecclesiastic and Secular Hegemony in Medieval Tibet, A Study of Tshal Gung thang*, Österreichische Akademie der Wissenschaften, philosophisch-historische Klasse, Denkschriften 361, Wien: Verlag der Österreichischen Akademie der Wissenschaften.

Takeuchi, T. (1995), "KH.TIB. 4 (XT–4): Contracts for the Borrowing of Barley," *Manuscripta Orientalia*, 1– 1, 49–51.

Takeuchi, T. 武内紹人 (2002), "Kigigunki kara seika jidai no chibettogo monjo to chibettogo shiyō" (帰義軍期から西夏時代のチベット語文書とチベット語使用) [The Tibetan Language and Tibetan Texts from the End of Tibetan Domination over East Turkestan Though the Tangut Period (9th–12th c.)]," *Tohōgaku* (東方学) [*Eastern Studies*], 104, 124–106.

Thupten Jinpa (tr.) (2008), *The Book of Kadam: The Core Texts*, Boston: Wisdom Publications.

Thupten Jinpa and Lopez Jr., D. S. (Tr.) (2014), *Grains of Gold: Tales of a Cosmopolitan Traveler by Gendun Chopel*, Chicago: University of Chicago Press.

Toh. = Kanakura, E. 金倉円照 et al. (eds.) (1953), *Chibetto senjutsu butten mokuroku* (西蔵撰述仏典目録) [*A Catalogue of the Tohoku University Collection of Tibetan Works on Buddhism*], Sendai: Tohoku daigaku bungakubu indo tetsugaku indo bungaku kenkyūshitsu (東北大学文学部印度哲学印度文学研究室) [The Seminary of Indology, Tohoku University].

Vorobyova-Desyatovskaya, M. I. (1995), "Tibetan Manuscripts of the 8–11th Centuries A.D. in the Manuscripts Collection of the St. Petersburg Branch of the Institute of Oriental Studies," *Manuscripta Orientalia*, 1–1, 46–48.

Part Two

Annotated Edition of the *Rgyal ba'i dben gnas Rwa sgreng gi bshad pa nyi ma'i 'od zer*

Introduction (1b1–7)

1. ཇི་ལྟར་བཞེངས་པའི་ལོ་རྒྱུས་ཀྱི་བཤད་པ། (1b7–22a8)

1–1. ལུང་བསྟན་པ། (2a2–2b6)

1–1–1. སངས་རྒྱས་ཀྱི་ [ཀྱིས་] ལུང་བསྟན་པ། (2a2–8)

1–1–1–1. སྤྱིར་རྒྱལ་ཁམས་སུ་དམ་པའི་ཆོས་ཇི་ལྟར་དར་བའི་ལུང་བསྟན། (2a2–6)

1–1–1–2. བྱེ་བྲག་ཏུ་རྭ་སྒྲེང་ལུང་བསྟན་པ། (2a6–8)

1–1–2. སྤྲུལ་པའི་རྒྱལ་པོ་ [པོས་] ལུང་བསྟན་པ། (2a8–2b3)

1–1–3. ཇོ་བོའི་བླ་མ་རྒྱུད་པས་ལུང་བསྟན་པ། (2b3–6)

1–2. སྤུས་ཕབ་པ། (2b6–14a5)

1–2–1. སྤུས་འབེབས་མཁན་གྱི་ཇོ་བོའི་ལོ་རྒྱུས། (2b6–9b5)

1–2–1–1. ཁྱིམ་ན་བཞུགས་པའི་ཚེ་བའི་ལོ་རྒྱུས། (2b8–3a7)

1–2–1–2. ཐར་པར་གཤེགས་པའི་ཚེ་བའི་ལོ་རྒྱུས། (3a7–5a7)

1–2–1–2–1. སྡེ་པ་གང་ལ་རབ་ཏུ་བྱོན་པ། (3b1–2)

1–2–1–2–2. བླ་མ་རྒྱུད་པ་དང་བཅས་པ་རྣམས་ལ་ཐེགས་པ་ཆེ་ཆུང་གི་ཆོས་གསན་པ། (2b2–5a5)

1–2–1–2–3. བོད་དུ་འབྱོན་ཁ་ན་གནས་གང་ན་གཞན་དོན་མཛད་པའི་ལོ་རྒྱུས། (5a5–7)

1–2–1–3. བོད་དུ་བྱོན་ནས་སངས་རྒྱས་ཀྱི་བསྟན་པ་ལ་ཕན་ཇི་ལྟར་བཏགས་པའི་ལོ་རྒྱུས། (5a5–9b6)

1–2–1–3–1. བོད་དུ་འབྱོན་དགོས་པའི་རྒྱུ་མཚན། (5a8–6b7)

1–2–1–3–1–1. བོད་དུ་སྤྱིར་སངས་རྒྱས་ཀྱི་བསྟན་པ་འཕེལ་འགྲིབ་ཇི་ལྟར་བྱུང་བ། (5b1–6b3)

1–2–1–3–1–2. དུས་དེ་ཙ་ན་ཇི་ལྟར་ཡོད་པ། (6b3–6)

1–2–1–3–2. བོད་ཀྱི་ [ཀྱིས་] ཇི་ལྟར་སྤྱན་དྲངས་པའི་ཚུལ། (6b8–8a7)

1–2–1–3–2–1. རྒྱལ་པོ་གང་གིས་བདག་རྐྱེན་མཛད་པ། (6b8–7a4)

1–2–1–3–2–2. ལོ་ཙ་གང་གིས་སྤྱན་དྲངས་པ། (7a4–8a2)

1–2–1–3–2–3. ཤུལ་ལམ་དུ་གང་དོན་མཛད་པའི་རིམ་པ། (8a2–7)

1-2-1-3-3. བོད་དུ་བྱོན་ནས་གཞན་དོན་ཇི་ལྟར་མཛད་པ། (8a7–9b6)

1-2-1-3-3-1. སྡེ་སྣོད་ཀྱི་ཆོས་གང་དུ་གསུངས་པ། (8a8–9a3)

1-2-1-3-3-2. སློབ་མ་ཇི་ལྟར་རྣམས་བྱོན་པ། (9a3–8)

1-2-1-3-3-3. བོད་དུ་ལོ་དུ་བཞུགས་པ། (9b1)

1-2-1-3-3-4. ཐ་མ་གནས་གང་དུ་མྱ་ངན་ལས་འདའ་ཚུལ་བསྟན་པ། (9b1–3)

1-2-1-3-3-5. དེ་དག་གི་སྐབས་སུ་མིང་ཇི་སྐད་གྲགས་པ། (9b3–5)

1-2-2. སྤྲུས་གང་ལ་ཕབ་པ་དགེ་བཤེས་སྟོན་པའི་ལོ་རྒྱུས། (9b6–13b4)

1-2-2-1. སྤྲུལ་གང་དུ་སྐུ་འཁྲུངས་པ། (9b7–10a7)

1-2-2-1-1. རིགས། (9b8–10a3)

1-2-2-1-2. རུས། (10a3)

1-2-2-1-3. ཡབ་ཡུམ། (10a3–4)

1-2-2-1-4. མཚན། (10a3–4)

1-2-2-1-5. སྐུ་འཁྲུངས་པའི་ས་དངོས། (10a4–7)

1-2-2-2. ཇོ་བོ་སེ་བཙུན་ལ་ཇི་ལྟར་བསྟེན་པ། (10a7–11a4)

1-2-2-3. འཕྲང་ཁ་བེར་ཆུང་དང་ཇི་ལྟར་མཇལ་བ། (11a4–12a4)

1-2-2-4. ཁྱད་པར་དུ་ཨ་ཏི་ཤ་ལ་ཇི་ལྟར་བསྟེན་པའི་ལོ་རྒྱུས། (12a4–13b4)

1-2-3. སྤྲུས་ཕབ་པའི་གནས། (13b5–14a5)

1-3. བཞེངས་པའི་ཚུལ། (14a6–22a8)

1-3-1. སྟོན་པ་རིན་པོ་ཆེ་ཡོན་མཆོད་ཀྱིས་ཕྱག་ལེན་མཛད་ནས་དབུ་རྩེ་གང་ལ་བཞེངས་པའི་ལོ་རྒྱུས། (14a7–18a3)

1-3-1-1. ཇོ་བོ་གཤེགས་ནས་རྭ་སྒྲེང་མ་བྱོན་བར་གྱི་ལོ་རྒྱུས། (14a8–15a4)

1-3-1-2. རྭ་སྒྲེང་བྱོན་ནས་བཞེངས་པའི་ཚུལ་དངོས། (15a4–17b5)

1-3-1-2-1. བརྟག་པ་མཛད་ཅིང་དགོན་པ་གོང་མ་དང་། སྟོན་པ་ཉིད་ཀྱི་གཟིམ་ཆུང་ཇི་ལྟར་བཞེངས་པ། (15a5–16a5)

1-3-1-2-2. དབུ་རྩེ་རིན་པོ་ཆེ་ལོ་གང་ལ་ཚུལ་ཇི་ལྟར་བཞེངས་པ། (16a5–17b1)

2–2–3. ཐུགས་ཀྱི་རྟེན། (29a4–31b2)

2–2–4. མཆོད་རྫས་ཀྱི་གྲངས། (31b2–32a1)

Conclusion (32a1–32a5)

Colophon (32a5–32a8)

Editorial signs

[1b1]	folio and line number
(1–1)	*sa bcad* number
abc (superscript)	upper inter lineally
abc (subscript)	under inter lineally
[illegible]	illegible
[illegible: a]	editor's supposition for the illegible part
[blank: a]	editor's supposition for the blank
a̲ (*abbreviations*)	*abbreviation* (*sbdus yig* or *skung yig*), only the first appearance
¦	broken shad
:	double dot
⋮	triple dot
×, +, ᔑ, ○, ∵	annotation marks (*mchan btags*)
+ a	supplement (footnote)
- a	erasion (footnote)

༄༅། །སྒྲིགས་དུས་བོད་ཡུལ་མིན་[1]པའི་སྐྲག་རྣམ་འདེར། །བསྟན་པའི་སྒྲོན་མེ་གསལ་པར་མཛད་ [illegible] རྣམས་ལ། །སྒྲིང་ནས་སྒྲོ་གསུམ་གུས་པས་ཕྱག་བགྱིད་དོ། །ཅེས་[2]པ་ [illegible] རྣམས་

གསུང་བར་ [illegible]

[1b1] ༄༅༅། །རྒྱལ་བའི་མདུན་ན་རྒྱལ་སྲས་བཟང་པོ་སྐྱོང་།།

ཁ་བ་ཅན་ན་དཔལ་ལྡན་མར་མེ་མཛད།།

དཔལ་[3]ལྡན་གནས་ན་ནམ་མཁའ་དྲི་མ་མེད།།

ཡིད་བཞིན་ནོར་བུ་ལྟ་བུར་ (ལྟུར་) གཞན་དོན་མཛད།།

[1b2] ཇོ་བོ་ (ཇོ་) ཨ་ཏི་ཤ་ལ་ཕྱག་འཚལ་ལོ་ (ཕྱོ) ||

ཡོངས་ཀྱི་དགེ་བའི་བཤེས་གཉེན་ཡོངས་ཀྱི་མགོན།།

རྒྱལ་བའི་གདུང་འཚོབ་གྱུར་པ་རྒྱལ་བའི་སྲས།།

རང་གཞན་ཡོན་ཏན་འབྱུང་གནས་རིན་པོ་ཆེ (རྀ) ||

བཤེས་གཉེན་སྟོན་པའི་སྐུ་ལ་ཕྱག་འཚལ་ལོ་ (ཕྱོ་ལོ) ||

[1b3] རྒྱལ་བས་ལུང་བསྟན་ཇོ་བོས་སྤྱུས་ཐབ་ཅིང་།།

སྟོན་པས་བཞེངས་པ་ལྷ་ཡིས་མཆོད་པའི་གནས།།

གཙུག་ལག་ཁང་ཆེན་རྭས་སྒྲེང་ (རྭ་སྒྲེང་) ཞེས་བྱ་བ།།

བཞེངས་པའི་ལོ་རྒྱུས་རྟེན་གསུམ་བཞུགས་པའི་ཚུལ།།

མདོ་ཙམ་བཤད་ [1b4] གྱི་[4]གསུས་པས་མཉན་པར་མཛོད།།

1 སྨན་

2 ཞེས་

3 དགའ་ ?

4 ཀྱིས་

དེ་ལ་བདེ་བ་བསྐྱེད་པའི་གཞི། སྡུག་བསྔལ་སྤོང་བའི་རྒྱུ། ཐར་པ་སྒྲུབ་པའི་ཐེ་ཚོམ་ (ཐེཾ) སྐྱས་[5]ཟླུག་ཏུ་འབྱིན་ པའི་ སྣང་པ། བཀྲ་ཤིས་ (བཀྲིས་) ཀྱི་དགོན་གནས། མཁས་བཙུན་ཀྱི་[6]འབྱུང་གནས། ཡིད་བཞིན་གྱི་[7]སློབ་གྲྭ༔ [1b5] ལྷུན་པ་སེལ་བའི་སྒྲོན་མེ༔ མཐོང་བ་ཙམ་གྱི་[8]དོན་ཡོད། ། ཐོས་པ་ཙམ་གྱི་[9]སྒྲིབ་པ་མཛད་[10]པ། །ལྷ་དང་། མི་དང་། ལྷ་མ་ཡིན་དང་ཀླུ་དང་རིགས་སྔགས་འཆང་དུ་མས་མཆོད་པའི་གནས་དང་བསྐུར་བའི་ཞིང་དུ་གྱུར་པ། [1b6] གྲུབ་པ་ཐོབ་པའི་རྣལ་འབྱོར་ (རྣོར་) པ་དང་། སྡེ་སྣོད་འཛིན་པ་བསམ་གྱིས་མི་ཁྱབ་པ་བྱོན་པ། ཕྱོགས་མཐའ་དག་ཏུ་སངས་རྒྱས་ཀྱི་བསྟན་པ་རྒྱ ས་ པར་མཛད་པས། ཀུན་ཀྱི་[11]ཕྱི་མོ་འམ། རྒྱ་མིག་བརྒྱ་ཙ་བརྒྱད་ཀྱི་མགོ་འ་ལྟ་བུར་གྱུར་པའི་གདན་ [1b7] ས་རིན་པོ་ཆེ་རྒྱལ་བའི་དབེན་གནས་ཆེན་པོ་རྣམ་སྣང་ཞེས་ཡོངས་སུ་ (ཡོངསྲུ་) གྱུར་པའི་བཤད་པ་ཡང་དོན་གཉིས་སུ་ (༢སུ་) ཤེས་པར་བྱ་དེ[12]། ཇི་ལྟར་བཞེངས་པའི་ལོ་རྒྱུས་དང་། དེ་ན་བཞུགས་པའི་རྟེན་རྣམས་ཀྱི་བཤད་པའོ། །

(1) ཇི་ལྟར་བཞེངས་པའི་ལོ་རྒྱུས་ཀྱི་བཤད་པ།

དང་པོ་ཇི་ལྟར་ (ཇྟིར་) བཞེངས་ [2a1] པའི་ལོ་རྒྱུས་ལ་གསུམ་ (༣) སྟེ༔ (1–1) ལུང་བསྟོན་[13]པ་དང་། (1–2) སྤུས་ཐབ་པ་དང་། (1–3) བཞེངས་པའི་ཚུལ་དངོས་སོ། །

(1–1) ལུང་བསྟོན་[14]པ།

དང་པོ་ལུང་བསྟན་པ་ལ་གསུམ་སྟེ། (1–1–1) སངས་རྒྱས་ (སརྒྱས་) ཀྱི་[15]བསྟན་པ་དང་ (1–1–2) སྤྲུལ་པའི་རྒྱལ་པོས་ (རྒྱཔོས་) ལུང་བསྟན་པ་དང་། (1–1–3) རྗེ་བོའི་བླ་མ་བརྒྱུད་པས་ལུང་བསྟན་ [2a2] འོ།[16] (1–1–1) དང་པོ་སངས་རྒྱས་ཀྱི་[17]ལུང་བསྟན་པ་ལ་གཉིས་སྟེ།

---

5 + །
6 གྱི་
7 གྱི་
8 གྱིས་
9 གྱིས་
10 འཛད་
11 གྱི་
12 སྟེ
13 བསྟན་
14 བསྟན་
15 ཀྱིས་
16 པའོ། །
17 ཀྱིས་

(1–1–1–1) སྤྱིར་རྒྱལ་ཁམས་སུ་ (ཁྱིཾསུ་) དམ་པའི་ཆོས་ཇི་ལྟར་དར་བའི་ལུང་བསྟན་དང་། (1–1–1–2) ཐེ་བྲག་དུ། རྣམ་སྤྲིན་ལུང་བསྟན་པའོ།།

(1–1–1–1) དང་པོ་ནི། སྤྱིར་སངས་རྒྱས་ཀྱི་མདོ་རྒྱུད་བསམ་གྱིས་མི་ཁྱབ་པ་ནས་ལུང་བསྟན་ [2a3] དུ་མ་ཡོད་མོད་ཀྱང་། ཁོ་བོས་ཐོས་ཚོད་ནི་འདི་དག་ལགས་སྟེ[18]: ཡུམ་རྒྱས་འབྲིང་གསུམ་ནས།

> བཅོམ་ལྡན་འདས་ (བཅོཾས) ཀྱི་[19]བཀའ་བསྩལ་པ།
> ཀུན་དགའ་བོ་ང་ཡོངས་སུ་མྱ་ངན་ (མྱངན་) ལས་འདས་ནས:
> ཤེས་རབ་ཕ་རོལ་ཏུ་ཕྱིན་པ་ [illegible] འདི་ལྷོ་ཕྱོགས་ཀྱི་རྒྱུད་དུ་ [2a4] སྤྱོད་པར་འགྱུར་རོ་ (འགྱུརོ) ||
> དེ་ནས་ཡུལ་བར་ཏ་ནིར་[20]འབྱུང་བར་འགྱུར་རོ།།
> དེ་ནས་བྱང་ཕྱོགས་སུ་འབྱུང་བར་གྱུར་[21]རོ།།
> བྱང་ཕྱོགས་ནས་བྱང་ཕྱོགས་ཀྱི་ཆ་དེ་ཉིད་དུ་རྒྱས་པར་འགྱུར་རོ།།[22]

ཞེས་པ་དང་། ཡང་འཇམ་དཔལ་ (འཇཾལ་) རྩ་བའི་རྒྱུད་ལས།

> ཁ་བ་ཅན་ [2a5] གྱི་རྒྱལ་ཁམས་སུ།།
> དད་ཅན་སྐྱེ་བོ་དཔག་མེད་འབྱུང་།།
> སྟོན་པའི་རིན་[23]སྲེལ་མཆོད་པར་འགྱུར།།

---

18 ཏེ

19 ཀྱིས་

20 ?

21 འགྱུར་

22 Cf. *Dge bshes ston pa'i rnam thar*: 184b4–5: མདོ་ལས། ཤེས་རབ་ཀྱི་ཕ་རོལ་ཏུ་ཕྱིན་པ་ནི་བྱང་དང་བྱང་གི་ཕྱོགས་སུ་རྒྱས་པར་འགྱུར་རོ་ཞེས་དང་།

23 རིང་

ཞེས་པ་དང་། ཡང་སྔ་[24]བརྒྱའི་ཐ་མ་ལ་གདོང་དམར་གྱི་ཡུལ་དུ་སངས་རྒྱས་ཀྱི་བསྟན་པ་རྒྱས་པར་འགྱུར་རོ་ཞེས་པ་ལ་སོགས་ (ལས྄ོ) པ་ལུང་བསྟན་ ཏི་མ་ [2a6] བཞུགས་མོད་ཀྱི། ཁོ་བོས་ (ཁོས་) དེ་ཙམ་ལས་དྲང་བར་མ་ནུས་སོ (ནུསོ) ||

(1–1–1–2) གཉིས་པ་ཐེ་བྲག་དུ་རུས་སྦྲེང་ཊཱི་ལྟར་ལུང་བསྟན་པ་ནི། འཇམ་དཔལ་བསྟན་པ་རོལ་པའི་རྒྱུད་ལས།།

ལྷ་བརྒྱ་དུས་ཀྱི་ཐ་མ་ལ།།
སངས་རྒྱས་བསྟན་པ་གར་[25]རྒྱས་པ།།
[2a7] བྱང་ཕྱོགས་ཁ་བ་ཅན་གྱི་རིའི་དབུས།།
སྨན་སྣ་སྣ་ཚོགས་ (སྣོད་) ཡོད་པའི་གུལ[26]།།
སྤོས་ཤིང་ནགས་ཚལ་རྒྱས་པའི་གནས།།
ཡི་གེ་ (ཡིགེ་) དང་པོ་ར་ལ་དེ་འོག་སྦྲེང་།།

ཞེས་དངོས་སུ་ (དངོསུ་) ལུང་བསྟན་པ་དང་། གཞན་ཡང་མདོ་རྒྱུད་རྣམས་ [2a8] ནས་ཟུར་ཀྱིས་ལུང་བསྟན་དུ་མ་ཡོད་མོད་ཀྱི། ཚིག་གིས་[27] (ཚིགིས་) གསལ་ཀ་[28]མི་འདུག་ལ་འདིར་མ་བཀོད་དོ།།

(1–1–2) གཉིས་པ་སྤྲུལ་པའི་རྒྱལ་པོས་ལུང་བསྟན་པ་ནི། འཕགས་པ་སྤྱན་རས་གཟིགས་ (གཟ྄ི) ཀྱི་སྤྲུལ་པ་རྒྱལ་པོ་སྲོང་བཙན་སྒམ་པོ་ (སྒཾཔོ་) [2b1] པོ་[29]ལ་ཁྲོ་གཉེར་ཅན་གྱི་སྤྲུལ་པ་བལ་མོ་བཟའ་ཁྲི་བཙུན་གྱིས་ཞུས་པ། སྤྲུལ་པའི་རྒྱལ་པོ་ཁྱེད་ལྷ་སྤྲུ་མི་བཞུགས་དང་ན་སངས་རྒྱས་ཀྱི་བསྟན་པ་གང་དུ་རྒྱས་པར་འགྱུར་ཞེས་ཞུས་པས། ལན་དུ། རྒྱལ་པོས་བཀའ་བསྩལ་པ།

ལྷ་ [2b2] བརྒྱ་དུས་ཀྱི་ཐ་མ་ལ།།

---

24 ལྷ་
25 དར་ ?
26 ཁུལ
27 - གིས་
28 ཁ་
29 - པོ་

སངས་རྒྱས་བསྟན་པ་གར་[30]རྒྱས་པ།།

ཁ་བ་ཅན་གྱི་རིའི་དབུས།།

སྤྱོས་ཤིང་ནགས་ཚལ་འབར་བའི་གསེབ།།

དྲི་མ་མེད་པ་རྒྱལ་བའི་གསུང་།།

རབ་རྣམས་འདུའ་ཞིང་མཆོད་པའི་གནས།།

སྤྲུལ་པའི་ [2b3] རྒྱལ་པོས་དེར་ལུང་བསྟན།།

ཞེས་གསུངས་སོ་ (གསུངསོ) ¦

(1–1–3) གསུམ་པ་ཇོ་བོའི་བླ་མས་ལུང་བསྟན་པ་ནི། ཇོ་བོ་བོད་དུ་འབྱོན་ཁར་འབྱོན་མི་འབྱོན་ཐུགས་ཐེ་ཚོམ་དུ་བཞུགས་པའི་གནས་སྐབས་སུ (སྐབསུ) ¦ ཇོ་བོ་ཉིད་ཀྱི་བླ་མ་པཎྜིཏ་དུ་ཏ་ར་ནག་པོ་ཞེས་བྱ་བ་ [2b4] མཆོག་གི་དངོས་གྲུབ་ (དངྲུབ་) མཉེས་[31]པ་མངོན་པར་ཤེས་པ་མངའ་བ་གཅིག་གི་ཞལ་ནས། ཁྱོད་བློ་ཐེ་ཚོམ་མེད་པར་བོད་དུ་སོང་དང་། སངས་རྒྱས་ཀྱི་བསྟན་པ་ལ་ཕན་ཐོགས་པར་འགྱུར། ཁྱོད་ལ་སློབ་མ་བུ་ཚ་བོ་མང་པོ་འོང་བར་འདུག ཁྱོད་ལ་གདན་ [2b5] ས་ལྷ་གཞོལ་བ། བྱང་སྐྱིབས་ས། རྩེ་ཤིང་དང་། ནགས་ཚལ་དུ་མ་ཡོད་པ་གཅིག་ (?) འོང་བར་འདུག། ཁྱོད་ཀྱི་བུ་ཚ་བོ་དེ་རྣམས་ཀྱི་གནས་གཞི་དང་། དགོན་པ་མང་པོ་བཞེངས་པར་འདུག་པས། དེའི་དུས་སུ་ (དུསུ་) འདི་དགོས་པ་ཡིན་གསུང་ [2b6] ནས་ས་སྤྱད་[32]རིན་པོ་ཆེ་འཕྲུལ་གྱི་མེ་ལོང་ (མེློང་) ཞེས་བྱ་བ་དེ་ཡང་གནང་བ་ལགས་པར་གདའ།།

(1–2) སྤྱུས་ཕབ་པ།

གཉིས་པ་སྤྱུས་ཕབ་པ་ནི། ཇོ་བོས་དགེས་བཤེས་ (དགེས་) སྟོན་པ་ལ་སྤྱུས་ཕབ་པ་ཡིན་ལ། འདི་ལ་གསུམ་སྟེ། (1–2–1) སྤྱུས་འབེབས་མཁན་གྱི་ཇོ་བོའི་ལོ་རྒྱུས་དང་། [2b7] (1–2–2) སྤྱུས་གང་ལ་ཕབ་པ་ དགེ་བཤེས་ སྟོན་པའི་ལོ་རྒྱུས་དང་། (1–2–3) སྤྱུས་ཕབ་པའི་གནང་[33]དངོས་སོ་ (དངོསོ) ¦

30 དར་ ?

31 བརྙེས་

32 དཔྱད་

33 གནས་

(1–2–1) དང་པོ་ཇོ་བོའི་ལོ་རྒྱུས་ལ་གསུམ་སྟེ: (1–2–1–1) ཁྱིམ་ན་བཞུགས་པའི་ཆེ་བའི་ལོ་རྒྱུས་དང་། (1–2–1–2) ཐར་པར་གཤེགས་པའི་ཆེ་བའི་ལོ་རྒྱུས་དང་། (1–2–1–3) བོད་དུ་བྱོན་ནས་ (བྱོནས་) སངས་རྒྱས་ཀྱི་བསྟན་ [2b8] པ་ལ་ཕན་ཇི་ལྟར་གཏགས་[34] པའི་ ལོ་རྒྱུས་སོ།།

(1–2–1–1) དང་པོ་ནི། རྒྱ་གར་ཤར་ཕྱོགས་ཟ་ཧོར་གྱི་ཡུལ་མི་ཁྱིམ་འབུམ་ཕྲག་ཉི་ཤུ་རྩ་ལྔ་ཡོད་པའི་དབུས་ན། རྒྱལ་པོའི་ཕོ་བྲང་ (ཕོང་) གསེར་ཀྱི་[35]རྒྱལ་མཚན་ཅན་ཅེས་བྱ་བ་ཡོད་དོ་ (ཡོདོ) ། །ཡུལ་དེའི་རྒྱལ་པོ་ [3a1] དགེ་བའི་དཔལ་བྱ་བ་ཡིན། དེའི་བཙུན་མོ་དཔལ་མོ་འོད་ཟེར་ (འོདེར) ཅན་བྱ་བ་སྟེ། ཡབ་ཡུམ་ (ཡུབ་) དེ་གཉིས་ལ་སྲས་གསུམ་སྟེ། དཔལ་གྱི་སྙིང་པོ་དང་། ཟླ་བའི་སྙིང་པོ་ (སྙིངོ) དང་། པདྨའི་སྙིང་པོའོ། །དང་པོས་བཙུན་མོ་ལྔ་ཁབ་ད་[36]བཞེས་པ་ལ་ [3a2] སྲས་དགུ་འཁྲུངས་པའི་ཆེ་ཤོས་ཐར་པར་གཤེགས་པ་ནི། པཎྜི་ཏ་རཏྣ་ཤྲཱི་[37]ཞེས་བྱའོ། །ཆུང་བ་པདྨའི་སྙིང་པོ་ཐར་པར་གཤེགས་པ་ཏེ་དགེ་སློང་ (དགྗོང) ཛྙཱ་ན་ཙནྡྲ་[38]ཞེས་བྱ་བའི་གྲུབ་པ་མཉེས་[39]པ་ཅིག་[40]བྱུང་སྟེ་ཕྱིས་བོད་དུ་བྱོན་ནས་འདས། [3a3] འབྲིང་པོ་རྒྱལ་བུ་ཟླ་བའི་སྙིང་པོ་ནི:[41] ཇོ་བོ་ཆེན་པོ་ (ཆེནོ) ལགས་སྟེ (ལགསྟེ) ¦ ཡུམ་ལ་འཁྲུངས་ནས་རིང་པོ་མ་ལོན་པར་རིན་པོ་ཆེའི་ཁྲིའི་སྟེང་ན་བཞུགས་པའི་དུས་ན། ཇོ་བཙུན་མ་སྒྲོལ་མ་ཞལ་གཟིགས་སྐད། ཡབ་ཡུམ་གྱིས་ཀྱང་མེ་ཏོག་ (མྟོག) [3a4] ཕུད་པ་ལ་སྤོ་སེར་ཡུ་བ་དང་བཅས་པ་གཅིག་མཐོང་སྐད།[42] དེ་ལྟར་བཞུགས་པའི་དུས་ན་རྒྱལ་པོའི་ཕོ་བྲང་དེའི་ལོངས་སྤྱོད་ (ལྤྱོད) ནི། རྒྱ་ནག་སྟོང་ཀུན་རྒྱལ་པོ་དང་འདྲ་བ་ཡོད་པ་ལས། ཇོ་བོ་ཉིད་འདོད་པའི་ཡོན་ཏན་ (ཡོྟན) ལྔ་ལ་མི་ལྟ་བར་སྒྲུ་རྩལ་དྲུག་ [3a5] བཅུ་རྩ་ (བཙྭ) བཞི་དང་། བཟོའི་བསྟན་ཆོས་དང་། གསོའ་བའི་བསྟན་ཆོས་དང་། སྒྲ་དང་། ཚད་མ་ལ་སོགས་པ་སློབ་ཅིང་མ[blank: ཐ]ར་ཕྱིན་པར་མཛད་དེ་ (མཛདེ) ¦ གུང་ལོ་ཉི་ཤུ་རྩ་གཅིག་གི་བར་དུ་བཞུགས་སོ། །དེ་ནས་རི་ནག་པོའི་ཁོང་སེང་གི་ [3a6] གཙུག་ལག་ཁང་དུ། བླ་མ་ར་ཧུ་ལ་གུ་པ་ཏ་བཛྲ་[43]ཞེས་བྱ་བའི་སྤྱན་མངར་[44]བྱོན་ནས་ཐེག་པ་ཆེན་པོ་གསང་སྔགས་ཀྱི་སྒོར་ཞུགས་སྟེ། དེ་ནས་བཟུང་སྟེ་བླ་མ་སྒྲུབ་ཐོབ་དང་མཁས་པ་མང་པོ་ལ་རྟེན་ནས་

---

34 བཏགས་

35 ཀྱི་

36 དུ་

37 Cf. *Rnam thar rgyas pa yongs grags*: 46, *Gsal ba'i sgron me*: 28b2: + མི་ཏྲ་

38 Cf. *Rnam thar rgyas pa yongs grags*: 46: ཙནྡྲ་

39 བརྙེས་

40 ཞིག་

41 ¦ ?

42 Cf. *Rnam thar rgyas pa yongs grags*: 47: ཡུམ་གྱིས་ཨུཏྤལ་སྔོན་པོ་སྐྱེས་མ་ཐག་ལྟ་བུའི་ཚུན་པོ་ཅིག་གཟིགས།

43 Cf. *Rnam thar rgyas pa yongs grags*: 48: རཱ་ཧུ་ལ་གུཔྟ་བཛྲ་

44 སྔར་

མཁས་པ་དང [3a7] སྒྲུབ་པའི་ཡོན་ཏན་དུ་མས་བརྒྱན་པར་མཛད་པའི་བླ་མ་ཨ་བ་[45]ཧྲུ་ཏི་པའི་ཕྱུགས་[46]ཕྱིར་ལོ་བཅུ་གཉིས་ (བཅིུས་) འབྲེངས་[47]ནས་བརྟུལ་ཤུགས་[48]ཀྱི་སྤྱོད་པ་མཐར་ཕྱིན་པར་མཛད་དེ[49]། །དེ་དག་ནི་ (དགེ་) ཕྱིམ་ན་བཞུགས་པའི་ཆེབའི་ལོ་རྒྱུས་སོ་ (རྒྱུསོ) ||

(1–2–1–2) གཉིས་པ་ཐར་པར [3a8] གཤེགས་པའི་ཆེབའི་ལོ་རྒྱུས་ལ་གསུམ་སྟེ། (1–2–1–2–1) སྡེ་པ་གང་ལ་རབ་ཏུ་བྱོན་[50]པ་དང་། (1–2–1–2–2) བླ་མ་བརྒྱུད་པ་དང་བཅས་པ་རྣམས་ལ་ཆོས་གསན་ཅིང་མཁས་པ་དང་བཙུན་པ་དང་། སྒྲུབ་[51]པའི་ཡོན་ཏན་དང་ལྡན་པར་མཛད་པ་དང་། (1–2–1–2–3) བོད་དུ་འབྱོན་ཁ་ [illegible: འཛོ] [illegible: ཏ] རི་[52]དགྲ་ལས་ རྣམ་པར་ (རྣོར་) རྒྱལ་བ: བྱང་ཆུབ་ (བྱུབ་) ཟང་[53]པོ་ རིག་པའི་ཁུ་བྱུག། ཨ་ཧྲུ་ཏི་པ[54]། རཏྣ་ལ་འགྱུ་པ་ཏ་ བཛྲ[55]། འདི་རྣམས་རབ་ཏུ་མ་བྱོན་[56]དུས་ཀྱི་བླ་མ་ཡིན་ནོ་ (ཡིནོ) || [3b1] ན་གནས་གང་ན་གཞན་དོན་མཛད་པའི་ལོ་རྒྱུས་སོ།།

(1–2–1–2–1) དང་པོ་སྡེ་པ་གང་ལ་རབ་ཏུ་བྱུང་བ་ནི། སྤྱིར་ཉན་ཐོས་རྩ་བའི་སྡེ་བཞི་ (ང་) ལས་གྱེས་པའི་སྡེ་བཅོ་བརྒྱད་ཡོད་པའི་ནང་ནས། དགེ་འདུན་ཕལ་ཆེན་པའི་སྡེ་པ་ལྷ་སངས་རྒྱས་ཡེ་ཤེས་ (ཡེས་) [3b2] ཞབས་ཀྱི་དཀར་[57]རྒྱུད་མཁན་པོ་ཤི་[58]ལ་རཀྴི་ཏ་ཞེས་བྱ་བ་གཅིག་ལས། མ་ཧཱ་བྷཱི་ཏ་རའི་གཙུག་ལག་ཁང་དུ་རབ་ཏུ་བྱུང་ནས་བཙུན་པའི་ཕྱུལ་ཏུ་ཕྱིན་པར་མཛད་དོ་ (མཛོད) ||

(1–2–1–2–2) གཉིས་པ། བླ་མ་རྒྱུད་པ་དང་བཅས་པ་རྣམས་ལ་ཐེགས་[59]པ་ཆེ་ཆུང་ (ཆེུང་) གི་ [3b3] ཆོས་གསན་པ་ནི། ཛོ་བོ་ལ་བླ་མ་རྒྱུད་པ་འདི་རྣམས་མངའ་སྟེ། ཐེག་པ་ཐུན་མོང་ (ཐོུང་) གི་རྒྱུད་པ་ནི། སངས་རྒྱས། འཇམ་དཔལ། སངས་རྒྱས་ཡེ་ཤེས་ཞབས། མར་མེ་མཛད་

---

45 Cf. *Rnam thar rgyas pa yongs grags*: 49: ཕ་

46 ཕྱུག་

47 འབྲངས་

48 ཞུགས་

49 དོ

50 བྱུང་

51 གྲུབ་

52 Cf. *Rnam thar rgyas pa yongs grags*: 78: ཛོ་ཏྣ་རི་

53 བཟང་

54 ཨ་ཝ་ཧྲུ་ཏི་པ

55 རཏྣ་ལ་གུཔྟ་བཛྲ

56 བྱུང་

57 བཀའ་

58 Cf. *Rnam thar rgyas pa yongs grags*: 55: ཤཱི་

59 ཐེག་

བཟང་པོ། ཡི་གེ་པ། ཀཎྞ་པ[60]། ཛྙ་[61]ན་ཤྲི་མི་ཏྲ[62]། དེ་ལ་ཇོ་བོས་གསན། [3b4] ཕ་རོལ་ཏུ་ཕྱིན་པའི་རྒྱུད་པ་ལུགས: ལྟ་བ་རྣམ་པར་དག་པའི་རྒྱུད་པ་དང་། སྤྱོད་པ་རྣམ་དག་པའི་རྒྱུད་པ་གཉིས་ལས། དང་པོ་ནི། འཕགས་པ་ཀླུ་སྒྲུབ[63]། ཟླ་བ་གྲགས་པ། རིག་པའི་ཁུ་བྱུག། ཨ་བ་དྷུ་ཏི་པ་ཆེ་བ། ཨ་བ་དྷུ་ཏི་བ་ཆུང་བ། [3b5] ཇོ་བོ། སྤྱོད་པ་རྣམ་པར་དག་པའི་རྒྱུད་པ་ལ། སངས་རྒྱས། བྱམས་པ། ཐོགས་མེད། དབྱིག་ཉེན[64]། འཕགས་པ་རྣམ་གྲོལ་སྡེ། སོ་སོ་ (སོ་) སྐྱི་བོ་རྣམ་གྲོལ་སྡེ། མཆོག་གི་ (མཆོག་) སྡེ། དུལ་བའི་སྡེ། རྣམ་པར་སྣང་མཛད་བཟང་པོ། སེང་གི་ (སེང་གེ་) བཟང་པོ། རིན་ཆེན་ (རིནེ) བཟང་པོ། [3b6] གསེར་གླིང་པ། ཇོ་བོ་རྗེ། གཉིས་པ་ནི། སངས་རྒྱས། འཇམ་དཔལ། ཤན་ ཏ་ ཏི་བ[65]། ཨེ་མ་ཧྲ་རི། དཔའ་པོ་ (དཔའོ་) ཇོ་རྗེ། གསེར་གླིང་པ། ཇོ་བོ། སེམས་བསྐྱེད་པའི་རྒྱུད་པ་ནི། བུདྡྷ་སྨྲི་ཏི། ཨ་སམ་ག། བ་སུ་བྷཾ་དྷུ། ཛི་ན་ཀ་ར། མ་ཏྲ་ཀུ་སུ་ལུ། ཀུ་སུ་ [3b7] ལུ་ཆུང་བ། རྣམ[66]གི་རྟི། ཇོ་བོ་ཨ་ཏི་ཤ་ཨོ།།[67]

གསང་སྔགས་ཀྱི་རྒྱུད་པ་ལ། གསང་སྔགས་མཐའ་དག་གི་རྒྱུད་པ་ལུགས་གཉིས་ལས། དང་པོ་ནི། སློབ་དཔོན་ (སློན་) ཀླུ་སྒྲུབ[68]། ཨ་རྱ[69]དེ་བ། མ་ཏི་ཙ་ལ། ཏི་ལ་ཛོ་ཀི[70]། ཙན་ཏི་ལ[71]། མཚྭ་ [3b8] ཤི་བྷ་ཏྲ[72]: པོ་དྷི་བྷ་ཏྲ[73]། ཤན་ཏི་བ[74]། ཇོ་བོ་རྗེ། གསང་བ་འདུས་པའི་རྒྱུད་པ་ལུགས་གསུམ་ལས། དང་པོ་ནི། རྒྱལ་པོ་ཨིན་དྲ་བོ་དྷི[75]། ཀླུ་མོ་རྣལ་འབྱོར་མ། བྲམ་ཟེ་ཆེན་པོ་ས་ར་ཧ། ན་ག་ སྦུ་ན[76]། ཙན་དྲ་ཀི་རྟི[77]། བིརྦ་སྦི་

---

[60] Cf. *Rnam thar rgyas pa yongs grags*: 68: ཀཎྛ་པ་ལ་

[61] ཛྙཱ་

[62] Cf. *Rnam thar rgyas pa yongs grags*: 68: ཛྙཱ་ན་ཤྲཱི་མི་ཏྲ་ཆེན་པོ་

[63] སྒྲུབ་

[64] གཉེན

[65] ཤཱནྟི་པ

[66] ཧྣ་མ

[67] Cf. *Rnam thar rgyas pa yongs grags*: 77: འཕགས་པ་བྱམས་པ། ཐོགས་མེད། དབྱིག་གཉེན། བློ་གྲོས་བརྟན་པ། ཀུ་སུ་ལུ་ཆེ་ཆུང་། གསེར་གླིང་པ། ཇོ་བོ་རྗེ།

[68] སྒྲུབ་

[69] ཨརྱ་

[70] Cf. *Rnam thar rgyas pa yongs grags*: 68: ཏི་ལ་ཡོ་གི

[71] Cf. *Rnam thar rgyas pa yongs grags*: 68, 74: ཙཾ་པི་པ་ལ་ཏ། or ཙཱ་རི་པ་ལ།

[72] Cf. *Rnam thar rgyas pa yongs grags*: 68: མཚྭ་ཤྲཱི་བྷ་ཏྲ་

[73] Cf. *Rnam thar rgyas pa yongs grags*: 68: བོ་དྷི་བྷ་ཏྲ་

[74] Cf. *Rnam thar rgyas pa yongs grags*: 68: ཤཱནྟི་པ་

[75] Cf. *Rnam thar rgyas pa yongs grags*: 69: ཨིནྡྲ་བོ་དྷི་

[76] Cf. *Rnam thar rgyas pa yongs grags*: 79: ནཱ་གཱ་རྫུ་ན་

[77] Cf. *Rnam thar rgyas pa yongs grags*: 70: ཙནྡ་ཀཱི་རྟི

ཧྲི78། [4a1] ཙཽ་ཡི་པ་ཏ79། རོལ་པའི་རྡོ་རྗེ། ས་འགེབས་80ཞབས། ཤན་ཏི་པ81། ཇོ་བོ་རྗེ། གཉིས་པ་ནི། སློབ་དཔོན་ཀླུ་སྒྲུབ82། ཟླ་བ་གྲགས་པ། བི་དྱཱ་ཀོ་ཀི་ལ83། ཀུ་སུ་ལུ་ཆུང་བ། ཇོ་བོ། གསུམ་པ་ནི། སངས་རྒྱས་ཡེ་ཤེས་ཞབས84། པདྨ་ [4a2] སཾ་བྷ་བ85། རྒྱལ་པོ་ཨི་ནྡྲ་བྷོ་དྷི། ལེགས་སྨིན་ཀ་ར86། རོལ་པའི་རྡོ་རྗེ (རྡོ་) | ས་འགེབས་87ཞབས། ཤན་ཏི་པ། ཇོ་བོ།88

མ་རྒྱུད་ཀྱི་རྒྱུད་པ་ལ། ལུ་ཨི་པ89། ཊང་ཀི་པ90། ཊ་ལི་པ91། བྲམ་ཟེ་འཛེ་ཏ་རི92། ཇོ་བོ། ཧྲི་93ཡོག་གི་རྒྱུད་པ་ལ་ [4a3] བུད་དྷ་ཛྙཱ་ན94། བུདྡྷ་གུ་ཧྱེ95། ཀུ་སུ་ལུ་ཆེ་བ། ཀུ་སུ་ལུ་ཆུང་བ། ཇོ་བོ།96 <u>གཤིན་རྗེ་གཤེད་ཀྱི་</u> (གཤིན་རྗེའི་) རྒྱུད་པ་ལ། ཀ་མ་ལ་ཤི་ཏ97། ནག་པོ་ཞབས་ཆེན་པོ། ཇོ་བོ་རྗེ། གསང་སྔགས་<u>ཕ་རོལ་</u> (ཕྱོལ་) ཏུ་ཕྱིན་པ་གཉིས་ཀ འི98 རྒྱུད་པ་ནི། ནག་ སྦུ་99 [4a4] ན། ཨ་ཙུ་རེ་བ། ཙནྡྲ་ཀ་རྟི100། ཏི་ལ་ཛོ་ཀི101།

---

78 Cf. *Rnam thar rgyas pa yongs grags*: 70: ཧྲི་ཙ་མི་ཏི་

79 Cf. *Rnam thar rgyas pa yongs grags*: 70: ཙཽ་ཡི་པ་ལ་ཏ

80 + པའི་

81 Cf. *Rnam thar rgyas pa yongs grags*: 70: ཤཱནྟི་པ་

82 སྒྲུབ་

83 Cf. *Rnam thar rgyas pa yongs grags*: 70: རིག་པའི་ཁུ་བྱུག

84 Cf. *Rnam thar rgyas pa yongs grags*: 70: + ཆེན་པོ་

85 Cf. *Rnam thar rgyas pa yongs grags*: 70: པདྨ་བ་

86 Cf. *Rnam thar rgyas pa yongs grags*: 70: ལྷུམ་ལེགས་སྨིན་

87 + པའི་

88 Cf. *Rnam thar rgyas pa yongs grags*: 70: སངས་རྒྱས་ཡེ་ཤེས་ཞབས་ཆེན་པོ། པདྨ་བ། རྒྱལ་པོ་ཨི་ནྡྲ་བོ་དྷི། ལྷུམ་ལེགས་སྨིན། རྒྱལ་པོ་སྤྱི་བོ་སྐྱེས། འཇམ་དཔལ་བཤེས་གཉེན། སངས་རྒྱས་ཡེ་ཤེས། ཀཾ་པ་ལའི་ཞབས། རོལ་པའི་རྡོ་རྗེ། ས་འགེབས་པའི་ཞབས། ཤཱནྟི་པ། ཇོ་བོ་རྗེ།

89 Cf. *Rnam thar rgyas pa yongs grags*: 70: ལཱུའི་ས་

90 Cf. *Rnam thar rgyas pa yongs grags*: 70: འདང་གི་པ་

91 Cf. *Rnam thar rgyas pa yongs grags*: 70: ཏཱ་རི་ཀ་པ་

92 Cf. *Rnam thar rgyas pa yongs grags*: 70: ཛེ་ཏཱ་རི

93 Cf. *Rnam thar rgyas pa yongs grags*: 70: ཀྱི་

94 Cf. *Rnam thar rgyas pa yongs grags*: 70: སངས་རྒྱས་ཡེ་ཤེས་

95 Cf. *Rnam thar rgyas pa yongs grags*: 70: སངས་རྒྱས་ཞི་བ་

96 Cf. *Rnam thar rgyas pa yongs grags*: 70: སངས་རྒྱས་ཡེ་ཤེས། སངས་རྒྱས་ཞི་བ། སངས་རྒྱས་གསང་བ། ཀུ་སུ་ལུ་ཆེ་བ། ཀུ་སུ་ལུ་ཆུང་བ། ཇོ་བོ་རྗེ།

97 Cf. *Rnam thar rgyas pa yongs grags*: 70: ཀ་མ་ལ་རཀྴི་ཏ

98 ཀའི་

99 ཛྙ

100 ཀཱིརྟི་

101 Cf. *Rnam thar rgyas pa yongs grags*: 74: ཏི་ལོ་ཡོ་གི

བི་རྣཱ་གོ་ཀི་ལྦྱ། ཛྙཱ་[102]ན་བོ་དྷི། མཉྫུ་ཤྲཱི་ཕ་ལ། རད་ན་ཨ་ཀ་ར། ཤན་ཏི་བ། ཇོ་བོ།[103] གྲུབ་ ཕ་ ཐོབ་པའི་རྒྱུད་ ཕ་ ལུགས་གཉིས་ལས། མཉྫུ་ཤྲི་ཕ་ལ། ཤན་ཏི་བ། [4a5] ཇོ་བོ། གཉིས་པ་ནི། ཨ་ཙ་ཙྭ[104]། མ་ཏྲཱ་བཛྲ་པ་ནི[105]། པདྨ་བ། རྒྱལ་པོ་ཨིནྡྲ་བྷཱུ་ཏི། [illegible] ལྷུམ་ལེགས་སྐྱིན་ཀ་ར[106]། ཛྙཱ་[107]ན་བོ་དྷི། ཙོ་ཡི་པ་ཏ[108]། བཛྲ་བོ་དྷི། མཉྫུ་ཤྲི་བཛྲ། ཤན་ཏི་པ[109]། ཇོ་བོ་ཆེན་པོ།།

བྱིན་གྱིས་ [4a6] བརླབས་པའི་རྒྱུད་པ་ལུགས་གཉིས་ལས། བཛྲ་ཧྲ་རི། ཕྲཛྙ་ཕ་ལ། ཛྙཱ་[110]ན་སིད་དྷི། ཏཾ་བྷི་བ། ཇོ་བོ།[111] གཉིས་པ་ནི། ཨ་ཙྭ།[112] བུདྡྷ་ཝྰ་ལིང་ཏ[113]། བུདྡྷ་ཛྙཱ་ན[114]། བུདྡྷ་ཤན་ཏི[115]། བུདྡྷ་གུ་ཧྱ[116]། ཀུ་སུ་ལུ་ཆེ་ཆུང་གཉིས: [4a7] ཇོ་བོ་ཆེན་པོ། གྲུབ་མཐའི་རྒྱུད་པ་ནི། མཉྫུ་ཤྲི། ཨ་བ་དྷུ་ཏི་བ། དྷི་པཾ་ཀ་ར[117]། ཤཱཀྱ་མི་ཏྲ[118]། རི་བོ་ཕ་ལ[119]། བཛྲ་ཧྲ་ཀི[120]། དགེ་སློང་བསོད་སྙོམས་པའི་ཞབས། ཁུ་སྦྱུག་ཞབས། ས་འགེབས་[121]ཞབས། [4a8] རད་ན་ཨ་ཀ་ར[122]། ཤན་ཏི་བ། ཇོ་བོ། གདམས་པ་སྣ་ཚོགས་པའི་རྒྱུད་ལུགས་གཉིས་ལ། དང་པོ་ནི། ཨ་ཙྭ་ནག་སྡུ་[123]ན། ཙན་ [illegible: ཏ] ཀི་ཏྲི། བི་རྣཱ་གོ་ཀཱི་ལྦྱ། ཨ་བ་དྷུ་ཏི་པ། གསེ་[124]གླིང་པ། ཇོ་བོ་རྗེ། གཉིས་པ་ནི། [4b1] སློབ་དཔོན་ཀླུ་

---

102 ཛྙཱ

103 Cf. *Rnam thar rgyas pa yongs grags*: 74: སྔགས་ཕ་རོལ་ཏུ་ཕྱིན་པ་གཉིས་ཀའི་བརྒྱུད་པ་ནི། སློབ་དཔོན་ཀླུ་སྒྲུབ་འཕགས་པ་ལྷ། བླ་བ་གྲགས་པ། ཏི་ལོ་ཡོ་གི རིག་པའི་ཁུ་བྱུག ཡེ་ཤེས་བྱང་ཆུབ། འཇམ་དཔལ་བཟང་པོ། རཏྣ་ཨཱ་ཀ་ར་ཤཱནྟི། ཨ་ཏི་ཤ་ཞེས་འབྱུང་། གཞན་ཡང་སློབ་དཔོན་ཀླུ་སྒྲུབ། ཨཱ་ཙ་དེ་བ། མ་ཏི་ཅི་ཏྲ། ཏི་ལོ་ཡོ་གི ཙ་ཏི་པ་ལ། མཉྫུ་ཤྲཱི་བྷ་དྲ། བོ་དྷི་བྷ་དྲ། ཤཱནྟི་པ། ཇོ་བོའོ།

104 ཨཱ་ཙཱ་ཙྭ་

105 Cf. *Rnam thar rgyas pa yongs grags*: 74: སློབ་དཔོན་ཆེན་པོ་ཕྱག་ན་རྡོ་རྗེ་

106 ལྷུམ་ལེགས་སྐྱིན་

107 ཛྙཱ

108 Cf. *Rnam thar rgyas pa yongs grags*: 68, 74: ཙོ་ཕི་པ་ལ་ཏ། or ཙའི་པ་ལ།

109 Cf. *Rnam thar rgyas pa yongs grags*: 74: ཤཱནྟི་པ་

110 ཛྙཱ

111 Cf. *Rnam thar rgyas pa yongs grags*: 74–76.

112 ཨཱ་ཙཱ་ཙྭ་

113 Cf. *Rnam thar rgyas pa yongs grags*: 76: སློབ་དཔོན་བུདྡྷ་པ་ལི་ཏ་

114 Cf. *Rnam thar rgyas pa yongs grags*: 76: སངས་རྒྱས་ཡེ་ཤེས་

115 Cf. *Rnam thar rgyas pa yongs grags*: 76: སངས་རྒྱས་ཞི་བ་

116 Cf. *Rnam thar rgyas pa yongs grags*: 76: སངས་རྒྱས་གསང་བ་

117 Cf. *Rnam thar rgyas pa yongs grags*: 78: མར་མེམཛད་བཟང་པོ་

118 Cf. *Rnam thar rgyas pa yongs grags*: 78: ཤཱཀྱ་བཤེས་གཉེན་

119 Cf. *Rnam thar rgyas pa yongs grags*: 78: རི་བོ་བཟང་པོ་

120 Cf. *Rnam thar rgyas pa yongs grags*: 78: རྡོ་རྗེ་མཁའ་འགྲོ་མ་

121 + པའི་

122 Cf. *Rnam thar rgyas pa yongs grags*: 78: རཏྣ་ཨཱ་ཀ་ར

123 སྡུ

124 གསེར་

གྲུབ[125]། འཕགས་པ་ལྷ། ཟླ་བ་གྲགས་པ། ཏི་ལ་ཡོ་གི། བློ་གྲོས་ (བློས་) ཡེ་ཤེས་བྱང་ཆུབ[126]། ཇོ་བོ།[127] དེ་རྣམས་རྒྱུད་པ་སོ་སོ་དང་སྦྱར་བའོ།།

རྩ་བའི་བླ་མ་ནི་འདི་རྣམས་ཡིན་ཏེ། གསེར་གླིང་པ། ཨ་བ་དྷུ་ཏི་པ། ཏཾ་བི་བ[128]། ཌོམྦྷི[129]ན་ [4b2] ཤྲཱི[130] ཆི་ ཧ། བྲམ་ཟེ་འཛེ་ཏ་རི[131]། ནག་པོ་ཞབས་ཆེན་པོ། ཀུ་སུ་ལུ་ཆུང་བ། ཀྵྨ་རཀྵི་ཏ། རཏྣ་ལ་གུ་པ་ཏ་བཛྲ། ན[132]རོ་པ། ཐྐ་མེད[133]ཨ་ཙ་ཙུ་ཆེན་པོ། བླ་མ་བསོད་སྙོམས་པ་ཆེན་པོ: རིག་པའི་ཁུ་བྱུག། དུ་ཏ་ར་ནག [4b3] པོ། པཎྜི་ཏ་མི་ཆེན་པོ: དག་གི་ (དགེ་) དབང་ཕྱུག་གྲགས་པ། མཁས་པ་ཆེན་པོ་ཧ་མཆོག། རདན་ཀིརྟི། གཤིན་ཆེན་ཛེ་བཤེད་ (གཤེནེད) ཀྱི་རྣལ་འབྱོར་པ། ཨ་བ་དྷུ་ཏི་པ་མངོན་པར་ཤེས་ཙན་ནེ་ (ཙནེ) །།

དེ་རྣམས་ཏེན[134]པའི་ཕྱིར་ལུས་ ངང་ སྲོག་ལ་ལྟོས་པ་མ་ [4b4] མཛད་པར་རྒྱ་གར་གྱི་ཡུལ་དབུས་ཆེན་པོ་དང་། ཤར་ཕྱོགས་དང་། ལྷོ་དང་། ནུབ་དང་། ཁ་ཆེའི་ཡུལ་དང་། ཨུ་རྒྱན་གྱི་ཡུལ་དང་། གསེར་གླིང་དང་། ཟངས་གླིང་དང་། ནགས་གླིང་ལ་སོགས་པ་རྣམས་སུ་བྱོན་ནས་མཉེས་པར་མཛད་དེ། [4b5] ཡོན་ཏན་མ་ལུས་པར་རྫོགས[135]པར་མཛད། ཇོ་བོ་ཉིད་ཀྱང་སློབ་མ་ཀུན་ལ་ཁྱེད་ཀྱི[136]དཀའ་ལས་སྤྱད་མ་དགོས་པར་ཆོས་ཟབ་མོ་ཐོས་པ་ངོ་མཚར་ཆེ་ཡི། ངས་བླ་མ་དམ་པ་ཚོལ[137]བའི་ཆེད་དུ་རྒྱ་མཚོ་ཆེན་པོར (ཆེནོར) ཡ[illegible: ང] [4b6] ལན་གསུམ་ཞུགས་གསུང་། གཞན་ཡང་རང་བཞིན (རངཞི) གྱི་ རྣལ་འབྱོར་མ་དང་། ཡི་དམ་ཀྱི[138]ལྷ་ལ་དངོས་སམ (དངོསཾ) རྨི་ལམ་དུ་ཆོས་གསན་པ་ཡང་བསམ་གྱིས་མི་ཁྱབ་ཏེ་བརྗོད་ལས་འདས་སོ།།

དེ་ལྟར་བླ་མ་རྣམས་ལ་སྡེ་སྣོད་ཀྱི་ཆོས་མཐའ་ [4b7] དག་གི་དོན་མ་ལུས་པ་ཐུགས་སུ་ (ཐུཏསུ) ཆུད་པས་རིག་པའི་གནས་ལྔ་ལ་མཁས་པའི་ཕུལ་དུ་ཕྱིན་པས། ཕྱི་རོལ་པའི་པཎྜི་ཏ་གདུགས་བཅུ་གསུམ་ཕུབ་པ་ཅིག་དང་། བརྒྱད་ཕུབ་པ་ཅིག་དང་། ལྔ་ཕུབ་པ་གསུམ[139]སྨྲ་ཚོད

125 སླབ་

126 Cf. *Rnam thar rgyas pa yongs grags*: 78: མ་ཏི་ཤྲི་ར། ཛྙཱ་ན་བོ་དྷི།

127 : ?

128 Cf. *Rnam thar rgyas pa yongs grags*: 79: ཊཾ་བི་པ་

129 ཌོཾ་

130 ཤྲཱི་

131 Cf. *Rnam thar rgyas pa yongs grags*: 79: ཛེ་ཏཱ་རི

132 ནཱ་

133 Cf. *Rnam thar rgyas pa yongs grags*: 79: ཡང

134 བསྟེན་

135 རྫོགས་

136 ཀྱིས་

137 འཚོལ་

138 ཀྱི་

139 + །

[illegible: ཡ་] [4b8] མཁས་པའི་ཕྱུལ་དུ་སྐྱོལ་བ་ཡང་ཐམ་པར་མཛད་ནས་ནང་པ་སངས་རྒྱས་པའི་བསྟན་པ་ལ་བཙུད་ནས།. སངས་རྒྱས་པ་ཕལ་ཆེ་བའི་ཐེ་ཚོམ་ཀྱི་[140]དྲྭ་བ་སེལ་བའི་གནས་སུ་གྱུར་པ་མཛད་དོ།།

བཙུན་པའི་ཡོན་ཏན་ནི (ཡོན྄ི)། འདུལ་བ་ [5a1] ཕ་རོལ་ཏུ་ཕྱིན་པ་དང་། གསང་སྔགས་ཀྱི་སྡོམ་པ་དང་། དམ་ཚིག་མ་ལུས་པ་རྣམས་རང་རང་གི་ལུགས་དང་མི་འགལ་ཞིང་། གཅིག་གིས་གཅིག་ལ་མི་གནོད་པར་ཉམས་སུ་བཞེས་ལ། བླ་མ་དམ་པས་བྱིན་གྱིས་ (བྱིནིས་) བརླབས་པ་ [5a2] རང་གི་སྒྲུབ་པའི་འབྲས་བུ་ཡི་དམ་གྱི་ལྷ་དཔལ་དགྱེས་པ་རྡོ་རྗེ་དང་། འཇིག་རྟེན་ (འཇིྟེན་) དབང་ཕྱུག་དང་། རྗེ་བཙུན་མ་སྒྲོལ་མ་དང་། དམ་ཚིག་གསུམ་བཀོད་པའི་རྒྱལ་པོ་དང་། དཔལ་འཁོར་ལོ་ (འཁོཪ་) སྡོམ་པ་ལ་སོགས་དུ་མའི་ཞལ་ཡང་གཟིགས་པ། གསང་སྔགས་པ་ [5a3] ལྟར་ན་བསྐྱེད་པའི་རིམ་པ་ལ་བསྟན་པ་ཐོབ་པ། ཕ་རོལ་ཏུ་ཕྱིན་པའི་གཞུང་ལྟར་ན་སྤྲུལ་པའི་སྐུ་ལ་དངོས་སུ་ཆོས་གསན་ཅིང་། བདག་གཞན་ (བདགཞན་) རྗེ་[141]བའི་བྱང་ཆུབ་ཀྱི་སེམས་རིན་པོ་ཆེ་ཐུགས་ལ་འཁྲུངས་སྟེ། སྦྱོར་བའི་ལམ་གྱི་ཡེ་ཤེས་ [5a4] བརྙེས་པ་མདོར་ན་བསམ་གྱིས་མི་ཁྱབ་པའི་ཡེ་ཤེས་བླ་མ་རྗེ་བཙུན་ཆེན་པོ་དཔལ་ལྡན་ (དཔལྡན་) མར་མེ་མཛད་ཅེས་གྲགས་པའི་ཡོན་ཏན་ནི་ནམ་མཁའི་ (ནཾཁའི་) མཐའ་དང་འདྲ་བས། བདག་ཅག་གི་ (ཅགི་) ཚད་བཟུང་བར་ག་ལ་ནུས་ཀྱང་། རང་གི་ནུས་ [5a5] ཚོད་ལ་ཆེ་ལོང་སྨོས་པ་ཡིན་ནོ།།

(1–2–1–2–3) གསུམ་པ་བོད་དུ་ ༡ བྱོན་ཁ་ན། གནས་གང་ན་གཞན་དོན་མཛད་ཅིང་བཞུགས་པ་ནི། རྒྱལ་པོ་ཆེན་པོ་དྷརྨ་པ་[142]ལའི་ཐུགས་དམ་ (ཐུཾཏ་) ཆུ་བོ་སྒཱ་[143]གའི་དྲམ་[144]བི་ཀ་མ་ལ་ཤཱི་ལ་ཞེས་བྱ་བའི་ [5a6] གཙུག་ལག་ཁང་ན་པཎྜི་ཏ་ལྔ་བཅུ་རྩ་བདུན་གྱི་ནང་ནས། གཙུག་གི་ནོར་བུ་ལྟ་བུར་གྱུར་སྟེ། ཐམས་ཅད་ (ཐཾད་) ཀྱི་[145]ཆོས་ཀྱི་ཞུ་ས། ཐེ་ཚོམ་གྱི་དྲ་བ་གཅོད་ས་མཛད་ཅིང་གནས་བརྟན་རད་ན་ཨ་ཀ་ར་དང་། རྒྱལ་པོ་ན་ཡ་པ་ [5a7] ལའི་དགོས་[146]ཀྱི་མཆོད་གནས་མཛད་ཅིང་: ལྔེ་མིག་བཅོ་བརྒྱད་ཙམ་གྱི་བདག་མཛད་ཡིན་[147]བཞུགས་སོ། །དེ་དག་ནི་ཐར་པར་གཤེགས་པའི་ཆེ་བའི་ལོ་རྒྱུས་སོ།།

140 གྲི་

141 བརྗེ་

142 ཕཱ་

143 གང་

144 འགྲམ་

145 ཀྲིས་

146 སྒྲོས་

147 ཀྲིན་

(1–2–1–3) གསུམ་པ་ནི། བོད་ཀྱི་བསྟན་པ་ལ་ཕན་ཇི་ལྟར་ [5a8] གདགས་[148]པའི་ལོ་རྒྱུས་ལ་གསུམ་སྟེ། (1–2–1–3–1) བོད་དུ་འབྱོན་དགོས་པའི་རྒྱུ་མཚན་དང་། (1–2–1–3–2) བོད་ཀྱིས་ཇི་ལྟར་སྤྱན་དྲངས་པའི་ཚུལ་དང་། (1–2–1–3–3) བོད་དུ་བྱོན་ནས་གཞན་དོན་ཇི་ལྟར་མཛད་པ་དངོས་སོ།།

(1–2–1–3–1) དང་པོ། བོད་དུ་འབྱོན་དགོས་པའི་རྒྱུ་མཚན་ལ་གཉིས་སྟེ (༢) | [5b1][149] (1–2–1–3–1–1) བོད་དུ་ ཕྱིར་ སངས་རྒྱས་ཀྱི་བསྟན་པ་ལ་འཕེལ་འགྲིབ་ཇི་ལྟར་བྱུང་བ་དང་། (1–2–1–3–1–2) དུས་དེ་ཙ་ན་ཇི་ལྟར་ཡོད་པའོ།།

(1–2–1–3–1–1) དང་པོ་ནི། བོད་དུ་སངས་རྒྱས་ཀྱི་[150]ཇི་ལྟར་འཕེལ་བ་དང་། འགྲིབ་པའི་ཚུལ་ནི། དེ་ལ་དང་པོ་བོད་ན་མིའི་འགྲོ་བ་ཡེ་ནས་མེད་ [5b2] པར་གནོད་སྦྱིན་གྱི་[151]བདག་བྱས་ཏེ་གནོད་སྦྱིན་གྱི་ཡུལ་བདུད་འཁར་[152]ནག་པོ་ཟེར་བ་བྱུང་སྐད། དེའི་རྗེས་ལ་ཀླུ[illegible: ས་] བཟུང་ནས་ཀླུའི་ཡུལ་འབོད་ཀྲ་གླིང་དགུ་ཟེར་སྐད། དེའི་རྗེས་ལ་བདུད་དང་སྲིན་པོས་བཟུང་ནས་ལྷ་ [5b3] མ་ཡིན་གྱི་ཡུལ་དུ་གྲགས་སོ༔ དེའི་རྗེས་ལ་འཕགས་པ་སྤྱན་རས་གཟིགས་ཀྱི་སྤྲུལ་པ་མ་སངས་རུ་དགུ་བྱ་བས་བཟ[illegible: ང་] ནས། མ་སངས་ཡུལ་དུ་གྲགས། དེའི་རྗེས་ལ་སྟོད་མངའ་རིས་བསྐོར་[153]གསུམ་རྫིང་འདྲ་བ་ན། རི་དགས་[154] [5b4] དང་གཅན་ཟན་[155]གྱི་[156]བཟུང་། སྨད་མདོའ་ཁམས་སྒང་གསུམ་ཞིང་འདྲ་བ་ན་འདབ་ཆག་ (ཆུག་)[157]ཇ་[158]དང་གླང་པོ་ཆེས་བཟུང་། བར་ [illegible: ད]བུས་རྩ་[159]རུ་བཞི་ཡུར་བ་འདྲ་བ་ན། སྤྲེའུ་དང་བྲག་སྲིན་མོས་བཟུང་ཡོད་པའི་སྐབས་སུ། འཕགས་པ་སྤྱན་ [5b5] རས་གཟིགས་ཀྱི་སྤྲུལ་པ་ཏ་ལུ་མ་ཏྭ་ལ་སྟོམ་པ་ཐོག་ནས་བཏང་ནས་བྲག་སྲིན་མོ་ཁབ་ཏུ་བཞེས་ནས།[160] བོད་དུ་ [illegible: མི]འི་འགྲོ་བ་ཇི་ལྟར་སྤེལ་བའི་ལོ་རྒྱུས་ནི་གཞན་དུ་རྒྱས་པར་ཤེས་པར་བྱའོ།།

---

148 བཏགས་

149 The folio 5b has a damage in the center part.

150 + བསྟན་པ་

151 ཀྱིས་

152 མཁར་

153 སྐོར་

154 དྭགས་

155 གཟན་

156 ཀྱིས་

157 ཆགས་

158 བྱ་

159 གཙང་

160 ː ?

དེ་ནས་རྒྱལ་[161]སིལ་མ་ [5b6] བཞི་བཅུ་ཞེ་གཉིས་བྱུ་བ་དང༌། རྒྱལ་ཕྲན་ལྔ་བཅུ་རྩ་གཉིས་བྱུ་བས་བཟུང་ནས་ཡུལ་ཡར་པོ་ཁ་བརྒྱད་དུ་གྲགས་སྐད༌། ཐ་མར་ཧྲི་གཉའ་ཁྲི་བཙན་པོའི་སྲས་སུ་རྒྱལ་བཙན་པོས་དབང་བྱས་ནས༌། སྤུ་[162]རྒྱལ་བོད་ཀྱི་རྒྱལ་ཁམས་ [5b7] ཞེས་མིང་དུ་གྲགས་སོ (གྲགསོ) ། །དེ་ནས་གཉའ་ཁྲི་བཙན་པོ་ནས་རྒྱལ་རབས་བདུན་དུ་བོད་དུ་ཆོས་དང་རིག་པ་གང་ཡང་མ་ [illegible: བྱོན]། ཁྲི་གུམ་བཙན་པོ་བྱ་བའི་རིང་ལ་བོན་འགྱུར་སྟེ[163]། དོན་ལ་ཆོས་འབྱོན་པའི་སྔ་ལྟས་ཡིན་ཟེར་ [5b8] བར་གདའ། དེ་ནས་རྒྱལ་རབས་བཅུ་དྲུག་ཙམ་དུ་ཆོས་མ་བྱོན། དེ་ནས་ལྷ་མཐོའ་དོ་རི་སྙན་ཤལ་[164]གྱི་རིང་ལ་དམ་ [illegible: པའི་] ཆོས་ཀྱི་དབུ་བརྙེས་ཀྱང་ཆོས་དང་བོན་དུ་དོ་ མ་ ཤེས་སྟེ། དཔྱེད་[165]མི་རབས་ +ལྔ་ ན་འདིའི་དོ་ཤེས་པ་འོང་གི་གསུང་ [6a1] ནས་སྤྲུལ་ པའི་ རྒྱལ་པོ་སྲོང་བཙན་བསྒམ་[166]པོ་ལུང་བསྟན། དེ་ནས་རྒྱལ་རབས་ལྔ་ན་སྤྲུལ་པའི་རྒྱལ་པོ་ (རྒྱལོ) སྲོང་བཙན་བསྒམ་[167]པོ་བྱོན་སྟེ། རས་འཕྲུལ་སྣང་ལ་སོགས་པའི་གཙུག་ལག་ཁང་མང་པོ་བཞེངས། ཇོ་བོ་ཤཀྱ་[168] [illegible: མུ་ནེ་] [6a2] སྤྱན་དྲངས་སྟེ། ཆོས་ཤས་གཅིག་ཡང་བསྒྱུར་དགེ་འདུན་གྱི་རྟེན་ནི་ (རྟེནི) མ་མཆིས་སོ (མཆིསོ) ། །དེ་ནས་མི་རབས་གསུམ་ན་སྤྲུལ་པའི་རྒྱལ་པོ་ཁྲི་སྲོང་ལྡེ་བཙན་བྱོན་ནས། བསམ་ཡས་ལ་སོགས་པའི་གཙུག་ལག་ཁང་མང་པོ་བཞེངས། ཆོས་བསམ་ [6a3] གྱིས་མི་ཁྱབ་པ་མང་པོ་བསྒྱུར། སློབ་དཔོན་བོ་དྷི་སཏྭ་དང་། སློབ་དཔོན་པདྨ་འབྱུང་གནས་ལ་སོགས་པའི་པཎྜི་ཏ་[169]བསམ་གྱིས་མི་ཁྱབ་པ་སྤྱན་དྲངས། དང་པོ་སད་པའི་མི་དྲུག་རབ་ཏུ་བྱུང་། དེ་ནས་ལྷ་བརྒྱ་ཙམ་རབ་ཏུ་བྱུང་སྟེ༔ [6a4] བསྟན་པ་རྒྱས་པར་མཛད། དེ་ནས་རྒྱལ་རབས་གཉིས་ན་སྤྲུལ་པའི་རྒྱལ་པོ་རལ་པ་ཅན་བྱོན་ཏེ་དམ་པའི་ཆོས་སྐད་གསར་ཆད་[170]ཀྱི་ཏན་[171]ལ་ཕབ། འོན་[172]ལྷུང་[173]རྡོ་དང་། ཐད་དམ་པའི་ལྷ་ཁང་ལ་སོགས་པ་བཞེངས། །དེ་ནས་ [6a5] རྒྱལ་པོ་དེའི་ཙུང་[174]པོ་དར་མའི་ཐུགས་སུ་འདྲེ་ཞུགས་ནས་བསྟན་པ་ནག་པོར་བྱས་པས་ལྷ་ལུང་དཔལ་གྱི་རྡོ་རྗེས་རྒྱལ་པོ་བཀྲོངས་སྟེ་ལོ་ཉིད་རྒྱ་ནག་རི་བོ་རྩེ་ལྔ་ལ་གཤེགས་སྟེ་སྐད། བར་སྐབས་དེར་དཔལ་ཆུ་བོ་རིའི་ [6a6] སྒོམ་

---

161 + ཕྲན་

162 སྤུ་

163 ཏེ་

164 Cf. *Bu ston chos 'byung*: 181: ལྷ་ཐོ་ཐོ་རི་གཉན་བཙན་

165 ལྔ་

166 སྒམ་

167 སྒམ་

168 ཤཱཀྱ་

169 པཎྜི་ཏ་

170 བཅད་

171 གཏན་

172 འུ་

173 ཤང་

174 གཙུང་

གྲ་[175]ནས། གཙང་རབ་གསལ། གཡོར་དགེ་འབྱུང་[176]། སྨ་བན་ཤཀྱ་མུ་ནེ་[177]གསུམ་གྱིས་འདུལ་བ་གྲེའུ་[178]རྒྱབ་གཅིག་བསྐལ་[179]ནས། མདོ་སྨད་དུ་བྲོས་པས། བྱང་ཆུབ་སེམས་དཔའི་སྤྲུལ་པ་ལས་སད་པའི་གང་ཟག [6a7] བླ་ཆེན་པོ་མུ་ཟི་[180]དགོངས་པ་རབ་གསལ་དང་འབྲལ་[181]། [illegible] རབ་ཏུ་བྱུང་ནས། ཏ་ཤང་གཉིས་ལ་ཁ་སྐོང་བཅོལ་ནས་འཐ་[182]འཁོབ་ཀྱི་ཆོས་གའི་ལུགས་སུ་ (ལུཊ་སུ་) བསྙེན་རྫོགས་མཛད་དེ། དན་ཏིག་[183]ཤེལ་གྱི་ལྷ་ཁང་དུ་ དགོན་པར་ བཞུགས་ [6a8] ནས་འགྲོ་དོན་མཛད༔ བླ་གོང་ཡེ་ཤེས་གཡུང་དྲུང་[184]། སྤུབས་སབས་ཤི་[185]། གྲུམ་ཤིང་གླག་ཅན་[186]གསུམ་གྱིས་རབ་ཏུ་བྱུང་ནས། ཕོང་གསུམ་གྱིས་མདོ་ཁམས་སུ་རབ་ཏུ་བྱུང་བ་མང་པོ་སྤེལ་ནས་བཞུགས་པའི་སྐབས་སུ་ [6b1] བོད་ནས་སད་མི་མི་དྲུག་གིས་ (དྲུགིས་) བྱོན་ཏེ། དབུས་ནས་ཐ་བཙུན་ཡེ་ཤེས་བློ་གྲོས་[187]། རག་ཤི་ཚུལ་ཁྲིམས་ (ཀྲིམས་) རྒྱལ་བ་[188]། ཀླུ་མེས་ཚུལ་ཁྲིམས། [illegible] འབྲིང་ཡེ་ཤེས་སྙིང་པོ་[189]། བཙང་[190] ནམ་ལ་།[191] སྟོན་རྡོ་རྗེ་དབང་ཕྱུག། ཚོང་བཙུན་ཡེ་ཤེས་སེང་གེ༔ དེ་ལྟར་མི་དྲུག་གིས།[192] [6b2] སྡོམ་པ་མནོས་ནས་བྱོན་པས། དབུས་རྩང་[193]དུ་མཁན་རྒྱུད་བརྩུགས་[194]སྟེ། ཐ་[195]། ཚོ། རག་ཚོ།

---

175 གྲུ་

176 Cf. *Bu ston chos 'byung*: 193: གཡོ་དགེ་འབྱུང་

177 Cf. *Bu ston chos 'byung*: 193: དམར་ཤཱཀྱ་མུ་ནི་

178 དྲེའུ་

179 བཀལ་

180 Cf. *Bu ston chos 'byung*: 193: གཟུ་

181 མཛལ

182 མཐའ་

183 Cf. *Bu ston chos 'byung*: 193: ཏན་ཏིག་

184 Cf. *Gsal ba'i sgron me*: 265b5: སྦ་གོང་ཡེ་ཤེས་གཡུང་དྲུང་

185 ?

186 Cf. *Gsal ba'i sgron me*: 265b5: གྲུམ་ཡེ་ཤེས་རྒྱལ་མཚན་

187 Cf. *Bu ston chos 'byung*: 194: སྦ་ཚུལ་ཁྲིམས་བློ་གྲོས

188 Cf. *Bu ston chos 'byung*: 194: རག་ཤི་ཚུལ་ཁྲིམས་འབྱུང་གནས

189 Cf. *Bu ston chos 'byung*: 194: འབྲིང་ཡེ་ཤེས་ཡོན་ཏན

190 གཙང་

191 ལོ་

192 གིས་

193 གཙང་

194 བཙུགས་

195 སྦ

ཀླུ་མེས། འབྲིང་ཚོ། རྩང[196]དུ་ལོ་ཆ། ཚོང་ཚོ་ཞེས་པའི་བཙུན་པ་མང་པོ་བྱོན་ནས་གཙུག་ལག་ཁང་ མང པོ་བཞེངས་སོ། [6b3] དེ་དག་ནི་བོད་དུ་སྤྱིར་སངས་རྒྱས་ཀྱི་བསྟན་པ་ལ་འཕེལ་འགྲིབ་ཇི་ལྟར་བྱུང་བའི་ལོ་རྒྱུས་ཙམ་མོ (ཙམོ) ||

(1–2–1–3–1–2) གཉིས་པ་དུས་དེ་ཙ་ན་ཇི་ལྟར་ཡོད་པ་ནི། མཁན་རྒྱུད[197]འཛིན་པ་དང༌། རབ་ཏུ་བྱུང་བའི་གཟུགས་བརྙན་མང་དུ་ཡོད་ཀྱང༌། [6b4] ཐེག་པ་ཆེ་ཆུང་གི་ཆོས་ཀྱི་དགོངས་པ་མ་ལོན་པས། ལག་ལེན་ལ་སོགས་པ་ལོག་པར་བྱེད་པ་དང༌། རང་བཟོ་དང༌། གཟུ་ལུམས་སུ (ལུཾསུ) སྤྱོད་ལ། རྒྱ་གར་ནས་ཀྱང་ཨ་ཙ་ར་གསེར་འདོད་ཁ་ཡར་བྱུང་ནས་ཆོས་ [6b5] གར་བདེ་བདེ་བྱས་པས། དེར་སྔགས་ལ་བརྟེན་ནས་འདུལ་བ་ཙ་ཕྱི། འདུལ་བ་བརྟེན་ནས་སྔགས་ཙ་ཕྱི། སངས་རྒྱས་ཀྱི་བསྟན་པ་སྐམ་ཐོག་འོག་གི (འོགི) ཉིམ་ལྟར་བྲ[illegible]ཤིག་གི (ཤིགི) བ་གཅིག་ལས་མེད་དོ (མེདོ) | |དེ་དག་ནི་དུས་དེ་ཙ་ན་ཇི་ལྟར [6b6] ཡོད་པའི་ལོ་རྒྱུས་ཟུར་ཙམ་མོ||

དེ་ལྟར་བོད་དུ་བསྟན་པའི་ཕེལ[198]འགྲིབ་དུ་མ་བྱུང་ཞིང༌། སྐབས་དེ་ན་འགྲིབས་པ་ཡང་མ་ཡིན། མ་འགྲིབས་པ་མ་ཡིན་པ་དེར་ཡོད་པས་ན། | དཔལ་ལྡན་ཨ་ཏི [6b7] ཤ་བོད་དུ་འབྱོན་དགོས་པའི་རྒྱུ་མཚན་དང་པོ་དེ་ཡིན་ནོ||

(1–2–1–3–2) གཉིས་པ་བོད་ཀྱི[199]ཇི་ལྟར་སྤྱན་དྲངས་པའི་ཚུལ་ལ་གསུམ་སྟེ། (1–2–1–3–2–1) རྒྱལ་པོ་གང་གིས་བདག་རྐྱེན་མཛད་པ་དང༌། (1–2–1–3–2–2) ལོ་ཙྪ་གང་གིས་སྤྱན་དྲངས་པ་དང༌། (1–2–1–3–2–3) ཤུལ[200]ལམ (ཤུལཾ) དུ་གང[201] [6b8] དོན་མཛད་པའི་རིམ་པའོ།

(1–2–1–3–2–1) དང་པོ་རྒྱལ་པོ་གང་གིས་བདག་རྐྱེན་མཛད་པ་ནི། རྒྱལ་པོ་མངའ་བདག་རལ་པ་ཅན་ནས་མི་རབས་དྲུག་ན། མངའ་རིས་སུ (རིསུ) ལྷ་བླ་མ་ཡེ་ཤེས་འོད་ཅེས་བྱ་བ [7a1] བྱུང་སྟེ། རྒྱལ་པོ་དེ་ནི་འཛམ་དཔལ་རྩ་བའི་རྒྱུད་དང༌། ལྷ་མོ་དྲི་མ་མེད [illegible: པའི] རྒྱུད་ལས་ལུང་བསྟན་པའོ། |རྒྱལ་པོ་དེས་ཇོ་བོ་སྤྱན་འདྲེན་པའི་ཆེད་དུ་བཀའ[202]ལས་དཔག་ཏུ་མེད་པ་སྤྱད་པ་ལས། ལོ་ཙྪ་བ་དང [7a2] གསེར

196 གཙང་

197 བརྒྱུད་

198 འཕེལ་

199 ཀྱིས་

200 བཤུལ་

201 + གཞན་

202 དཀའ་

ཕལ་ཆེ་བ་བརླག་ཅིང་སྤྱན་མ་འགྲེངས[203]། སྤྱིར་ནི་བསྟན་པའི་སྒོ་བ་མང་དུ་མཛད། ཕྱིས་ཁོང་རང་གསེར་བསྒྲུབ་དུ་བྱོན་པས་གར་ལོག་གི་ (ལོགི་) རྒྱལ་པོས་བརྩོན[204]་དུ་བཟུང་། ལྷ་བླ་མ་བས་བསླུ་བར་བཞེད་ [7a3] པ་མ་ལྷུས[205]པར་གར་ལོག་གི་རྒྱལ་པོའི་ཡུལ་དུ་དཀོན་མཆོག་གསུམ་ (དཀོགསུཾ་) གྱི་སྐྱབས་དང་བཅས་བཞིན་དུ་འདས་སོ (འདསོ) ། །དེ་ནས་ལྷ་བླ་མ་བ་བྱང་ཆུབ་འོད་ཀྱི[206]་བདག་རྐྱེན་མཛད་དེ། སྤྱན་འདྲེན་པའི་ཕྱིར་དཀའ་བ་དཔག་ཏུ་མེད་པ་སྤྱད་དོ (སྤྱདོ) ། ། [7a4] དེ་དག་ནི་རྒྱལ་པོ་གང་གིས་བདག་རྐྱེན་མཛད་པའོ།།

(1–2–1–3–2–2) གཉིས་པ་ཕོ་ཉ་གང་གིས་སྤྱན་དྲངས་པ་ནི། ལོ་ཙྪ་བ་ནག་ཚོ་ཚུལ་ཁྲིམས་རྒྱལ་བས་སྤྱན་དྲངས་ཏེ། ལྷ་བླ་མ་བས་གསེར་ལིང་བ་ཆེན་པོ་གཅིག་གི[207]་སྣ་དྲངས་པའི་ [7a5] གསེར་མང་དུ་སྣྲངས[208]་ནས། འཁོར་ལྔ་དང་བཅས་སྟེ་ཧྲི་ཀ་མ་ལ་ཤྲཱི་ལའི་གཙུག་ལག་ཁང་ ཏུ་ བྱོན། ལོ་ཙྪ་བ་རྒྱ་བརྩོན་འགྲུས་ (བརྩོྂས་) སེང་གེ་དེ་ན་བཞུགས་པས་ཀུང་རོགས་མཛད་ནས: ཇོ་བོ་ལ་དབུ་ཙྪས་ན་མཇལ་[illegible: གྱུ་] [7a6] གང་བ་གཅིག་ཡོད་པ་དེའི་སྟེང་དུ་གསེར་ལིང་བ་དེ། དབུས་སུ་ (དབུསུ) བཞག། གསེར་སིལ་མ་དེ་རྣམས་མཐའ་མར་ཚོམ་བུ་བཀོད་ནས་ཕུལ་ནས། བོད་ལ་ཐུགས་རྗེས་ (ཐྱེས་) བཟུང་ནས་འབྱོན་པར་ཞུ་ཞུས་པས། བོད་ཀྱི་རྒྱལ་པོ་ [7a7] དེས་ངར་གདན་འདྲེན་པའི་ཕྱིར་བཀའ[209]ལས་མང་པོ་བྱས། ཁོའི་མི་དང་གསེར་མང་པོ་ ཡང་ གྲོན: རྒྱལ་པོ་དེ་ལ་ཡང་ང་ངོ་གནོང་བར་ཡོད་དེ་ (ཡོདེ) འོན་ཀྱང་ངས་བརྟག་པ་གཅིག་བྱའི། དེའི་བར་ +ཏུ་ གསེར་ཚོགས་ཀྱིས་གསུང་: [7a8] དེ་ནས་ཇོ་བོས་དེ་ནུབ་རྗེ་བཙུན་མ་སྒྲོལ་མ་ལ་གསོལ་བ་འདི་ལྟར་བཏབ་སྐད། བདག་གི་བོད་དུ་ཅིན[210]ན་སངས་རྒྱས་ཀྱི་བསྟན་པ་ལ་ཕན་ཐོགས་སམ་མི་ཐོགས། རྒྱལ་པོ་བྱང་ཆུབ་སེམས་དཔའི་ཐུགས་དགོངས་སྐོང་སམ་མི་སྐོང་། [7b1] རང་གི་ཚེ་སྲོག་གི་ (སྲོགི) བར་ཆད་དུ་འགྱུར་རམ་ (འགྱུརཾ་) མི་འགྱུར། ཞེས་གསོལ་བ་བཏབ་པས: སྒྲོལ་མའི་ཞལ་ནས། ལྷ་ཕྱོགས་སུ་ཁྱེར་གྱི་གྲོང་དུ་སོང་དང་། དེ་ནས་ལུང་བསྟོན[211]པ་གཅིག་འོང་གི་གསུང་། སང་ནང་པར་སུ་ཁྱེར་དུ་ [7b2] བྱོན་ནས་གྲོང་གི་དབུས་སུ་ལྷ་ཁང་གཅིག་འདུག་པའི་ནང་དུ་མཇལ་ ཤུལ་ ནས་གསོལ་བ་འདེབས་ཞིང་བཞུགས་སྐད། དེ་ཙ་ན་རྣལ་འབྱོར་མ་རལ་པ་ས་ལ་ཁེད་པ་ཅིག་བྱུང་། དེ་ལ་སྔར་བཞིན་གསོལ་བ་བཏབ་པས: རྣལ་འབྱོར་མའི་ [7b3] ཞལ་ནས། ཁྱོད་ལུས་དང་། སྲོག་ལ་མི་ལྟ་བར་བོད་དུ་སོང་དང་། སངས་རྒྱས་ གྱི་ བསྟན་པ་ལ་ཕན་ཐོགས་རྒྱས་པར་བྱེད་ཅིང་རྒྱལ་པོ་བྱང་ཆུབ་སེམས་དཔའི་ (སེཾདའི་) ཐུགས་དགོངས་ཀྱང་

203 རྫངས་

204 བརྩོན་

205 བསླུས་

206 ཀྱིས་

207 གིས་

208 དྲངས་

209 དཀའ་

210 ཕྱིན་

211 སྟོན་

ཟློགས་[212]པར་འགྱུར་རོ། །ཁྱད་པར་དུ་ཨུ་པ་སི་ཀ་གཅིག་དང་འཇལ་[213]ནས་དེ་ལ་ [7b4] བརྟེན་ནས་ཕན་ཐོགས་པར་འགྱུར། །བོད་དུ་མ་བྱོན་ན་ལོ་དགུ་བཅུ་གོ་ལྔ་ཐུབ་ལ། བོད་དུ་བྱོན་ན་བདུན་བཅུ་རྩ་གསུམ་ལས་མི་ཐུབ་གནང་ངོ་ (གནངོ་) ། །དེའི་སྐབས་སུ་སངས་རྒྱས་ཀྱི་བསྟན་པ་ལ་ཕན་ཐོགས་ན་ཆེ་རང་[214]ཐུང་ཡང་ཐུང་སྙམ་པའི་ [7b5] ཐུགས་གོངས་[215]བྱུང་སྐད། དེ་ནས་ལོ་ཚྭ་བ་ལ་ངབོད་དུ་འགྲོ་ན་འདིའི་ཆོས་འཕྲོ་ཆོ་འདུལ་བ་དང་། གཏད་གཉེར་ལ་ཡུན་རིངས་[216]འགོར་པར་འདུག་པས་དེའི་ལོང་ཡོད་དམ་མེད་གསུང་། དེ་ཡོད་ལགས་ཞུས་པས༑ འོ་ན་ [7b6] ཁྱེད་རང་དེའི་བར་དུ་སློབ་གཉེར་གྱིས་གསུང་ནས། དེ་ནས་ཇོ་བོས་བོད་དུ་འབྱོན་པའི་ཕྱིས་[217]རྣམས་མཛད། སློབ་མ་རྣམས་ཀྱི་ཆོས་འཕྲོ་སྔན་[218]མ་ཆོ་ཐོན་པར་མཛད། །ཕྱི་མའི་ཕྲོ་[219]མ་བཙུགས། ལྡེ་མིག་བཅོ་ [7b7] བརྒྱད་པོ་རྣམས་ཀྱང་རིམས་[220]ཀྱིས་གཏད་གཉེར་མཛད་དེ། གཞན་དག་མིག་བྲིད་པའི་ཕྱིར་དཔལ་རྡོ་རྗེ་གདན་ལ་སོགས་པ་རྣམས་སུ་ (རྣམསུ་) ཕར་གཤེགས་ཚུར་གཤེགས་མཛད། །དེ་ལྟར་མ་མཛད་ན་རྒྱ་གར་བས་བོད་དུ་མི་གཏོང་བས་སོ། ། [7b8] དེ་ནས་དཔལ་རང་བྱུང་མཆོད་པ་ལ་འགྲོ་གསུང་བ་ལ། གནས་བརྟན་རད་ན་ཨ་ཀ་རས་ཆོར་ནས༑ ལོ་ཚྭ་བ་ལ་ཁྱེད་བོད་སློབ་གཉེར་ལ་མ་ཡོངས་[221]པར་ཇོ་བོ་སྤྱན་འདྲེན་པར་འོངས་ནས་འདུག [8a1] ཇོ་བོ་ཡང་ལྷག་པའི་བསམ་པས་བཞུད་པར་དགོངས་ནས་འདུག་སྟེ། ངས་བཅག་ན་ཚོགས་[222]སྟེ། ད་ཁྱེད་བོད་སྙིང་རྗེ་བས་ལོ་གསུམ་གཡར་གཞུག་གི་ (གཞུགི་) དེ་ནས་ཕྱིར་སྤྱན་དྲོངས་ཤིག མ་དྲངས་ན་ངང་དང་དམ་ཚ[223] [8a2] མེད་དོ་གསུང་༑ དེ་དག་ནི་ཕོ་ཉ་གང་གིས་སྤྱན་དྲངས་པའི་ལོ་རྒྱུས་ཟུར་ཙམ་མོ།[224]

(1–2–1–3–2–3) གསུམ་པ་ཤུལ་[225]ལམ་དུ་གཞན་དོན་མཛད་པའི་རིམ་པ་ནི༑ ཇོ་བོའི་ཞལ་ནས༑ ལོ་ཚྭ་བ་ལ་གསེར་དེ་ཁྱེར་ལ་ཤོག་གསུང་ (ཤོགསུང་) ༑ གསེར་དེ་རྣམས་ [8a3] བཞིར་དགོས་ནས་ཆ་གཅིག་རྡོ་རྗེ་གདན་དུ་མཆོད་པ་དངོས[226]། ཆ་གཅིག་བྷི་ཀ་མ་ལ་ཤཱི་ལའི་དགེ་

212 ཛློགས་

213 མཇལ་

214 རིང་

215 དགོངས་

216 རིང་

217 ཆས་

218 སྔོན་

219 འཕྲོ་

220 རིམ་

221 ཡོང་

222 ཚོག་

223 ཚིག་

224 ༎

225 བཤུལ་

226 བསྔོས

འདུན་ལ་དངོས[227]། ཆ་གཅིག་ཇོ་བོའི་བླ་མ་རྣམས་ལ་དངོས[228]། ཆ་གཅིག་རྒྱལ་པོ་ནི་ཡ་པ་ལ་གཏད་ནས་ཇོ་བོ་ཉིད་ཀྱི་བླ་མཆོར་དོང་[229]། [8a4] དེ་ནས་གཏད་གཉེར་ཐལ་ཆེ་བ་གནས་བརྟན་རད་ན་ཨ་ར་ལ་མཛད་ནས། བོད་དུ་བྱོན་ཏེ་དེའི་ཤུལ་[230]ལམ་དུ་རྒྱ་གར་མཐའ་འཁོབ་གྱི་[231]ཆོས་སློན་གཅིག་གིས་ལྷ་ཁང་བཞེངས་པའིས་ཚོག་མཛད། སུ་སྟེགས་ [8a5] ཀྱི་སྟོན་པ་བཙྡོ་ལྤ་བཏུལ། དེ་ནས་བལ་ཡུལ་དུ་བྱོན་ཏེ། ཤུལ་[232]ལམ་དུ་བྱུང་བའི་ནོར་སླས་[233]ཀྱིས་ཐང་ཐྱི་ཧྲས་ཞེས་པའི་གཙུག་ལག་ཁང་གཅིག་བཞེངས། དེ་ནས་རིམས་[234]ཀྱིས་བོད་དུ་བྱོན་ནས་སྤྱུ་རངས་འཐོ་ [8a6] འཕིང་[235]གི་གཙུག་ལག་ཁང་དུ་ཕྱགས་[236]ཕབ་པོ (ཕབ་) | |དེ་དག་ནི་ཤུལ་[237]ལམ་དུ་འགྲོ་བ་མང་པོའི་དོན་མཛད་པའི་ལོ་རྒྱུས་ཟུར་ཙམ་སོ། |དེ་རྣམས་ཀྱིས་ཇོ་བོ་བོད་དུ་སྤྱན་ཇི་ལྟར་དྲངས་པའི་ལོ་རྒྱུས་ཆེ་ལོང་སྟན་[238] [8a7] ཟིན་ཏོ:

(1-2-1-3-3) གསུམ་པ་བོད་དུ་བྱོན་ནས་གཞན་དོན་མཛད་པའི་རིམ་པ་དངོས་ལ་ [illegible] ལྔ་སྟེ། (1-2-1-3-3-1) སྔེ་སྟོད་ཀྱི་ཆོས་ [illegible: གང] དུ་གསུངས་པ་དང: (1-2-1-3-3-2) སློབ་མ་ཇི་ལྟ་བུ་རྣམས་བྱོན་པ་དང༔ (1-2-1-3-3-3) བོད་དུ་ལོ་དུ་བཞུགས་པ་དང༔ (1-2-1-3-3-4) ཐ་མ་ [8a8] གནས་གང་དུ་མྱ་ངན་ལས་འདའ་ཚུལ་བསྟན་པ་དང༔ (1-2-1-3-3-5) དེ་ དག་ གི་སྐབས་སུ་མིང་ཇི་སྐད་གྲགས་པའོ།།

(1-2-1-3-3-1) དང་པོ་བོད་དུ་ཆོས་གང་གསུངས་པ་ནི། ཇོ་བོས་སྤུ་རངས་མཐོའ་ལྡིང་གི་གཙུག་ལག་ཁང་དུ་ [8b1] ཕྱགས་[239]ཕབ་ནས༔ རྒྱལ་པོ་ལྷ་བླ་མ་བས་ཞུ་བ་མཛད་ནས། བོད་ཀྱི་རྒྱལ་ཁམས་འདིར་ཆོས་ཟབ་ [illegible] པོ་དང༔ མཆོར་མཆོར་པོ་ལས་ཀུང་ལས་རྒྱུ་འབྲས་ཀྱི་ཆོས་ཀྱིས་བསྐྱང་བར་ཞུ་ཞེས་པ་དང༔ སྔེ་སྟོད་ [8b2] མཐའ་དག་གི་དོན་བསྡུས་པ་བླ་མ་ཉིད་ཀྱིས་སྐྱུ་ཉམས་སུ་ (ཉིསུ་) བཞེས་པའི་

---

227 བསྙོས

228 བསྙོས

229 དོར

230 བཤུལ་

231 ཀྱི་

232 བཤུལ་

233 རྫས་

234 རིམ་

235 Cf. *Gsal ba'i sgron me*: མཐོ་ལྡིང་།

236 ཕྱག་

237 བཤུལ་

238 བསྟན་

239 ཕྱག་

བསྟན་ཆོས་གཅིག་བརྩམ་པར་ཞུ་ཞེས་པ་དང་། གསང་བ་འདུས་པའི་ལྷ་བཅུ་དགུའི་གཙོ་བོ་འཇིག་རྟེན་དབང་ཕྱུག་གིས་ (ཕྱུགིས་) མཛད་པའི་བསྒྲུབ་[240]ཐབས་གཅིག་ཞུ་ཞེས་ [8b3] པ་དང་། གཞན་ཡང་བོད་ཀྱི་ལོག་པར་རྟོགས་[241]པ་ མཐའ་དག་ ཇི་ལྟར་ཡོད་པ་རྣམས་ཇོ་བོའི་སྤྱན་དུ་ཞུས་པས། ཇོ་བོའི་ཞལ་ནས། ཆོས་ལ་ ལ་ ལས་རྒྱུ་འབྲས་ལས་ཟབ་པ་ཡེ་མེད་སྐད། ལས་རྒྱུ་འབྲས་ལས་བརྩམས་ [8b4] པའི་ཆོས་མང་དུ་གསུངས། བོད་ཀྱི་ལོག་པར་རྟོག་པ་མཐའ་དག་གི་གཉེན་པོར་གཞུང་བྱང་ཆུབ་ལམ་ཀྱི་[242]སྒྲོན་མ་གསུངས (སུ) ། དེའི་སྐོག་[243]ཆོས་སུ་ (ཆོསུ་) ལམ་ཀྱི་[244]རིམ་ པ་ གནང་། ལྷ་བླ་མ་བ་ལ་གསང་བ་འདུས་པའི་དཀྱིལ་འཁོར་ (དཀྱིར་) དུ་དབང་བསྐུར། [8b5] དེའི་གཙོ་བོ་ (གཙོཾ) འཇིག་རྟེན་དབང་ཕྱུག་གིས་མཛད་པའི་བསྒྲུབ་[245]ཐབས་མཛད་ནས་གནང་། གཞན་ཡང་རྟེན་རབ་གནས་མེད་པ་ལ་རབ་གནས་མཛད། ཡོན་བསྔོ་བ་མེད་པ་ལ་བསྔོ་བ་མཛད། ཁྱིམ་པ་རྣམས་ [8b6] ཟ་ཕྱུག་དང་བསྙེན་གནས་ལ་བཀོད། རབ་ཏུ་བྱུང་བ་རྣམས་འདུལ་ཁྲིམས་ལ་བཀོད། སེམས་བསྐྱེད་ (སྐྱེཾདེ) དང་བསླབ་བྱ་ལ་བཀོད། བསྔགས་[246]པ་རྣམས་དབང་དང་དམ་ཚིག་ལ་བཀོད། མདོར་ན་སངས་རྒྱས་ཀྱི་བསྟན་པ་རིན་པོ་ཆེའི་ [8b7] གསོལ་[247]ཕྱིན་ཅི་ལོག་པ་ ལ་ བཀོད། བོད་ཀྱི་ཐེ་ཚོམ་ ཀྱི་[248] ནུ་བ་མ་ལུས་པ་གསལ་[249]ཏེ། ཕུ་རངས་སུ་ལོ་གཅིག་བཞུགས: དེ་ནས་གནས་སྐབས་དེར་གནས་རྟན་[250]རད་ན་ཨ་རའི་ཁོར་ཞག་ཐེམ་ནས་ཕྱིར་རྒྱ་གར་ལ་ [illegible: བཞུད།] [8b8] ཕྱིས་ཅིག་ཀྱང་མཛད་པའི་སྐབས་སུ། དགེ་བཤེས་སྟོན་པ་དང་འཛལ་[251]ནས་བོད་དབུས་རྩང་[252]གི་ས་ཆར་སྤྱན་དྲངས་ནས། གཙང་གི་ཉན་ཚོ་[253]གནས་དང་། ལ་བསྟོད་[254]དང་། བསམ་ཡས་དང་། ཐང་པོ་ཆེ་དང་། [illegible] [9a1] ཀྱི་ལྷ་ཁང་ཀ་རུ་དང་། སྙིའི་རྒྱ་ཕིབས་དང་། ར་ས་འཕྲུལ་སྣང་དང་། ཡེར་པ་དང་། ལན་པའི་སྤྱིལ་བུ་དང་། གཉེ་ཐང་[255]དང་། དེ་རྣམས་སུ་ (རྣཾསུ་) བཞུགས་སྐྱེ་གདུལ་བྱ་རྣམས་ལ་དམ་པའི་

---

240 སྒྲུབ་

241 རྟོག་

242 གྱི་

243 སྐོག་

244 གྱི་

245 སྒྲུབ་

246 སྔགས་

247 སྲོལ་

248 གྱི་

249 བསལ་

250 བརྟན་

251 མཇལ་

252 གཙང་

253 Cf. *Gsal ba'i sgron me*: 107b2: མཚོ་

254 སྟོད་

255 Cf. *Gsal ba'i sgron me*: སྙེ་ཐང་

ཆོས་སྡེ་སྣོད་རིན་པོ་ཆེ་རྣམ་པ་ [9a2] གཞུང་དང་། གདམས་ངག་མ་ལུས་པ་གང་ལ་གང་མཆམ་[256]པ་བསྟན་ཏེ། འགྲོ་བ་མཐའ་དག་དང་དངོས་བརྒྱུད་པས་མ་སྨིན་པ་རྣམས་སྨིན་པར་མཛད། སྨིན་པ་རྣམས་གྲོལ་ནས་མཐར་ཕྱིན་པར་མཛད་དོ། །དེ་དག་ནི་ [9a3] སྡེ་སྣོད་ཀྱི་ཆོས་གང་དང་གང་དུ་གསུངས་པའི་ལོ་རྒྱུས་ཟུར་ཙམ་མོ།།

(1–2–1–3–3–2) གཉིས་པ་སློབ་མ་ཧེ་ལྷ་བུ་ (ལྷུ་) རྣམས་བྱོན་པ་ནི། སྤྱིར་ཆོས་འཕྲེལ་ཡོད་པ་མང་དུ་བྱོན་མོད་ཀྱང་། ཡོངས་སུ་གྲགས་པའི་ཆེན་པོ་རྣམས་འདི་རྣམས་ལས། [9a4] མངའ་རིས་སུ་ལྷ་བླ་མ་བ་བྱང་ཆུབ་འོད། ལོ་ཆུང་བ་རིན་ཆེན་བཟང་པོ. ལོ་ཆུང་བ་བརྒྱ་[257]བརྩོན་འགྲུས་སེང་གེ། ལོ་ཆུང་བ་ནག་ཚོ་ཚུལ་ཁྲིམས་རྒྱལ་བ། ལོ་ཆུང་བ་དགེ་ བ་ བློ་གྲོས། ལོ་ཆུང་བ་ཤཱཀྱ་བློ་གྲོས། ཀར་སྟོན་ཆེ་ཆུང་གཉིས། བསྒོམ་[258] [9a5] ཆེན་གཞོན་ནུ་ (གཞོནུ) ཚུལ་ཁྲིམས། གནས་རྟན་[259]གསེར་བཟོའ་ལ་སོགས་པ་མང་དུ་བྱོན། བཙང་[260]སྟོད་ནས། ལེང་[261]མི་ལོ་ཆུང་བ། འབྲོག་མི་ལོ་ཆུང་བ་དང་། ཙང་[262]སྨད་ནས། འགར་དགེ་བ་དང་། ལོ་ཆུང་བ་འགོས་ཁུག་ [9a6] པ་ཧྲ་[263]ཙ་[264]གཉིས། དབུས་ནས་ཡོལ་ཆོས་ཀྱི་འབྱུང་གནས། ཡོལ་ཐོག་འབེབས། སྤྱིང་[265]ཁ་པ། བང་སྟོན་གནས་ཁངས་ཕུག་པ། ཞང་བཙུན་ཡེར་པ་བ། ཀ་བ་ཤཱཀྱ་དབང་ཕྱུག[266]། རྣལ་འབྱོར་ བ་ ཕྱག་ཁྲི་ [9a7] མཆོག། ལྟོགས་ཀྱི་རབ། ལྷ་བཙུན་པོ་དེ་ར་ཙ་འོད། འཁམས་[267]ནས་དགེ་བཤེས་ཕྱག་དར་སྟོན་པ། རྣལ་འབྱོར་ བ་ ཆེན་པོ། རྣལ་འབྱོར་ཀྱི་[268]དབང་ཕྱུག་དཔལ་ལྡན་དགོན་པ་བ། བྱམས་པའི་བློ་གྲོས. གང་དང་འདྲན་[269]བླ་མེད་ [9a8] པ་ནི: དབུས་ནས་ཕྱ་རོག་འབྲོམ་གསུམ་མོ། དེ་དག་ལ་སོགས་པ་བསམ་གྱིས་མི་ཁྱབ་པ་གཅིག་བྱོན་ཏེ། ཆེ་ལོང་ཙམ་བརྗོད་པ་ཡིན་ནོ། །དེ་དག་ནི་སློབ་མ་ཧེ་ལྷ་བུ་རྣམས་བྱོན་པའི་ལོ་རྒྱུས་ཟུར་ཙམ་མོ།།

---

256 འཚམ་

257 རྒྱ་

258 སྒོམ་

259 བརྟན་

260 གཙང་

261 གར་ ?

262 གཙང་

263 Cf. *Gsal ba'i sgron me*: 69b5: ཧྲས་

264 བཙས་

265 སྤྱིང་ ?

266 Cf. *Gsal ba'i sgron me*: 81b3: ཀླ་བ་ཤཱཀྱ་དབང་ཕྱུག

267 ཁམས་

268 གྱི་

269 འགྲན་

(1–2–1–3–3–3) [9b1] གསུམ་པ་བོད་དུ་ལོ་དུ་བཞུགས་པ་ནི༑ གུང[270]ལོ་དྲུག་བཅུ་རྩ་གཅིག་ཏའི་ལོ་ལ་བོད་དུ་བྱོན་སྟེ། ལོ་ཕྱུར་སོ་བཅུ་གཉིས་བོད་དུ་བཞུགས་སོ (བཞུགསོ) །[271] དེ་དག་ནི་ལོ་དུ་བཞུགས་པའོ།[272]

(1–2–1–3–3–4) བཞི་པ་གནས་གང་ན་མྱ་ངན་ལ་འདས་ [9b2] པ་ནི༑ གཉེའ་ཐང་དུ་གུང[273]ལོ་བདུན་བཅུ་རྩ་གསུམ་ཀྱི་[274]སྟེང་དུ་ཏའི་ལོ་དབྱུག་གུ་ (དབྱུགུ) ཟླ་བའི་ཚེས་བཙོ་བརྒྱད་ལ་མྱ་ངན་ལས་འདའ་བའི་ཚུལ་བསྟན་སྟེ༑ དགའ་ལྡན་དུ་མགོན་པོ་ (མགོཾན་) བྱམས་པའི་སྤྱན་མངར[275] [9b3] གཤེགས་སོ (གཤེཏསོ) : དེ་དག་ནི་འདས་པའི་ཚུལ་བསྟན་པའོ།།

(1–2–1–3–3–5) ལྔ་པ་དེ་དག་གི་སྐབས་སུ་མི་[276]ཇི་སྐད་གྲགས་པ་ནི། དང་པོ་མངའ་རིས་སུ་ལས་རྒྱུ་འབྲས་ཀྱི་ཆོས་མང་དུ་གསུངས་པས༑ ལས་རྒྱུ་འབྲས་པ་བྱ་བར་ [9b4] གྲགས༑ བར་དུ་གཙང་རོང་ལ་སོགས་པ་རྣམས་སུ་དབུས་རྩང[277]གི་མི་ཆེན་རྣམས་ལ་སེམས་བསྐྱེད་མཛད་ཅིང་། བྱང་ཆུབ་སེམས་ཀྱི་ཕན་ཡོན་ཁོ་ན་གསུངས་པས༑ བྱང་ཆུབ་སེམས་ཆོས་པར་གྲགས། །དེ་ནས་ [9b5] གཉེའ་ཐང་དུ་སྐྱབས་འགྲོའི་ཕན་ཡོན་མང་དུ་གསུངས་པས: སྐྱབས་འགྲོ་བར་གྲགས་སོ (གྲཏསོ) | །དེ་དག་ (དེག་) ནི་མིང་ཇི་སྐད་དུ་གྲགས་པའོ།།

དེ་རྣམས་ཀྱི་བོད་དུ་བྱོན་ནས་སངས་རྒྱས་ཀྱི་བསྟན་པ་ལ་ཕན་ཇི་ལྟར་ [9b6] གདགས་[278]པའི་ལོ་རྒྱུས་སོ། །དེ་ལྟར་དོན་གསུམ་གྱིས་རྣམ་སྦྱོང་བཞེངས་པའི་སྤྲུལ་འབབས་ +མཁན་ ཀྱི་[279]ཇོ་བོའི་ལོ་རྒྱུས་ཅུང་ཟད་བརྗོད་པའོ།།

---

270 དགུང་

271 །།

272 །།

273 དགུང་

274 གྱི་

275 སྔར་

276 མིང་

277 གཙང་

278 བཏགས་

279 གྱི་

(1–2–2) གཉིས་པ་སྤུས་གང་ལ་ཕབ་པ་དགེ་བཤེས་སྟོན་པའི་ལོ་རྒྱུས་ལ་བཞི་སྟེ (ང་སྟེ) | (1–2–2–1) [9b7] ཡུལ་གང་དུ་སྐུ་འཁྲུངས་པ་དང¦ (1–2–2–2) ཇོ་བོ་སེ་བཙུན་ལ་ཇི་ལྟར་བསྟེན་པ་དང¦ (1–2–2–3) འཕྲང་ཁ་བེར་ཆུང་དང་ཇི་ལྟར་འཇལ[280]བ་དང¦ (1–2–2–4) ཁྱད་པར་དུ་ཨ་ཏི་ཤ་ལ་ཇི་ལྟར་སྟེན[281]པའི་ལོ་རྒྱུས་སོ།།

(1–2–2–1) དང་པོ་ཡུ[illegible: ལ་] [9b8] གང་དུ་སྐུ་འཁྲུངས་པའི་ལོ་རྒྱུས་ལ་བཞི[282]སྟེ། (1–2–2–1–1) རིགས་དང་། (1–2–2–1–2) རུས་དང¦ (1–2–2–1–3) ཡབ་ཡུམ་དང¦ (1–2–2–1–4) མཚན་དང¦ (1–2–2–1–5) སྐུ་འཁྲུངས་པའི་ས་དངོས་སོ།།

(1–2–2–1–1) དང་པོ་རིགས་གང་ཡིན་པ་ནི: སྤྱིར་བོད་ལ་མི་རིགས་ཇེའུ་དང [9b9] ཁྱིང[283]པོ་གཉིས་ཡིན་པ་ལས¦ འདི་ནི་ཇེའུ་ཡི་རིགས་སོ། །ཇེའུ་ལ་ཡང¦ ལྟོང་དང་སྟོང་གཉིས་ཡོད་པ་ལས: སྟོང་གི་ཇེའུ་ལགས། །སྟོང་ལ་ཇེ་བཞི་ལོལ་བརྒྱད་ཡོད་པ་ལས། ཡི[284]གེ་སྟེ [illegible: མཛོ་] [10a1] ཇེ¦ གཙང་ཇེ¦ ཐོད་དཀར (ཐོད་ཀར) ཇེ¦ ཉག་ཉེ་ཐོམ་ཐོམ་ཇེ [illegible: ¦] ཅོག་ལ་རམ་པོ་ཆེའོ (པོའ)། | ལོལ་བརྒྱད་ལ། སྒྲོ་དང། ལ་གྲོ་གཉིས¦ སུ་རུ་དང་གནང་གཉིས¦ ཟ་ར་དང་ཟུ་ར་གཉིས¦ རམ་དང་གཡམ་པ་གཉིས་ [illegible] གསར་བ་ཡང་ཟེར། སྟེ¦ བརྒྱད་དོ (བརྒྱདོ) [illegible: ¦] དེའི་ནང་ནས་ [10a2] ཡི་གེ་སྟེ་མཛོ་ཇེ¦ དེ་ལ་ཕ་ལྔ་ཡོད་པ་ལས¦ ལྷང་ལྟོ་དང¦ [285][illegible: ལྷང་] ཟུར་འགོ་ ལྷང་ཁ[286]འཁོར¦ ལྷང་ལྷང་རྨའོ: དེ་ནང་ནས་ལྷང་ཁ་འཁོར་ཡིན་ནོ། འཁོར་རམ་སྟག་པོ་ཆེའི་སྤྱིལ་གྱི་བུ་གསུམ་ལས: དང་མི་དང་གཙང: ཐང་པ་རྩ [10a3] ར་སྨ་ལྟོ¦ རྣ་ཕྱུག་རྣ་པའོ། །དེའི་ནང [illegible] མཚན[287] [illegible: པ[288]] བཞེད¦ དེའི་ཆུང་རྒྱུད་སྟག་ཐུད་ཅེས་བྱའོ།།[289]

(1–2–2–1–2) གཉིས་པ་རུས་ནི་འཁོར་ཡིན་ནོ།

---

280 མཇལ་

281 བསྟེན་

282 ལྔ་

283 རྒྱལ་ ?

284 - ཡི་ ?

285 dot-line annotation mark

286 + །

287 ཚན་

288 Cf. *Gsal ba'i sgron me*: 84a6–84b1: སྟུ་བ་ ?

289 Cf. *Gsal ba'i sgron me*: 84a6–84b1: གདུང་རུས་ནི་ཇེའུ་རིགས་ཀྱི་ནང་ཚན་འཁོར། དེའི་ནང་ཚན་སྟུ་བ། དེའི་ནང་ནས་སྟག་གསུམ་ལགས།

(1–2–2–1–3) གསུམ་པ་ཡབ་ཡུམ་ནི་ཡབ་འཁོར་ལོ་སྡོམ་ཧེ་རུ་ཀ་ཤེན་[290]བྱ་བ་བོན་ཤིན་ཏུ་མཁས་པ་ལགས་ [10a4] སྐད¦ ཡུམ་ཁྲུ་འོད་བཟའ་ལན་གཅིག་[291]བྱ་བ་ལགས།

(1–2–2–1–4) བཞི་པ་ཡབ་ཡུམ་དེ་གཉིས་ ཀྱི་ སྲས་འབྲུག་གྲགས་ཅེས་བྱའོ།།

(1–2–2–1–5) ལྔ་པ་སྐུ་འཁྲུངས་པའི་ས་དངོས¦ གནམ་ཁྲེ་མ་ལུང་[292]དུ་ཤིང་ཕོ་འབྲུག་ལ་སྐུ་འཁྲུངས་ནས། གུང་[293]ལོ་བཅུ་བཞིའི་ (ངའི་) [10a5] བར་དུ་བཞུགས་སོ། །དེའི་བར་དུ་ཐང་ལྷས་བར་ཆད་བྱ་བར་བརྩམས་པར་གདའ¦ དེ་ཟའི་རྒྱལ་པོ་ཟུར་ཕུད་ལྔ་པ་ཡིན་ཟེར་བ་ལ¦ དར་[294]གཅིག་ན་ཁོང་གི་སློམ་འོག་ན་སྒྲུར ཕ་ ལྷ་བུའི་སྒོག་ཆགས་སུ་སྤྲུར་ནས་གནོད་པར་མ་ནུས་ [10a6] སྐད¦ དེའི་དུས་སུ་ཡུམ་དེ་འདས་ཡབ་དེས་མ་ཡར་གཅིག་བླངས¦ དེ་དང་ཅུང་ཟད་མ་མཐུན་པས། འདིར་འདིའི་སྡིག་རྐྱེན་བྱེད་པ་ལས་གཞན་དུ་འགྲོན་དགོངས་ནས¦ གུང་[295]ལོ་བཅོ་ལྔ་ལ་ཡབ་དང་འགྲོགས་ནས་ [10a7] གཞུ་གཉེ་མདོར་བྱོན¦ དེར་གཡུང་དྲུང་སྲས་[296]བྱ་བའི་བསྟུགས་[297]པ་གཅིག་ལ་ཡི་གེ་ལ་སོགས་པ་སློབ་གཉེར་མཛད་ཡིན་ལོ་གཉིས་བཞུགས་སོ། །དེ་དག་ནི་ཡུལ་གང་དུ་སྐུ་འཁྲུངས་པའོ།།

(1–2–2–2) གཉིས་ ཕ་ རྗེ་བོ་སེ་བཙུན་ལ་ཇི་ལྟར་སྟེན་[298] [10a8] པ་ནི། རྗེ་བོ་སེ་བཙུན་དབང་ཕྱུག་གཞོན་ནུ་སྐད་པ¦ གྲུམ་ཡེ་ཤེས་རྒྱལ་མཚན་ (རྒྱན་) ཀྱི་[299]མཁན་པུ་ཡིན་པ། སྡེ་སྣོད་ཀྱི་ཆོས་མང་དུ་མཁྱེན་པ¦ གྲུབ་པའི་ཡོན་ཏན་དུ་མ་དང་ལྡན་པ་བདག་གཞན་རྗེ་[300]བའི་བྱང་ཆུབ་[illegible: ཀྱི་] [10b1] སེམས་དང་ལྡན་པ་གཅིག¦ མཁོམས་[301]ཡུག་ཐང་ན་བཞུགས་པ་ལ། རྒྱ་གར་དུ་བཞུད་པར་དགོངས་ནས¦ བལ་ཡུལ་བར་དུ་བྱོན་པ་ལ¦ རྒྱ་གར་ ན་ ཁོང་རང་ལས་མཁས་པ་མེད་ཅིང¦ སྐུ་སྲོག་གི་བར་ཆད་དུ་སོང་དགོས་ [10b2] ནས¦ ཕྱིར་བྱོན་པའི་

---

[290] Cf. *Gsal ba'i sgron me*: 84a6: སྐུ་ག་ཤེན་ཡག་གཞེར་འཕེན་

[291] Cf. *Gsal ba'i sgron me*: 84a6: ཁྲུ་འོད་བཟའ་ལན་གཅིག་མ་

[292] Cf. *Gsal ba'i sgron me*: 84a6: སྟོད་ལུང་གི་ཕུ་རྟ་སྒྲེ་མོ་

[293] དགུང་

[294] དལ་

[295] དགུང་

[296] Cf. *Gsal ba'i sgron me*: 84b2: དགེ་བཤེས་གཡུང་ཆོས་དགོན་

[297] སྟུགས་

[298] བསྟེན་

[299] གྱི་

[300] བརྗེ་

[301] ཁམས་

གཤུལ་[302]ལམ་ཀྱི་[303]གཞུ་སྐྱེ་མོར་ཞལ་འཛལ[304]། དེའི་དུས་སུ་དགེ་བཤེས་སྟོན་པ་དེ། ཇོ་བོ་སེ་བཙུན་ལ་ཐུགས་དད་པ་འཁྲུངས་ནས།[305] ཕྱགས་[306]ཕྱི་ལ་འབྲིད་པར་ཞུས་པས། དབུ་རའི་ཕྱི་ལ་ཕྱིན་ན། [10b3] སེ་བཙུན་གྱིས་[307]མི་རྐུས་ཐེར་ནས་འོང་བས། སང་ཕོད་ཤོག་གསུང་། དེའི་ཕྱིར་ལོ་གུང་[308]ལོ་བཅུ་བདུན་ལ་བབ་པོ་ཚན་གཅིག་དང་འགྲོགས་ནས་[309]མཁམས་[310]སུ་བྱོན་ཏེ། ཡུག་ཐང་དུ། ཇོ་བོ་སེ་བཙུན་ཀྱི་[311]སྤྱན་མངར་[312]འཛལ་[313] [10b4] ཏེ། <u>དགེ་བསྙེན་</u> (དེགེན) ཀྱི་[314]སྡོམ་པ་མནོས། སྡེ་སྣོད་ཀྱི་ཆོས་མང་ གསན་པས། སེ་བཙུན་ཀྱི་[315]སྤྱན་མངར་[316]འགྲོམ་སྟོན་པ་བློ་ནོར་པོར་གྲགས། ཁུ་དང་རྔོག་གཉིས་ཀུང་ཁོང་གི་སློབ་མ་ཡིན་པར་གདའ། ཁུ་རྔོག་ [10b5] འགྲོམ་གསུམ་དུ་ཁོང་གི་སྤྱན་མངར་[317]གྲགས། ཁྱད་པར་དུ་དགེ་བཤེས་སྟོན་པ་དེ། བླ་མ་ལ་གུས་ཤིང་ཐུགས་ཀྱི་སྐྱིལ་[318]དང་མཁྱེན་པ་རྒྱ་མཚོ་ལྟ་བུར་ཟབ་ལ། སྐུ་ལུས་ཀྱི་སྟོབས་ཀུང་བསམ་གྱིས་མི་ཁྱབ་པ་མངའ་བས། [10b6] ཇོ་བོ་སེ་བཙུན་ཀྱི་[319]ནོར་སྣམས་[320]ཕྱི་ནང་བར་གསུམ་ཐམས་ཅད་ཀྱི་གཉེར་ཁ་དང་། འཕྲུལ་ཀྱི་[321]ཞབས་ཏོག་གང་དགོས་ཐམས་ཅད་མཛད་པས། སེ་བཙུན་ཐུགས་ཤིན་དུ་མཉེས་ནས། སློབ་མ་གཞན་གང་དང་ཡང་མི་སློམ་[10b7] པར་མཛད་དེ། ཆོས་དང་མན་ངག་མ་ལུས་པ་གནང་བ་ལགས། དེའི་དུས་སུ་པཎྜི་ཏ་སྨྲྀའི་ཚེར་མ་བྲ་བ་གཅིག་བྱོན་པ་ལས། དེས་སེ་བཙུན་གྱི་བླ་མཆོད་མཛད་པས། དགེ་བཤེས་སྟོན་པ་ལ་ལོ་ཙྪ་ [10b8] བསླབས: གཞན་ཡང་མན་ངག་མང་དུ་ཞུས། དགེ་བཤེས་སྟོན་པའི་

---

302 བཤུལ་

303 གྱི་

304 མཇལ་

305 : ?

306 ཕྱག་

307 གྱིས་

308 དགུང་

309 Cf. *Gsal ba'i sgron me*: 85a1: ཚོང་པ་དང་གྲགས་ཏེ་

310 ཁམས་

311 གྱི་

312 སྔར་

313 མཇལ་

314 གྱི་

315 གྱི་

316 སྔར་

317 སྔར་

318 དཀྱིལ་

319 གྱི་

320 རྫས་

321 གྱི་

ཞལ་ནས༔ ང་ +ལ་ བླ་མ་པཎྜི་ཏ་སྨྲའི་ཆོས་རམ་བྲ་བ་ཤིན་ཏུ་བཀའ་དྲིན་ཆེ༔ ཕྱི་ས་ ཇོ་བོ་དང་འཇལ་[322]བའི་དུས་ན་ལོ་རྩེ་ [illegible: གཞུག་མ་] [11a1] སློབ་མ་དགོས་གསུང་ (དགོསུང་) ། དེ་ལྟར་ཇོ་བོ་སེ་བཙུན་ཀྱི་[323]སྤྱན་མངར་[324]ལོ་ཉི་ཤུ་བཞུགས་སོ། །དེ་ནས་ཇོ་བོ་སེ་བཙུན་དེ་ལ་མངོན་ཤེས་མངའ་བས༔ དགེ་བཤེས་སྟོན་པ་ཇོ་བོ་དང་འཇལ་[325]ན་བསྟན་པ་ལ་ཕན་ པ་ དགོངས་ན[illegible: ས་] [11a2] ཕྱིད་དབུས་སུ་ཡབ་ལ་འཇལ་[326]འགྲོ་དགོས་པ་མེན་[327]ནམ་ (མེནཾ) གསུང་། དེའི་དུས་སུ་མངའ་རིས་སུ་ཇོ་བོ་རྗེ་སྐྱད་པའི་པཎྜི་མཁྱེན་པ་ནམ་མཁའ་དང་མཉམ་པ་གཅིག་བྱོན་ལོ་ཟེར་བའི་ཁ་སྐད་ (ཁསྐད) ཐོས་པས༔ ང་དབུས་སུ་འགྲོ་བའི་དུས་པཎྜི་ཏ་དང་ [11a3] འཇལ་[328]ན་ཆོས་ཞུ་བར་ཞུ་ཞུས་པས: དེ་ལྟར་མཛོད་གཅིག་གསུང་ནས: ཇོ་བོ་སེ་བཙུན་གྱིས་ཆོས་དཔེའ་རྟ་ཁལ་གཅིག་དང༔ འཁོར་གཉིས་དགོས་པའིམཐུན་རྐྱེན་ (པའི་ཐྱེན) མང་དུ་གནང་ནས་དབུས་སུ་བྱོན་ནོ་ (བྱོནོ) ། །དེ་དག་ནི་སེ་བཙུན་ [11a4] ལ་ཇི་ལྟར་སྟེན་[329]པའི་ལོ་རྒྱུས་ཟུར་ཙམ་སོ།།

(1–2–2–3) གསུམ་པ་འཕྲུང་ཁ་བེར་ཆུང་དང་ཇི་ལྟར་འཇལ་[330]བའི་ལོ་རྒྱུས་ནི༔ དེ་ལྟར་འཁམས་[331]ནས་དབུས་སུ་བྱོན་པའི་ཤུལ་[332]ལམ་དུ༔ སོག་ཆུ་ ཁ་ སླེབ་པའི་དུས་སུ༔ ཁང་པ་ཅིག་ན་ [11a5] འདུག་པས༔ དེར་བྱོན་ཙ་ན། དེ་ན་ཞང་འཕྲུང་ཁ་བེར་ཆུང་བེར་ཆེན་ཀྱི་[333] འདས་པའི་ འདབ་དང༔ སྲིད་གཙོད་པའི་སྟོན་མོ་བྱེད་ཀྱིན་འདུག་སྐད༔ དེར་འཕྲུང་ཁ་བར་[334]ཆུང་ན་རེ: ཕྱོད་ཆོས་གྲྭ་[335]ནས་འོངས་ [11a6] པའི་རིགས་གཅིག་འདུག་པས༔ དེ་ནས་ང་ལ་ཕྱག་གྱིས་གཅིག་[336]ཟེར༔ དགེ་བཤེས་སྟོན་པས་ཕྱག་ཕྱ་འབྱུགས་པ་འདྲ་བ་ཅིག་མཛད༔ དེ་ནས་དེ་ནུབ་དེར་བཞུགས་པ་ལ༔ ཞང་འཕྲུང་ཁ་བེར་ཆུང་དེ༔ སྔགས་དང་ [11a7] མངོན་པ་གཉིས་ཀ་ལ་མཁས་པ་ཡིན་པས: ཕལ་ཆེ་བ་སློག་[337]གླིངས་[338]བྱས་ཚོར་

---

322 མཇལ་

323 ཀྱི་

324 སྔར་

325 མཇལ་

326 མཇལ་

327 མིན་

328 མཇལ་

329 བསྟེན་

330 མཇལ་

331 ཁམས་

332 བཤུལ་

333 ཀྱི་

334 བེར་

335 གྲྭ་

336 ཤིག

337 བསྒྲོ་

338 གླིང་

གཙོད་པ་ཡིན་པར་གདའ་བ་ལ: དགེ་བཤེས་སྟོན་པ་ལ་ཡང་ཆོས་ཀྱི་མོལ་པ་མང་དུ་མཛད་ལ། དགེ་བཤེས་སྟོན་པའི་ [11a8] བཏུལ་ཡ་ནོན་པར་གློ་ཐེ་ཚོམ་དུ་གྱུར་ནས། དགེ་བཤེས་སྟོན་པ་ལ་དད་པ་སྐྱེས་སྟེ། ཁྱེད་འཁམས[339]ན་འབྲོམ་སྟོན་པ་བྱ་བ་གཅིག་ཡོད་ཟེར་བ་དེ་ཡིན་ནམ་ (ཡིནཾ་) ཟེར། ཡིན་མོད་གསུངས་པས། གདན་ལས་ལངས་སྟེ། [11b1] དགེ་བཤེས་སྟོན་པ་ལ་འབོལ་དང་བྲུམ་ཟེའི་གདན་ལ་བཞུགས་སུ་བཅུག ཁོང་རང་གི་ཆིབས་བཟང་པོ་གཅིག་གི་མཐུར་མདའ་དར་ཡུག་ལ་བྱས་ནས་ཕྱག་དུ་ཕུལ། ཕྱག་ཕྱ་འབྱུགས་པ་འདྲ་བ་གཅིག་མཛད་ནས་དང་པོ་ [11b2] ཕྱག་བླངས་པའི་བཟོད་གསོལ་མཛད་ [illegible: པས]། དེ་ནས་སྒྲོ[340]གླིངས[341]བྱས་པའི་བཟོད་གསོལ་ཡང་མཛད་ནས། དེ་དགེ་བའི་བཤེས་གཉེན་ (གཤེཉེ་) རིན་པོ་ཆེ་ཁོ་བོའི་བླ་མཆོད་མཛད་པ་ཞུ། ངལ་རྣམ་སྨྲིང་ཟེར་བའི་དགོན་པ་བྱ་བ་ [11b3] ལེགས་པོ་གཅིག་ཡོད་པས། དེར་དགོན་པ་ཕྱིག་པར་ཞུ་ཞུས་པས། དགེ་བཤེས་སྟོན་པའི་ཞལ་ནས། ཁྱོད་འབྲུག་དཔོན་གཅིག་གི་བླ་མཆོད་ངས་མི་ཡོང་གསུངས་ནས་མ་གནང་། ཡང་ཡང་ཞུ་བ་ཕུལ་ [11b4] བས། དགེ་བཤེས་སྟོན་པའི་ཞལ་ནས། ད་ཁྱོད་ཀྱི་ཡོད་མདོའི་འཁར[342]དེ་ལྷ་ཁང་དུ་བསྒྱུར: ཤ་ཟན་དང་། ཙམ[343]ཟན་ཀྱི[344]འབྲུག་པ། ཤང་གཟིགས་དང་མདོའ་སྟག་གི་འབྲུག་པ་བསྡུམ་ན། ངས་བླ་མཆོད་ [11b5] བྱ་ཡི་གསུང་། དེར་ཕྱིགས་དེ་དག་ [345]རིམས[346]ཀྱིས[347] ཕུལ་ནས་བླ་མཆོད་བྱེད་པར་ཞལ་ཀྱིས[348]བཞེས་སོ (བཞེསོ) ། །དེ་ནས་ཡར་ལ་[illegible] འགྲོགས་ནས་བྱོན་སྟེ། རྣམ་སྨྲིང་གི་དགོན་པ་གཟིགས། རོག་ཐོམ་སྒྱུར་དུ་ཆོས་ཞག་ཤས་ཀྱང་གསུངས: [11b6] དེའི་དུས་སུ་མངའ་རིས་སུ་ཇོ་བོ་རྗེ་སྐད་པའི་པཎྜི་ཏ་གཅིག་བྱོན་ལོ་བྱ་བ་གསན་པས། དེས་ཐུགས་ཕྱོགས་པར་གྱུར་ནས། དངས་མངའ་རིས་སུ་པཎྜི་ཏ་དང་འཛལ[349]ལ་དེ་ནས་དགོན་པ་ཕྱིག་པར་ཆད་མཛད། དེའི་དུས་སུ་ [11b7] ཡོད་མདོའིས་ཆོག་མཛད་ནས་འཕན་ཡུལ་དུ་བྱོན་ནས། [350]དབང་[351] ཡང་གུང་གསུམ་དབང་ཕྱུག་རྒྱལ་མཚན་དང་། ཀ་བ་ཤཀྱ[352]དབང་ཕྱུག་དང་། ཞ[353]སྣ་ནམ་རྡོ་རྗེ་དབང་ཕྱུག་ལ་སོགས་པ་རྣམས་ལ་ཕྱག་

---

339 ཁམས་

340 བགྲོ་

341 གླེང་

342 ཁར་ ?

343 རྩམ་

344 གྱི་

345 dot-line annotation mark

346 རིམ་

347 གྱིས་

348 གྱིས་

349 མཛལ་

350 dot-line annotation mark?

351 ?

352 ཤཱཀྱ་

353 ཞང་

འཚལ། [11b8] དགེ་བཤེས་ཀ་བ་ལ་ [354]རྒྱ་ལ་[355] མངའ་རིས་ཀྱི་པཎྜི་ཏ་དེ་སྤྱན་དྲངས་ན། དེའི་བདག་རྐྱེན་ཁྱེད་ཀྱིས་མཛོད་ལ་བོད་ཀྱི་མི་ཆེན་རྣམས་བྱོན་ཅིག ངས་ཁྱེད་ལ་ཡི་གེ་གཏང་[356]ངོ་ (ཡིགེཏངོ) ¦ ཞེས་པའི་རྐོག་[357]ཆ་མཛད་དེ: ཐུགས་སྨོམ་ (ཐུགསྨོཾ) [12a1] ལ་སྐྱིལ་[358]ཆེ་བ་རྒྱལ་པོ་སོགས་དར་བའི་དུས་ན་ཡིན་ ཱི གུང་བློན་པོ་ (བློན) ཕེར་བའི་ཐུགས་ཚད་ཙམ་མངའ་བ་ལ་གསུང་སྐད: དེ་ནས་གནམ་དུ་བྱོན་ནས་ཡབ་དང་འཇལ། དེ་ནས་བྱང་ལམ་ ལ་ བྱོན་པའི་དུས་སུ། ལམ་ཁ་ [illegible: ཐག་] [12a2] གཅིག་བྱུང་ནས་གང་ལ་འགྲོ་མ་ཤེས་པའི་སྐབས་སུ། རྒྱལ་པོ་དཔེའ་དཀར་བཙུན་ཆུང་ཞ་[359]རྒྱབ་ལག་མ་གོན་པ་དྲེའུ་གཅིག་ལ་ཞོན་པ་གཅིག་དུ་བྱུས་ནས། ཤུལ་[360]ལམ་འདི་ལ་འབྱོན་པར་ཞུ་ཟེར་ནས་མ་ཚད་ [12a3] སྐྱུལ་[361]ནས། དསྐུ་ཁམས་བདེ་བར་བཞུད་ཅིག སྣ་ནམ་དང་ཤུད་སུ་ གཉིས་ འབྲུག་པ་ལངས་ཡོད་ངའི་འགྲོ་དགོས་པར་སྣང་ཟེར་ནས་ས་ཚུབ་[362]གཅིག་དུ་བྱུས་ནས་སོང་སྐད། དེ་ནས་ཡང་ལམ་ཁ་བྲག་གཅིག་བྱུང་ངེ: [12a4] ཡང་རྒྱལ་པོས་སྐྱུང་[363]གཅིག་ཏུ་སྤྲུལ་ནས་ཤུལ་[364]ལམ་སྣ་དྲངས་སྐད། དེ་ནས་ཕུ་རངས་སུ་བྱོན་ནོ། དེ་དག་ནི་འཕྲང་ཁ་བེར་ཆུང་དང་ཇི་ལྟར་འཇལ་[365]བའི་ལོ་རྒྱུས་སོ།།

(1–2–2–4) བཞི་པ་ཁྱད་པར་དུ་ཨ་ཏི་ཤ་ལ་ཇི་ལྟར་སྟེན་[366]པའི་ལོ་རྒྱུས་ [12a5] ནི: དེའི་དུས་སུ་ཇོ་བོ་བོད་ནས་ཕྱིར་རྒྱ་གར་ལ་བཞུད་ཕྱིས་[367]མཛད་པའི་སྐབས་སུ། སྤུ་རངས་བརྒྱའ་བཞི་[368]བྱ་བ་ན་བཞུགས་ནས་ཡོད་སྐད། དེའི་དུས་སུ་ཇོ་བཙུན་མ་སྒྲོལ་མའི་ཞལ་ནས། དེ་ལྟ་[12a6] ཞག་གསུམ་ (ཞགསུཾ) གྲོ་[369]དང་བཞིའི་ནང་པར་བོད་ཀྱི་ཨུ་པ་སི་ཀ་ཆེན་པོ་ཡོང་བར་ཡོད་པས་དེ་ནས་དེ་ལ་བྱིན་གྱིས་ (བྱིཾཉིས)

---

354 dot-line annotation mark

355 ?

356 བཏང་

357 ཤོག་

358 དཀྱིལ་

359 ཞུ་

360 བཤུལ་

361 བསྐྱལ་

362 འཚུབ་

363 རྐྱང་

364 བཤུལ་

365 མཇལ་

366 བསྟེན་

367 ཕྱིས་

368 Cf. *Gsal ba'i sgron me*: 87a5: རྒྱལ་ཞིང་

369 འགྲོ་

བརྡེབས་[370]ཅིག་གསུང་། དེ་ནས་ཇོ་བོས་ཀྱང་དཔལ་གསང་བ་འདུས་པའི་དཀྱིལ་འཁོར་བཞེངས་ནས་བྱམ་ [illegible: བཅས་] [12a7] དགོས་པའི་ཡོ་བྱད་ལྷ་གོན་མཛད་ནས་བཞུགས། ཞག་གསུམ་དུ་སོང་བའི་ནང་པར་བྱ་ར་གཅིག་མཛད་ནས། ངའི་ཨུ་པ་སི་ཀ་ ༼ དུང་མ་སླེབ། ཇོ་མོ་སྒྲོལ་མ་བརྙན་ཅན་གསུང་ངམ་གསུང་ཡི་བྱ་ར་གཅིག་ [12a8] མཛད། དེ་ཡོན་བདག་ཅིག་གིས་ (ཅིགིས་) ཇོ་བོ་གྲོ་ལ་གདན་དྲངས། དེ་ཉིད་དུ་དགེ་བཤེས་སྟོན་པས་ཕེབས་ནས། ཡོན་བདག་དེའི་ཁང་པར་ཞལ་འཛལ[371]། སྐྱོ་བ་དཔག་ཏུ་མེད་པ་ནས་ཀྱི་[372]ལས་ཀྱི་[373]འབྲེལ་ [12b1] པ་ཅན་དུ་གྱུར་པའི་སྟོབས་ཀྱིས་ཅིག་གི་[374]ཅིག་ངོ་ཤེས་པར་གྱུར་ཏོ།[375] དེར་དགེ་བཤེས་སྟོན་པས་དད་དཀར་པོ་ཡུག་གཅིག་ཕྱག་རྟེན་དུ་ཕུལ་ནས་ཞུ་བ་གསུམ་ཕུལ་བ། དལྷ་རྒྱ་གར་ན་ངོ་མཚར་ཅན་ཇི་ལྟ་བུ་བཞུགས། ངས་དེ་ [12b2] སྔ་ཆོས་འདི་ཙོ་ཤེས། བླ་མ་འདི་དག་བསྟེན་པ་ལམ་དུ་སོང་མ་སོང་། དཇོ་བོ་ཉིད་ཀྱི་སྤྱན་མངར[376]སྣང་ན་ཇི་ལྟར་མཆི་ཞུས་པས། ཇོ་བོའི་ཕྱག་དགེ་བཤེས་སྟོན་པའི་དབུའ་ཐོག་ཏུ་བཞག་ནས་བཀྲ་ཤིས་ཀྱི་ཚིགས་སུ་ [12b3] བཅད་པ་མང་པོ་གསུངས་སོ། །དེ་ནས་ཇོ་བོའི་ཞལ་ནས། རྒྱ་གར་ན་ངོ་མཚར་བ་མང་པོ་བཞུགས། ངབོད་དུ་འོང་ [illegible: བའི་] དུས་ཤར་ཕྱོགས་ཟླ་ག་ལ་ན་ཉིན་རེ[377]གྲུབ་ཐོབ་རེ་འགྲོན་ཡིན་ཡོད་དོ། །ཁྱོད་ཀྱི་དེ་སྔའི་ཆོས་དེ་ཚོ་ལམ་དུ་ [12b4] མི་འགྲོ། བླ་མའི་ཞབས་ཏོག་དེ་རྣམས་ལམ་དུ་སོང་ནས་འདུག: དཁྱོད་ངའི་དྲུང་དུ་སྡོད། ངའི་ལྷ་མོ་སྒྲོལ་མས་ཁྱོད་ལུང་བསྟན་པ་ཡིན། ངའི་དཀར[378]རྒྱུད་འདི་ལ་བྱིན་རླབས་གཞན་དང་མི་འདྲ་བ་ གཅིག་ ཡོད་གསུང་ནས། དེའི་ [12b5] ནུབ་མོ་ཇོ་བོས་དགེ་བཤེས་སྟོན་པ་ལ་དཔལ་གསང་བ་འདུས་པའི་དཀྱིལ་འཁོར་ཀྱི་[379]དབུས་ཀྱི་གཙོ་བོ་འཇམ་དཔལ་རྡོ་རྗེས་མཛད་ནས་དབང་བསྐུར། དེ་ནས་བཟུང་སྟེ་དགེ་འདུན་ཕལ་ཆེན་པའི་ལུགས་ཀྱི་ནུབ་ཡོལ་བས་ཆོད་པར་བཞེད་ [12b6] པས། ཡོལ་བས་བར་བཅད་དེ་ (བཅདེ་) དབུས་སྤུས་ (དབུསྤུས་) སླེབ་ནས་ཆོས་དང་རིགས[380]པ་མ་ལུས་པ་གནང་། ཐེག་པ་ཆེན་པོ་གསང་སྔགས་ཀྱི་སྟོམ་པ་མ་ལུས་པ་རྣམས་དང་། ཕ་རོལ་ཏུ་ཕྱིན་པའི་ལམ་གྱི་གདམས་པ་ཐུན་མོང་མ་ཡིན་རྣམས་གནང་། [12b7] མན་ངག་གི་ (ངགི་) ཀ་བ་ལིའི་ལྡེ་མིག་ཡང་དགེ་བཤེས་སྟོན་པ་ལ་གནང་། ལོ་ཆུང་བ་ནག་ཚོ་ཚུལ་ཁྲིམས་རྒྱལ་བ་ལ་སོགས་པ་གཞན་རྣམས་ལ་ཡེ་མི་སྟོད། དེ་ནས་དགེ་བཤེས་སྟོན་པས། ཇོ་བོ་ལ་བོད་ན་རབ་ཏུ་བྱུང་བ་འདི་ཙམ་

370 རྡེབས་

371 མཛལ

372 - ཀྱི་

373 ཀྱིས་

374 གིས་

375 ||

376 སྔར་

377 རེར་

378 བཀའ་

379 གྱི་

380 རིག་ ?

བཞུགས་ [12b8] འདི་ཐམས་ཅད་ཇོ་བོ་ལ་དད་པ་ལགས་པས། ཕྱིར་རྒྱ་གར་ལ་མི་འབྱོན་པར་བོད་ལ་ཐུགས་རྗེ་གཟིགས་ནས་འབྱོན་པར་ཞུ་ཞུས་པས། དགེ་འདུན་དེ་ཙམ་ཡོད་ན་དེ་རྣམས་ཀྱི་ནང་ནས་དགྲ་བཅོམ་ (དགྲོཾ) པ་ཡོང་བར་བཅོམ་ལྡན་འདས་ཀྱིས་ལུང་བསྟན་པ་ཡིན་[381] [13a1] དགེ་འདུན་རྣམས་དད་ཅིང་གྲོས་ཡོད་ན། ལོ་བོས་དགེ་འདུན་གྱི་[382]བཀའ་མི་ཆོག་པར་དམ་བཅས་པ་ལགས་གསུང་ནས། བོད་ཀྱི་ཕྱོགས་ཀྱི་དགེ་འདུན་ལ་ཕྱག་མཛད། དེར་དགེ་བཤེས་སྟོན་པས་འབྲོམ་གསུམ་པ་དབང་ཕྱུག་ [illegible: མགོན་] [13a2] ལ་བཀའ་ཤོག་སྫངས་[383]སྟེ། དགེ་བཤེས་ཀ་བའི་ཕྱག་ཏུ་གཏད། དེ་ནས་བོད་ཀྱི་མི་ཆེན་རྣམས་བཀའ་དྲོས་[384]མཛད་དེ། ཇོ་བོ་སྤྱན་འདྲེན་དུ་བྱོན། བཀའ་ཤོག་གི་ (ཤོགི) ནང་དུ་ཁུ་མ་ཚུད་པས་ཐུགས་ཁྲོས་ཏེ་སྟོན་ལ་རྒྱུགས་པས། བོད་ལ་སྤྱན་འདྲེན་ [13a3] པ་ལ་ཕན་པར་བྱུང་སྐད། བོད་ཀྱི་མི་ཆེན་རྣམས་ཀྱིས་གཙང་གི་ཉན་ཚོ་གནས་བརྙིང་[385]དུ་སྤྱིབ་[386]ཆོས་མང་པོ་ཞུས་དེ་ནས་དབུས་སུ་གདན་དྲངས་སོ་ (དྲངསོ) ། །དགེ་བཤེས་སྟོན་པ་མིན་ན་ ཇོ་བོ་ ན་ཕྱིར་རྒྱ་གར་ལ་དེའུ་ཤོར་སྐད། དེ་ནས་ཇོ་བོའི་ [illegible: ཕྱགས་[387]] [13a4] ཆི་[388]ལ་དཔལ་བསམ་ཡས་སུ་བཞུགས་པའི་དུས་སུ། ཞང་འཕྲང་ཀ་བེར་རྒྱུང་གིས། སེ་ཟླ་བ་དང་། ཟིར་ཁུ་དབང་དེ་གཉིས་པོ་ཉར་སྫངས་[389]ནས: དགེ་བཤེས་སྟོན་པ་ལ་ད་འབྱོན་པར་ཞུ་ཞུས་པས། སྟོན་པའི་ཞལ་ནས། ངཇོ་བོ་བཞུགས་ [13a5] རིང་མི་ཡོང་། དེ་ནས་འོང་གིས། དེའི་བར་དུ་ཁྱོད་མཆོད་གནས་འདི་ལ་གྱིས་ཆོས་འདི་རྣམས་ལ་སོམས་གསུང་ནས་ཐུགས་དམ་འཛམ་དཔལ་རྡོ་རྗེ་དང་། ཆོས་གདམས་ངག་ཚོགས་བཅད་མ་དེ་ཚོ་བསྐུར་བ་ལགས་སྐད། དེ་ལྟར་ཕྱགས་[390]ཕྱི་ལ་བཞུགས་ [13a6] ནས་ཆོས་དང་མན་ངག་ (སྔག) མ་ལུས་པ་ཞུས། ཞབས་ཏོག་དང་ཞབས་འབྲིང་དཔག་ཏུ་མེད་པ་མཛད་དེ། ཇོ་བོ་ཡང་ཤིན་ཏུ་མཉེས་ནས་ང་ལ་སློབ་མ་ཁྱོད་འདྲ་བ་གཅིག་རྒྱ་གར་ན་ཡང་ཡོད་གསུང་། ཇོ་བོ་ཡེར་པར་བཞུགས་དུས་གདུང་ཆོས་ [13a7] ཀྱི་ཡུལ་དང་། ཁ་ཆེ་གསེར་ཁར་བྱོན་ནས་སྨས་[391]ཀྱི་དངོས་པོ་མང་པོ་བསྒྲུབས་ནས། ཡེར་པ་ལྷ་རི་སྙིང་པོའི་འགྱུལ་[392]དུ་གསེར་ཞོ་དགུ་དགུ་ལ་སྲང་རེ་རེར་བྱས་པའི་གསེར་སྲང་རྒྱ་[393]རྩ་བརྒྱད་ལ་ནོར་སྣ་གཅིག་ཏུ་བྱས་པའི་ནོར་སྣ་རྒྱ་[394]རྩ་ [13a8] བརྒྱད་ཀྱི་འབུལ་བ་ཡང་བྱས། མངའ་

381 + །

382 གྲི་

383 བརྫངས་

384 གྲོས་

385 རྙིང་

386 སྤྱིབས།

387 ཕྱག་

388 ཕྱི་

389 བརྫངས་

390 ཕྱག་

391 སྨས་

392 མགུལ་

393 བརྒྱ་

394 བརྒྱ་

རིས་སུ་ཞལ་འཇལ་[395]བའི་ཉིན་བར་ཡོན་བདག་དེས་དྲངས་བའི་མར་ཚོལ་པ་དེས། དེ་ནུབ་དབུས་[396]སྤུས་སུ་ (སྤུསུ་) མར་མེ་མཚན་ཐུབ་གཅིག་བྱས་ ནས་ ཕུལ། དེ་ནས་བཟུང་སྟེ་ད་ལྟ་རྣས་སྒྲིང་ན་གདུང་བཞུགས་ [13b1] པ་ཡན་ཆད་ལ། རྩེ་མར་ཀྱི་[397]མར་མེ་མཚན་ཐུབ་དེ་འཆད་མ་མྱོང་། །[398]ཉིན་རེ་ལ་ཇ་སྲུག་[399]འདྲེས་མ་ལན་གསུམ་ལས་བྱས་པའི་ཆབ་ཚ་ཐེངས་གསུམ་འདྲེན་པ་འཆག་མ་མྱོང་སྐད། དགེ་བཤེས་སྟོན་པས་ཇོ་བོ་ལ་སློབ་དཔོན་ [13b2] ཀླུ་སྒྲུབ་[400]ལུགས་ཀྱི་དབུ་མའི་རྟོགས་པ་ཕུལ་བས། ཕྱག་ཐལ་མོ་སྦྱར་ནས་ཁྱོད་ལྟ་བུའི་བསོད་ནམས་ (སོཾན་) ཆེན་པོ་བོད་ན་བཞུགས་འདུག་པ[401]། ཁོ་བོ་བོད་དུ་ཡོང་མི་དགོས་པར་འདུག་པ་གསུང་སྐད། གཞན་ཇོ་བོའི་མངའ་ཐང་ཐམས་ཅད་ [13b3] དགེ་བཤེས།[402] སྟོན་པའི་ཕྱག་དུ་རྫིལ་ཀྱིས་[403]བྱུང་བས་ཁུ་ལ་སོགས་པའི་སློབ་མ་གཞན་དག་ལ་མི་མགུ་པར་ཡོད་པར་གདའ། ཤེས་རབ་ཀྱི་ཕ་རོལ་ཏུ་ཕྱིན་པ་བརྒྱད་སྟོང་པ་ལ་སོགས་པ་དང་། འགྲེལ་པ་ཆུང་བ་དང་། མན་ངག་གི་ (ཐུགི་) སྒྲུབ་ [13b4] ཐབས་མང་པོའི་ འགྱུར་ ཡང་མཛད་དོ། །དེ་རྣམས་ཀྱིས་ཨ་ཏི་ཤ་ལ་ཇི་ལྟར་བསྟེན་[404]པའི་ལོ་རྒྱུས་སྨོས་པའོ། །དེ་ལྟར་དོན་བཞིས་རྣས་སྒྲིང་བཞེངས་པའི་སྐུས་གང་ལ་ཕབ་པ་དགེ་བཤེས་སྟོན་པའི་ལོ་རྒྱུས་ཟུར་ཙམ་བརྗོད་པའོ།།

(1–2–3) [13b5] གསུམ་པ་སྐུས་ཕབ་པའི་གསུང་དངོས་ནི་འདི་ཡིན་ [illegible: ཏེ|] ¦ ཇོ་བོ་གཉེ་ཐང་དུ་སྐུ་གཤེགས་ཁའི་དུས་སུ། སྤྱིར་ཡང་སློབ་མ་རྣམས་ལ་ཆོས་ +གསུངས་ ཚད་ཞལ་ཆེམས་སུ་ (ཆེཾསུ་) གསུང་སྟེ (གསུངསཏེ) ¦ ཁྱད་པར་ (ཁྱར་) དུ་དགེ་བཤེས་སྟོན་པ་ལ། ཇོ་བོའི་ཞལ་ནས་ [13b6] སྟོན་པ་རིན་པོ་ཆེ་དུས་གསུམ་ ཀྱི་[405] སངས་རྒྱས་ཐམས་ཅད་ཀྱི་གཤེགས་ པའི་ ཤུལ་མཁས་པ་ཆེན་པོ་ཀླུ་སྒྲུབ་[406]དང་། ཐོགས་མེད་ནས་བརྒྱུད་པའི་ཤིང་རྟ་ཆེན་པོའི་བསྒྲོལ[407]། སངས་རྒྱས་ཀྱི་སྟན་[408]པ་རིན་པོ་ཆེ་ལེགས་པར་ (ལེར་) བཟུང་བ་འདི་ཁྱོད་

395 མཇལ་

396 དབུ་

397 གྱི་

398 - །

399 བསྲེག་

400 སྒྲུབ་

401 པས

402 - ¦

403 གྱིས་

404 བསྟེན་

405 གྱི་

406 སྒྲུབ་

407 སྒྲོལ་

408 བསྟན་

ལ་ལེགས་པར་གཏོད་པ་ཡིན་ནོ། [13b7] དེ་ཡང་སངས་རྒྱས་ཀྱི་སྟན་[409]པ་དགེ་འདུན་ཀྱི་[410]སྡེ་ལ་རག་ལུས་ལ། དགེ་འདུན་ཀྱི་[411]སྡེ་གཙུག་ལག་ཁང་ལ་རག་ལུས་པས། ཁྱོད་ཀྱིས་གཙུག་ལག་ཁང་གཅིག་བཞེངས་ཅིག་[412]གསུང་སྐད། དེར་དགེ་བཤེས་སྟོན་པའི་ཐུགས་[13b8] ལ་ཅི་[413] ལྷ་ ཏིང་གིས་སོང་ནས། སླར་ཞུ་བ་ཕུལ་བ། ཁོ་བོ་ལ་དེ་སྐད་བཀའ་མི་བསྩལ་བར་ཞུ། སྤྱིར་ཡང་བོད་ལ་སྐྲ་ཅན་བསོད་ནམས་ཆུང་། ཁྱད་པར་དུ་ཁོ་བོ་འཇིག་རྟེན་གྱི་ཤེས་ ×ཆེ རྒྱུ་མི་བདོག། དེ་ལྟར་མི་ཆོས [14a1] ལ་རྟེན་[414]ནས་བྱེད་དགོས་པ་ཡིན་ལ། ཁོ་བོའི་མི་ཆོས་སྐད་སྙིད་འགག་ཡོད་པ་ཡང་བྱུང་ཙ་གིར་ལུས་པས། ཁོ་བོས་སྒྲུབ་པར་མི་ནུས་པས་དེ་སྐད་མི་གསུང་བར་ཞུ་ཞུས་པས། ཡང་ཇོ་བོའི་ཞལ་ནས: [14a2] ངན་[415]རེ་ཟེར་བ་ཡིན་གྱིས་ལས། ཅིས་ཀྱང་དགེ་འདུན་ཀྱི་[416]སྡེ་གཅིག་ཚུགས་ཅིག་[417]འདི་ལ་བྱེད་པ་པོ་གཅིག་ཡོང་བ་ཡིན་གསུང་། དེར་དགེ་བཤེས་སྟོན་པས་ཀྱང་ཞལ་ཀྱིས་[418]བཞེས་སྐད། འདིའི་སྐབས་སུ། རྣལ་འབྱོར་པ་ཆེན་པོ [14a3] དཔལ་ལྡན་དགོན་པ་བ་དང་། ཁོང་རང་ལ་དཔོན་ས་ཟུང་ཟེར་བ་རེ་ནས། ཨ་ཏི་ཤའི་དེ་ལྟར་བགྱི་ཞུལ་[419]པས། ཇོ་བོའི་ཞལ་ནས་འཇིག་རྟེན་བློས་ཐོང[420]། ཆོ་གཞུག་འབྲོམ་སྟོན་པ་དང་མ་བྲལ་བར་གྱིས་གསུང་། དེར [14a4] ཁོང་རྣམ་པའི་ཐུགས་ལ་བླ་མ་མཉམ་པོར་སྟེན་[421]ཡོན་ཏན་ཡང་ང་རང་ཆེ་བ་ལ་མཉམ་པའི་ཐུགས་གོངས་[422]བྱུང་བ་ལ། ང་རྒྱལ་མ་བྱེད་པར་འབྲོམ་སྟོན་པ་ཆེན་པོའི་གྲོགས་གྱིས་ལོ་འགྲོ་བ་མང་པོའི་དོན་བྱེད་དགོས་པ་ཡིན: [14a5] ངས་ཁོ་བྱིན་གྱིས་བརླབས་ནས་ཡོད་པ་ཡིན་གསུང་སྐད། དེ་དག་ནི་སྨྲུས་ཐབ་པའི་གསུང་དངོས་སོ། དེ་ལྟར་དོན་གསུམ་གྱིས་ཇོ་བོས་དགེ་བཤེས་སྟོན་པ་ལ་སྨྲུས་ཐབ་པའི་ལོ་རྒྱུས་ཙུང་ཟད་བསྟན་ཏོ།།

---

409 བསྟན་

410 ཀྱི་

411 ཀྱི་

412 ཤིག་

413 ལྷི་

414 བརྟེན་

415 ག་ ?

416 ཀྱི་

417 ཤིག་

418 ཀྱིས་

419 ཞུས་

420 ཐོངས

421 བསྙེན་

422 དགོངས་

(1–3) བཞེངས་པའི་ཚུལ།

[14a6] དོན་གསུམ་པ་ཇི་ལྟར་བཞེངས་པའི་ལོ་རྒྱུས་དངོས་ལ་གཉིས་ཏེ། (1–3–1) སྟོན་པ་རིན་པོ་ཆེ་ཡོན་མཆོད་ཀྱིས་ཕྱག་ལེན་མཛད་ནས་དབུ་རྩེ་གང་ ལ་ བཞེངས་པའི་ལོ་རྒྱུས་དང་། (1–3–2) དེའི་རྗེས་སུ་གང་ཟག་གང་ ངང་ གང་གིས་ཕྱག་ལེན་ [14a7] མཛད་ནས་དབུ་རྩེ་གཞན་རྣམས་བཞངས་[423]པའི་ལོ་རྒྱུས་སོ།།

(1–3–1) དང་པོ་ལ་གསུམ། (1–3–1–1) ཇོ་བོ་གཤེགས་ནས་རྣས་སྤྲེང་[424]མ་བྱོན་བར་གྱི་ལོ་རྒྱུས་དང་། (1–3–1–2) རྣས་སྤྲེང་[425]བྱོན་ནས་བཞེངས་བའི་ཚུལ་དངོས་དང་། (1–3–1–3) ལོ་དུར་སློབ་མ་སྐྱུངས་[426] [14a8] ནས་སྨྱོ་རན་ལས་འདའ་བའི་ཚུལ་བསྟན་པའོ།།

(1–3–1–1) དང་པོ་ནི། ཇོ་བོ་གཉེ་ཐང་ན་སྐུ་གཤེགས་ཁའི་རྗེས་སུ། དགེ་བཤེས་སྟོན་པའི་ཐུགས་གོངས་[427]ལ། ཇོ་བོས་[428]ཐུགས་གོངས་ (ཐུཏ་གོངས་)[429]བསྐང་བའི་ཕྱིར་གཙུག་ལག་ཁང་གཅིག་ [14b1] གཉེ་ཐང་ན་བཞེངས་སམ་ (བཞེངསཾ་) དགོངས་པ་ལ། སངས་སྟོན་ལ་སྟད་[430]པ་ཆེད་པོ་མི་འདུག ཇོ་བོའི་ཕྱག་དཔེའ་དང་རྟེན་གསུམ་རྣས་[431]དགེ་འདུན་རྨ་ཚོ་ཀུན་ལོང་དབང་ཟེར་ཡིན་འདུག་པས་སྐབས་དེར་ཤིན་ཏུ་ཐུགས་མ་བདེ་ནས། [14b2] ཇོ་བོས་ཀུང་ལོ་བོས་མི་འགྲུབ་པའི་བྱ་བ་ལ་གཏད། བོང་ཐོར་ལ་ཚལ་[432]སྐལ་སླམ་དུ་དགོངས་པའི་དུས་སུ། རྗེ་བཙུན་མ་སྒྲོལ་མའི་ཞལ་ནས། ཁྱོད་དེ་ཙམ་དུ་ཐུགས་མི་བདེ་མི་དགོས། ཁྱེད་ཀྱི་བྱ་བ་ཐམས་ཅད་ངས་སྒྲུབ་[433]པ་ [14b3] ཡིན་གྱི་གསུང་། དེས་ཐུགས་བདེ་འབོལ་ཀྱིས་[434]སོང་བའི་སྐབས་སུ། དགེ་བཤེས་ཀ་བས་བྱོན་ཏེ། ཐམས་ཅད་ཀྱི་བགོ་བཤའ་དང་། བསྐྱི་[435]གོད་[436]མཛད་དེ།

423 བཞེངས་

424 + ལ་

425 + ལ་

426 བསྐྱུངས་

427 དགོངས་

428 བོའི

429 དགོངས་

430 གཏད་

431 རྣམས་

432 ཚ་

433 བསྒྲུབ་

434 གྱིས་

435 སྐྱེས་

436 འགོད་ or བགོས་

ཀ་བ་དེ་ཁྱུ་ཇོག་འཁྲོམ་གསུམ་ལ་སོགས་པ་ཀུན་གྱི་[437]ཐུགས་གཏོད་པ་ཡིན་པར་འདུག [14b4] དགེ་བཤེས་ཁྱུ་སྟོན་ལ་ཇོ་བོ་ཤཀྱའི་གསེར་སྐུ་གཅིག་ཕུལ། ཇོག་ལ་མཆོད་རྟེན་བརྒྱད་པ་གཅིག་དང་། སྒྲོལ་མའི་སྐུ་གཅིག་ཕུལ། འཁར་བསིལ་དང་། ལུགས་[438]སྐུ་ཆང་ཆུང་ཁ་ཡར་དང་། ཆོས་སྒྲོལ་མཛད་གཅིག་རྣམས་གཉེ་ཐང་དུ་ [14b5] བཞུགས། དེ་ནས་དགེ་བཤེས་སྟོན་པ་ལ་ཕའི་ནུས་པ་བུ་ལ་དགོས་པ་ཡིན་པས། ཇོ་བོའི་གདུང་འདི་རྣམས་ཁྱོད་ཚོགས་གྱིས[439]། རྒྱ་དཔེའ་ལོ་ཙྪ་བ་ལ་དགོས་པས། ཕྱག་དཔེའ་འདི་རྣམས་ཀྱང་ཁྱོད་ཚོགས་གྱིས་[440]གསུང་། ཇོ་བོའི་ཐུགས་དམ་ [14b6] རྟེན་[441]ཆེ་ཤོས་བླ་མ་གསེར་གླིང་པའི་གདུང་ཁང་དངུལ་གདུགས་ཅན་ཆུང་བ་འདི་ཡིན་པས་འདི་ཡང་ཁྱོད་གྱིས་[442]གསུང་ (གྱིསུང་) ནས། དགེ་བཤེས་སྟོན་པ་ཉིད་ཇི་ལྟར་བཞེད་པ་རྣམས་ཕུལ། གཞན་ཡང་སྐྱི་[443]དགོད་[444]གང་ལ་གང་འོས་ [illegible] [14b7] སྐད། དེ་ནས་དགེ་བཤེས་སྟོན་པས་དགུན་དེ་གཉེ་ཐང་རང་དུ་བཞུགས། སོས་ཀ་གཉེ་ཐང་ནས་ ཇོ་བོའི་ སྨྲ་དཀར་ནག་གཉིས་ཡོད་པ་བསྐལ[445]། གདུང་དང་། ཕྱག་དཔེའ། ཐུགས་དམ་རྣམས་སྤྱན་དྲངས་ཇོ་བོའི་བླ་མཆོད་བཞི་ཁྲིད་ནས་སྟོད་ [illegible: ལུ]ངས་ [14b8] ལ་ལམ་དོན་ནས་གནམ་བྱེ་མ་ལུང་དུ་བྱོན། དེའི་ཕྱུགས་ཆེ[446]ལ་ཇོ་བོའི་དམ་ཅན་ཤ་ཟ་མ་མཆོད་[447]ཀྱང་བྱོན། དེ་ནས་གནམ་ཀྱི་[448]བྱེ་མ་ལུང་དུ་ལྷ་ཁང་བཞེངས་པའི་ཐུགས་གོངས་[449]ཡོད་པ་ལས། ཁྱི་སྟོན་བྱོ་ཡེ་[450]བྱ་བས་ [15a1] ཕྱག་དོག་བྱས་ནས་བཞེངས་དབང་མ་བྱུང་བར་ཡོད་པའི་སྐབས་སུ། ཉིན་གཅིག་ [451]སྟོ་[452] སྐྱོ་སངས་ལ་བྱོན་པའི་ཤུལ་[453]ལམ་དུ། སྤྲང་པོ་གཅིག་ ངང་ ཕྲད། གང་ནས་འོངས་དྲིས་པས། ཀླུང་[454]ཤོད་རོང་ནས་འོངས་ཟེར། དེ་ཕྱོགས་ན་ཁ་སྐད་ཅི་འདུག [15a2] དྲིས་པས། གཞན་ཇི་མི་འདུག་ཞང་འཕྲང་ཀ་བེར་ཆུང་གི་བུ་ཇོ་སྲས་ཆོས་

437 གྱི་

438 ཀླུགས་

439 ཀྱིས

440 ཀྱིས་

441 རྟ་

442 ཀྱིས་

443 སྐྱིས་

444 འགོད་ or བགོས་

445 བཀལ

446 ཕྱུག་ཕྱི་

447 མཆེད་ See 31b6.

448 གྱི་

449 དགོངས་

450 Cf. *Gsal ba'i sgron me*: 100b3–4: ཁྱི་སྟོན་ཇོ་སྲས་

451 dot-line annotation mark

452 ?

453 བཤུལ་

454 ཀླུང་

ཧོག་[455]ཅེས་བྱ་བའི་ཆོས་པ་ཅིག་ཡོད་པ། དགེ་བཤེས་སྟོན་པའམ་ཅིག་ཡོད་པ་གདན་འདྲེན་དུ་ཕྱིན་པས་འཕན་ཡུལ་རན་ཆུས་ཁྱེར་ནས་ [15a3] ཤི་ཟེར་སྐད། ཁ་སྐད་ཆེ་འོ་གསུང་། དེ་ནས་ཐུགས་ལ་རྩེ་ལྷངས་ཀྱིས་གྲུར་ནས་རྩུར་བྱོན་པར་དགོངས་པའི་དུས་སུ། ཞང་འཕྲང་ཀ་བེར་ཆུང་གི་བུ་ལྷུན་པོ་བྱ་བས་སྤྱན་དྲངས་སྟེ།། རྣམ་སྲིད་དུ་ལུག་གི་ (ལུགི་) ལོ་ལ་བྱོན་ནས་ཕྱུགས་[456] [15a4] ཕབ་པོ: དེ་དག་ནི་ཇོ་བོ་འདས་ ནས་ རྣམ་སྲིད་[457]མ་བྱོན་པར་གྱི་ལོ་རྒྱུས་སོ།།

(1–3–1–2) གཉིས་པ་རྣམ་སྲིད་དུ་བྱོན་ནས་བཞེངས་པའི་ཚུལ་དངོས་ལ་གཉིས་སྟེ། (1–3–1–2–1) དང་པོ་རྟག་[458]པ་མཛད་ཅིང་དགོན་པ་གོང་མ་དང་། སྟོན་པ་ཉིད་ཀྱི་གཟིམས་[459]ཆུང་ཇི་ལྟར་ [15a5] བཞེངས་པ་དང་། (1–3–1–2–2) གཉིས་པ་དབུ་རྩེ་རིན་པོ་ཆེ་ལོ་གང་ལ་ཚུལ་ཇི་ལྟར་བཞེངས་པའོ།།

(1–3–1–2–1) དང་པོ་ནི། རྣམ་སྲིད་དུ་བྱོན་ནས་སའི་རྟག་[460]པ་མཛད་དེ། དེ་ལ་སྤྱིར་ལུང་པའི་ཤར་ཡངས་པ། ནུབ་དོག་པ། ཕུ་ཤར་ལ་སྟན་[461]པ[illegible: འི་][462] [15a6] མདའ་ནུབ་ལ་བསྟན་པ། ལྷོ་གཞོལ་བ། བྱང་སྐྱིབས་པ། སའི་འབྱུ་བ་ཆེ་ཞིང་ཁ་དཀར་བ། ཕྱོགས་ཀྱི་རི་རྣམས་ཀྱང་རྒྱལ་སྲིད་རིན་པོ་ཆེ་སྣ་བདུན་འདྲ་བ་འདུག་སྟེ། དེ་ཡང་རྒྱབ་རི་རིའི་རྒྱལ་པོ་རྩེ་རྗེ་འཆིང་དཀར་བ་ནི [15a7] ལྷུན་འཁྱུག་ལ་ངོས་ཡངས་པ། རྒྱལ་པོ་ལ་ཕོད་བཅིངས་སྟེ་གདན་ལ་བཞུགས་པ་འདྲ། ཤར་ན་སྟག་རི་དམག་ [illegible: དཔོན་] རིན་པོ་ཆེ་ལག་ན་གོ་མཚོན་ཐོགས་པ་འདྲ་བ། ཤར་ལྷོ་མཚམས་ན་ཁེའུ་རི་རྟ་མཆོག་རིན་པོ་ཆེ་ཉེལ་ལྡོངས་ [15a8] ལ་རྩ་ཟ་བ་འདྲ་བ། ལྷོ་ན་ཛ་ཚ་རྟ་གཡག་གི་རི་བློན་པོ་གྲོས་ལ་འདུ་བ་འདྲ་བ། ལྷོ་སྣད་ན་རི་བཙུན་ཕྱུག་མོ་བཙུན་མོ་བྲང་ ཆབ་ ཅན་དར་དཀར་གྱི་[463]གུ་ཟླ་གསོལ་བ་འདྲ་བ། ལྷོ་ནུབ་མཚམས་ན་གླང་རི [15b1] གླང་པོ་རིན་པོ་ཆེ་ཆུ་འཐུང་བ་འདྲ་བ། ནུབ་ན་སྟོད་ཕུར་མོའི་བྲག་ནོར་བུ་རིན་པོ་ཆེ་འོད་འབར་བ་འདྲ་བ། ཕོ་བོང་ཐོང་[464]འཁོར་ལོ་རིན་པོ་ཆེས་ལ་

455 གྲགས་ ? See 20a2.

456 ཕྱུག་

457 + ལ་

458 བརྟག་

459 གཟིམ་

460 བརྟག་

461 བསྟན་

462 Cf. *Dge bshes ston pa'i rnam thar*: 182b2: པས་

463 གྱི་

464 ཕ་བོང་ཐང་

གཉིང་བ་འདྲ། གཞན་ཡང་ཧྲུག་གཡག་གི་ལྷ་བཞི་ ཡང ཚོང་སྟེ། ཤར་ཀྱི་[465]ཕྱུག་འཚོལ་སྣང་གི་ལམ་སྟག་ [15b2] སྐྱ་བོ་ཁ་ཡིད་བཞིན་ (ཅན་) གྱི་ནོར་བུ་ཕྱིར་བ་འདྲ་བ། ལྷོའི་འབབ་ཆུ་གཡུ་འབྲུག་སྔོན་མོ་སྟན་པའི་སྒྲ་སྒྲོག་པ་འདྲ་བ། ནུབ་ཀྱི་བྱ་མཆུ་མོ་ཐང་བྱ་དམར་མོ་མཛེས་པའི་གཤོག་པ་སྒྲུང་བ་འདྲ་བ། བྱང་གི་བྲག་ [15b3] ནག་པོ་རྡུལ་[466]སྦྲུལ་འཁྱིང་བ་འདྲ་བ་འདུག གཞན་ཡང་ས་གཞི་དེར་བསྟོད་པ་ཙམ་གྱིས་ས་སྨུམ་ལ་ཞག་ཆགས་ (ཆུ) པ། སའི་འབྲུ་བ་ཆེ་བ་རྒྱས་པ[467]བུ་སློབ་ཀྱི་སར་བཟང་བ། ཆུ་མིག་དབྱར་མི་ཆེ་དགུན་མི་ [15b4] ཆུང་བའི་ཆུ་མིག་མང་པོ་ཡོད་པ། ཤིང་སྣ་ཚོགས་སྐྱེས་པ། ཁྱད་པར་དུ་ཤུགས་[468]པའི་ནགས་ཚལ་ཀྱི་[469]གཞི་ཐིངས་ནས་འདུག་སྟེ། དེ་ཙ་ན་ཤུག་པ་ཆེ་བ་གཡག་གྲུས་[470]ཙམ་ཆུང་བ་ར་ལུག་ཙམ་དུ་གདའ་སྐད། མེ་ཏོག་ [15b5] སྣ་ཚོགས་སྐྱེས་པ། བྱ་སྣ་ཚོགས་སྐད་སྙན་པ་སྒྲོག་[471]པ། སའི་འོག་ན་ཀླུའི་རྒྱལ་པོ་ནེའུ་ལུང་པ་ལ་སོགས་པའི་ཕོ་བྲང་དུ་མ་ཡོད་བ[472]། དེ་དག་ཀུང་ཆོས་ལ་མོས་པ་འབབ་[473]ཞིག་འདུག་སྐད། དེར་ས་བཞི་[474]དེར་སྟོད་[475]པ་ཙམ་གྱིས་ཉམས་དགའ་ [15b6] བའི་གནས་ཕུན་སུམ་ཚོགས་པར་མཁྱེན་ནས། རྨ[476]ལམ་གྱི་རྟག་[477]པ་མཛད་པས་རྩེ་རྗེ་འཆིང་དཀར་བ་མར་ཀྱི་[478]ཕྱུང་པོར་སོང་བ་རྨིས། [479]ཕ་བོང་ཐང་རྡོ་རྗེ་རིན་པོ་ཆེས་ཁེངས་པ་རྨིས་ ×དབུ་རྩེ་ཀ་གཉིས་མ་ཅན་དེ་ན་གསེར་ཀྱི་[480]མཆོད་རྟེན་ཤིན་ཏུ་མཐོ་བ་ལ་སོགས་པ་གཅིག་ [15b7] འདུག་པ་ལས་འོད་ཟེར་འཕྲོས་ཏེ་སོང་བའི་སྣ་ལ[481]། དབུ་རྩེ་འབག་ཕྱི་ར་[482]སེར་ལྷག་གེ་ (ལྷགེ་) བ་ མང་པོ་

---

465 ཀྱི་

466 རྡུས་

467 + །

468 ཤུག་

469 ཀྱི་

470 རྒྱུ་

471 སྒྲོགས་

472 པ

473 འབབ་

474 གཞི་

475 བསྟོད་

476 རྨི

477 བརྟག་

478 ཀྱི་

479 no annotation mark, under the eighth line

480 ཀྱི་

481 same as སྣེ་མོ་ལ་

482 གན་ཛི་ར or གཉྫི་ར

བྱུང་ནས་བོད་ཀྱི་རྒྱལ་ཁམས་ཐམས་ཅད་དུ་ཁྱབ་པ་རྨིས། ནང་པར་རྣལ་[483]སད་པ་དང་: སུམ་པ་མཐྱེ [484]ཆ ན་[485]བྱ་བ་དང་། རྣལ་འབྱོར་ཆེན་པོ་དང་། [15b8] གཉིས་ཀྱིས་རྨིལམ་ཀྱི་[486]རྟག་[487]པ་བཟང་ངམ་ཞུས་པས: ཤིན་ཏུ་བཟང་བར་གདའ་གསུང་སྐད། དེ་ནས་དང་པོ་ཇོ་བོའི་བླ་མཆོད་རྣལ་འབྱོར་པ་རྣམས་བཞིའི་གཞུགས་[488]གནས་སུ་གཉན་གྲོང་ནས་གཞུ་མདོམ་ལྔ་བརྒྱ་འཇལ་[489]བའི་སར་ [16a1] དགོན་པ་གོངམ་བཞེངས་སྟེ (བཞེངསྟེ)། དེའི་རྩར་ནུབ་ཕྱོགས་སུ་རྣལ་འབྱོར་ཆེན་པོའི་གཟིམས་[490]ཁང་བཞེངས་སྟེ། དེའི་ཡོན་བདག་ པེར་རྒྱུད་ དགྲ་བཅོམ་གྱིས་བྱས། དེའི་རྩར་རྣལ་འབྱོར་པ་དགོན་པ་བ་ཆེན་པོའི་གཟིམས་[491]ཁང་བྱ་སྟེ། ཡོན་ [16a2] བདག་པེར་རྒྱུད་ལྷུན་པོས་བྱས། དེའི་རྩར་རྣལ་འབྱོར་པ་ཤེས་རབ་ (ཤེབ་) རྡོ་རྗེའི་གཟིམས་[492]ཁང་བྱས་ཏེ། ཡོན་བདག་པེར་རྒྱུད་ཤཱཀྱ་གྲགས་ཀྱིས་བྱས། དེའི་ཤར་དུ་རྣལ་འབྱོར་པ་བྱམས་ པའི་ བློ་གྲོས་ཀྱིས་[493]གཟིམས་[494]ཁང་བྱ་ཏེ། ཡོན་བདག་པེར་རྒྱུད་ [16a3] བླ་བ་ཁ་སེར་ཀྱིས་[495]བྱས། དེ་རྣམས་ཕྱི་ལྷུགས་རི་གཅིག་གིས་བསྐོར་ཏེ་ཡོན་བདག་ཞང་ཟྲུང་པ་བཞིས་བྱས། ཤར་ཕྱོགས་གཡུ་དཔོའི་རྒྱུད་ཀྱི་[496]བྱས། ལྷོ་ཕྱོགས་རྡོ་རྗེ་སླིང་གིས་བྱས་[497]ནུབ་ཕྱོགས་གཡུ་བརྟན་གྱིས་བྱས། [16a4] བྱང་ཕྱོགས་འདོང་དུས་བྱས། ཕྱི་སྒོ་ཤར་དུ་བལྟ་བ། སྒོ་ནས་བློ་འབེན་གང་ཙམ་ན་བཀོད་མའི་ཆུ་ཡོད་པ། དེ་ནས་ཀླུའི་རྒྱལ་པོ་ནེའུ་ལུང་པའི་ཕོ་བྲང་གི་སྟེང་དུ། དགེ་བཤེས་སྟོན་པའི་གཟིམས་[498]ཁང་ཆུང་ཆུང་གཅིག་བཞེངས་ [16a5] སྟེ། དེ་རྣམས་སུ་བྲང་ཁང་གེར་མ་གཅིག་བཏབ་སྐད། དེ་རྣམས་ནི་དང་པོ་སའི་རྟག་[499]པ་མཛད་ཅིང་དགོན་པ་གོངམ་དང་། སྟོན་པ་ཉིད་ཀྱི་གཟིམས་[500]ཁང་ཇི་ལྟར་བཞེངས་པའི་ལོ་རྒྱུས་བསྟན་ཏོ:།

---

483 མནལ་

484 dot-line annotation mark

485 མཐུ་ཆེན་

486 ཀྱི་

487 བརྟག་

488 བཞུགས་

489 མཇལ་

490 གཟིམ་

491 གཟིམ་

492 གཟིམ་

493 ཀྱི་

494 གཟིམ་

495 ཀྱིས་

496 ཀྱིས་

497 + །

498 གཟིམ་

499 བརྟག་

500 གཟིམ་

(1–3–1–2–2) གཉིས་པ་དབུ་རྩེ་རིན་པོ་ཆེ་གང་ལ་ [16a6] ཚུལ་ཇི་ལྟར་བཞེངས་པའོ། །དེ་ལ་གསུམ་སྟེ:[501] (1–3–1–2–2–1) ཐོག་མར་སྟོན་པ་སྨྲ་ངན་ལས་འདས་ནས་བསྟན་རྩིས་ཀྱི་ལོ་སྤྱིར[502]བསྒྲངས[503]ནས་དེ་ཉིད་ཀྱི་[504]ལོ་ངོས་བཟུང་བ་དང་། (1–3–1–2–2–2) སའི་དམིགས[505]ཇི་ལྟར་བརྟལ[506]ནས་བཟོར་ཕྱིད་ཇི་ [16a7] ལྟ་བུར་བཞེངས་པ་དང་། (1–3–1–2–2–3) དེ་ལ་རབ་ཏུ་གནས་པ་མཛད་པའི་ཚུལ་ལོ་ (ཚུལོ) ||

(1–3–1–2–2–1) དང་པོ་སྤྱིར་སྟོན་པ་ཤཱཀྱ་ཐུབ་པ་གྲོང་ཁྱེར་ (གྲོང་ར་) རྩ་མཆོག་ཏུ་སྨྲ་ངན་ལས་འདའ[507]བའི་ཚུལ་བསྟན་ནས་ལོ་གསུམ་སྟོང་དང་སུམ་བརྒྱ་དགུ་བཅུ་རྩ་གསུམ་ [16b1] ལ་ཇོ་བོ་བོད་དུ་རྒྱུ་ཕོ་རྟའི་ལོ་ལ་ [illegible: ཐོ་དུ] བྱོན་སྟེ་དགུང་ལོ་བཅུ་གཉིས་བོད་དུ་བཞུགས་སོ། །ཤིང་པོ[508]རྟ་ལ་གཉེ་ཐང་དུ་འདས་པའི་ཚུལ་བསྟན། དེ་ནས་ཤིང་མོ་ལུག་ལ་སྟོན་པས་ལྷས་སྒྲིང་དུ་བྱོན་ནས: མེ་མོ[509]སྦྲེའུ་ལ་དགོན་པ་ [16b2] གོང་མ་དང་། གཟིམས[510]ཁང་ཀུན་ [illegible] བཞེངས། དེ་ནས་མེ་མོ་བྱའི་ལོ་ལ་དབུ་རྩེ་རིན་པོ་ཆེ་བཞེངས་ཏེ། སངས་རྒྱས་སྨྲ་ངན་ལས་འདས་ནས་ལོ་སུམ་སྟོང་དང་བཞི་བརྒྱ་དང་བདུན་སོང་བའི་དུས་ཡིན་པར་གདའ། དེ་ལོ་ངོས་བཟུང་བའོ།།

(1–3–1–2–2–2) [16b3] གཉིས་པ་སའི་དམིགས[511]ཇི་ ལྟ་ བུ་བརྟལ[512]ནས་བཟོ་ཕྱིད་ཇི་ལྟ་བུ་བཞེངས་པ་ནི། ཇོ་བོའི་གདུང་དང་ཕྱག་དཔེར་རྣམས་གྲེའུ[513]རིག་པ་ཅན་གཅིག་ ལ་ བསྐལ[514]ནས་ས་འཚོལ་དུ་བཏུག་པས། ནེའུ་ལྷུགས་ལྷིགས་ཡོད་པ། མེ་ཏོག་ཤང་ཤང་ [16b4] ཐིབ་སེ་སྐྱེས་པ་གཅིག་ཏུ་ཉལ་སྐད། དེ་ནི་དབུ་རྩེ་ཀ་གཉིས་མ་དེའི་ས་གཞི་ ༢ འོ། །དེ་ན་རྒྱུ་མིག་ཆེ་བ་གཉིས་འདུག སྐྱེར་པ་ཕུང་པོ་གཉིས་འདུག

501 ¦ ?

502 ཕྱིར་

503 བགྲངས་

504 ཀྱིས་

505 མིག་

506 བརྩལ་

507 འདས་

508 ཕོ་

509 ཕོ་

510 གཟིམ་

511 མིག་

512 བརྩལ་

513 དྲེའུ་

514 བཀལ་

དེའི་སྐྱེར་ཕུང་རྩ་བ་ནས་སྟོན་[515]པས། སྐལ་པ་ ལྡོང་[516] དང་། སྤྲུལ་སྐུ་ཚོགས་གྱིས་[16b5] བྱུང་སྐད། ཆུ་མིག་སྤུབས་[517]ཏེ་འོག་ཏུ་དྲངས་སྐད་(དྲང་སྐད)། ས་གཞི་ལ་ས་ཆོག་ཕུན་སུམ་འཚོགས་[518]པ་མཛད་དོ། །དཔལ་གསང་བ་འདུས་པའི་དཀྱིལ་འཁོར་ཀྱི་[519]ཐིག་གདབ: སའི་ལྷ་མོ་དང་། ཀླུའི་རྒྱལ་པོ་ལ་སོགས་པའི་གཏེར་ [16b6] དང་བཅའ་ཁ་ཐམས་ཅད་ས་དཔྱད་རིན་པོ་ཆེ་འཕྲུལ་ཀྱི་[520]མེ་ལོང་ནས་འབྱུང་བ་ལྟར་མཛད: ཛོ་བོའི་གདུང་དང་། དངུལ་གདུགས་ཅན་ཆུང་བ་དང་། འཇམ་དཔལ་དོ་རྗེ་ལ་སོགས་པ་རྣམས་བཞུགས་པར་མཛད། ཛོ་བོའི་གུར་དཀར་ [16b7] ཕུབ། ས་འདུལ་ལ་བརྒྱད་སྟོང་ མཛོའ་ འགྲེལ་གསུངས། དེ་ནས་ཀ་བདུ་ང་[521]གི་རྒྱུ་ལ་ [illegible] ཛོ་བོའི་ [illegible: ནདཔྲར་ཡུལ་] ནས་སྒྲིང་ཤར་ཕྱོགས་སུ་རྒྱང་གྲགས་གཉིས་འཇལ་[522]བའི་ས་ན། གསེར་མ་དང་། གཡུ་མ། དངུལ་མ། འཚོང་[523]མ་ཞེས་བྱ་བའི་ཤུག་ [17a1] པ་ཆེན་པོ་ཀླུའི་རྒྱལ་པོའི་ཕོ་བྲང་གནས་པ་ཡོད་པ་ལས། དེའི་ཀླུ་དེ་དག་ཁྲིའུ་བཞོན་[524]ནུར་ (བཞོནནུར) སྤྲུལ་ནས། གསེར་མ་དང་། དངུལ་མ་གཉིས། དགེ་བཤེས་སྟོན་པ་ལ་ཕུལ་སྐད། དེའི་དུས་སུ་ཅིག་པ་མཁན་པོ་ [17a2] དང་། ཤིང་བཟོའ་བ་དང་མ་འཆམ་སྟེ། ཅིག་མཁན་ན་རེ། ངའི་ཅིག་བ་མེད་ན་ཤིང་བཟོའ་ +པས་[525]ངག་ [blank] ཆེ་ +དོན་མེད་ཟེར། དེར་ཤིང་བཟོའ་བས་ཅིག་པ་ལ་མ་ལྟོས་པར་ཕྱོགས་བཞིར་ཀ་བ་གཉིས་སྟེ་བརྒྱད: ཟུར་ [17a3] བཞི་ལ་བཞི་སྟེ། བཅུ་གཉིས། དབུས་སུ་གསེར་མ་དང་གཡུ་མ་གཉིས་བརྩུགས་[526]སྟེ། ཀ་བ་བཅུ་བཞི་བཙུགས་[527]ནས་སྟེང་དུ་རྒྱ་ཕིབས་ལ་སོགས་པ་བྱ་[528]ཏེ་བཟོའ་ཁྱད་བསམ་གྱིས་མི་ཁྱབ་པ་བྱས་སོ། ཀ་བའི་བར་ [17a4] རྣམས་སྤང་ལེབ་དང་ཤིང་ཕྱུན་གྱི་[529] བཀག་[530]ཏེ། དེ་ལ་འཇིམ་པའི་ཞ་[531]མ་ལེགས་པར་བྱས། དེ་ལྟར་ [illegible] མཛད་པའི་བཟོའ་བོ་ནི་ཛོ་བོ་བེ་རི་རྐྱོར་བ་བྱ་བ་ལགས་སྐད། དེ་ལ་དབུ་རྩེ་རིན་པོ་ཆེའི་ནང་ [17a5] ན་ཀ་བ་གཉིས་ཕྱོགས་མཚམས་ན་ཀ་བ་བཅུ་གཉིས་ཡོད་པ། སྒོ་ནི་རྒྱ་སྒོ་ལྷོ་ལ་བསྟན་པ། རྒྱ་ཕིབས་ཀྱི་

515 བརྟེན་
516 ལྡོང་
517 བསྤུབས་
518 ཚོགས་
519 ཀྱི་
520 ཀྱི་
521 གདོང་
522 མཇལ་
523 མཚོང་
524 གཞོན་
525 བས་
526 བཙུགས་
527 བཙུགས་
528 བྱས་
529 གྱིས་
530 བཀབ་
531 ཞལ་

སྙིང་ན་གསེར་ཀྱི་[532]འག་ལྦི་ར་[533]དང་; གཡས་གཡོན་ན་ནམ་མཁའ་ལྡིང་གིས་མཛེས་ [17a6] པར་བྱས་པའོ། །དེ་ནས་དེའི་ཁྱམས་སྟོད་ན་ཀ་བ་བཅུ་གཉིས་ཕིབ་[534]ནས་ཡོད། དེའི་མན་ཆད་བྱེད་པ་པོ་གཅིག་འོང་གི་གསུང་ནས་འཕྱོར་བཞག་སྐད། དེ་དག་ནི་ས་དམིགས་[535]རྩལ་[536]ནས་བཟོའ་ཁྱད་ཇི་ [17a7] ལྟ་བུར་བཞེངས་པའི་ཚུལ་ལོ།།

(1–3–1–2–2–3) གསུམ་པ་དེ་ལ་རབ་ཏུ་གནས་པ་མཛད་པའི་ཚུལ་ནི། །གཙུག་ལག་ཁང་གི་ཞལ་བསྒྲོས་ཀྱི་རིམ་པ་རབ་ཏུ་གནས་པའི་གདམ་[537]ངག་ནས་ཇི་ལྟར་འབྱུང་བ་ལྟར་ [17a8] སློན་པ་རིན་པོ་ཆེ་ཉིད་ཀྱི་གྲོགས་མཆེད་རྣལ་འབྱོར་ པ་ རྣམས་པས་མཛད་ནས་ཕུན་སུམ་ཚོགས་[538]པ་མཛད་དོ། །དེ་དག་ནི་རབ་ཏུ་གནས་པ་མཛད་པའི་ཚུལ་ལོ། །དེ་རྣམས་ཐམས་ཅད་མེ་མོ་བྱའི་ལོ་ལ་ཚར་བར་མཛད་དེ། [17b1] དེ་ལྟ་བུའི་གཙུག་ལག་ཁང་དེ་ནི་ལོ་གང་ལ་ཚུལ་ཇི་ལྟར་བཞེངས་པའི་ལོ་རྒྱུས་བསྟན་ཟིན་ཏོ།།

དེ་ལྟར་ཞང་འཕྲང་ཁ་ཕེར་ཆུང་ཡབ་སྲས་ཀྱིས་ཡོན་བདག་མཛད་དེ། །[539]དགེ་བཤེས་སློན་པས་ [17b2] མཆོད་གནས་མཛད་ནས་ཇོ་བོའི་ཐུགས་དགོངས་བསྐང་བའི་ཕྱིར། ཐྲི་ [+ཀ] མ་ལ་ཤི་ལའི་གནས་ཆུང་ལྟ་བུར་བཞེངས་སྟེ[540]། །བོད་ཀྱི་སྡེ་པ་གང་གི་ཡང་ཕྱོགས་སུ་མ་སོང་བ; བོད་ཀྱི་ཇོ་ཛེ་གདན་གཅིག་ཡོད་པར་འདུག [17b3] སྣ་མི་རག ཀླུ་མི་མེས; འབྲིན་མི་ཚོ; རག་མི་ཚོ; ལོ་མི་ཚོ; ཚོང་མི་ཚོ [illegible: ¦] བོད་ཁ་བ་ཅན་ཡོངས་ཀྱི་སྤྱིའི་མཆོད་གནས་སངས་རྒྱས་ ཀྱི་ བསྟན་པ་མི་ནུབ་པའི་རྒྱལ་མཚན; མི་ [17b4] འགྱུར་བའི་སྲོག་ཤིང་དུ་བཞེངས་པ་ལགས་སོ (ལགསོ) ། །དེ་དག་ནི་རྣམ་སྙིང་དུ་བྱོན་ནས་བཞེངས་པའི་ཚུལ་དངོས་སོ། །

[541]ཇོ་བོ་འཇམ་དཔལ་རྡོ་རྗེ་ ×དཉུལ་གདུགས་ཅན་ ×ཆུང་ ×དང་། སྒྲོལ་མ་གསུང་བྱོན་མ་ གསེར་ལྷ་ལྷུ་ལ་སོགས་པའི་ལོ་རྒྱུས་ནི་རྟེན་བཤད་ ཆུང་བའི་ བསྐབས་[542]སུ་ཤེས་ [17b5] པར་བྱའོ།།

---

532 ཀྱི་

533 གན་ཛི་ར་ or གཉྫི་ར་

534 ཕུབ་

535 མིག་

536 བཙལ་

537 གདམས་

538 ཚོགས་

539 - །

540 ཏེ

541 no annotation mark

542 སྐབས་

(1–3–1–3) གསུམ་པ་ལོ་དུར་སློབ་མ་བསྐྱངས་ནས་མྱ་ངན་ལས་འདའ་བའི་ཚུལ་བསྟན་པ་ནི། དེ་ལྟར་དགེ་བའི་བཤེས་གཉེན་སྟོན་པ་རིན་པོ་ཆེ་སྐད་པ་ཐུགས་ཀྱི་སྐྱིལ་[543]དང་མཁྱེན་པ་རྒྱ་མཚོར་ [17b6] ལྡན་པ་དེས། རྣས་སྒྲིང་དུ་ཇོ་བོའི་བསྐྱོལ་[544]བཟང་གི་བསྟུགས་[545]ནས་བཞུགས་ཡོད་པའི་དུས་སུ། སྤྱིར་ཡང་ལས་ཚན་རྒྱ་[546]བཙུ་བྲ་བ་བྱོན་པ་ལགས་སྐད་ (ལགསྐད) । ཁྱད་པར་དུ་སྐུ་མཆེད་རིན་པོ་ཆེ་རྣམས་[547]པ་གསུམ་ [17b7] བྱོན། ཁམས་པ་ལུང་པ། སྟོན་བཙན་ན་མགོའ་བ། ལྷ་ཙང་སྟོན་པ། སྐྱི་རབ་བཙོན་[548]ནུ་འོད་ཟེར། ལྷ་མི་ཤེས་རབ་གཡུང་དྲུང་ (གཡུང) ། ཀ་བ་རྒྱ་གར། རུག་པའི་ཞང་ཆེན་པོ། མཁན་པོ་ཡེ་ [17b8] རྒྱལ། བྲག་དཀར་ཇོ་བཙུན། ཀམ་ཡུང་བ་བ། ཀ་སྐྱོག་པ། ཡོང་རྫོང་རྣལ་འབྱོར་པ། མཐའ་བཞི་བསྒོམ་[549]པ། སྟིང་[550] [illegible] པ་ལ་སོགས་མང་པོ་སྨིན་ཅིང་གྲོལ་ཏེ། སངས་རྒྱས་ཀྱི་བསྟན་པ་ [18a1] གཙང་སྦྲ་དང་། ཕྱི་རྗེས་སུ་གཟིགས་པའི་སྒོ་ནས་བསྐྱངས་སོ། །དེ་ལྟར་ ལོ་ དགུའི་བར་དུ་འགྲོ་བ་སྨིན་པའི་ལས་མཛད་དེ། ཡི་དམ་ (ཡིདྃ་) ཀྱི་[551]ལྷ་དུ་མའི་ཞལ་ཡང་གཟིགས་སྐད། དེ་ནས་གུང་[552]ལོ་དྲུག་བཅུ་ [18a2] ཐམ་པ་ལ་ཆུ་མོ་ཡོས་བུའི་ལོ་བྲི་[553]ཟླ་པའི་ཚེས་ཉི་ཤུ་ (ཉི) ལ། སེ་བའི་དུང་སྐད་དཀར་སྒྲེར་ཡོད་པའི་དུས་དེར་སྐུ་གཤེགས། །དེ་དག་ནི་ལོ་དུར་སློབ་མ་བསྐྱངས་ནས་མྱ་ངན་ལས་འདའ་བའི་ཚུལ་ [18a3] བསྟན་ པའི་ ལོ་རྒྱུས་ཟུར་ཙམ་མོ། །དེ་ལྟར་དོན་གསུམ་གྱིས་སྟོན་པ་རིན་པོ་ཆེ་ཡོན་མཆོད་ཀྱིས་[554]ཕྱག་ལེན་མཛད་ནས་བཞེངས་པའི་ལོ་རྒྱུས་བསྟན་ཟིན་ནོ་ (ཟིནོ) ||

(1–3–2) གཉིས་པ། དེའི་རྗེས་སུ་གང་ཟག་དང་གང་ [18a4] གིས་ཕྱག་ལེན་མཛད་ནས། དབུ་རྩེ་གཞན་རྣམས་བཞེངས་པའི་ལོ་རྒྱུས་ལ་དྲུག་སྟེ། (1–3–2–1) ཀ་གཉིས་མའི་ཁྲམས་སྨད་གང་གིས་མཛད་པ་དང་། (1–3–2–2) དབུ་རྩེ་ཀ་བ་བཅུ་དྲུག་མ་གང་གིས་བཞེངས་པ་ [18a5] དང་། (1–3–2–3) ཀ་བ་ཉི་ཤུ་རྩ་བཞི་མ་གང་གིས་བཞེངས་པ་དང་། (1–3–2–4) ཀ་བཞི་མ་གང་གིས་བཞེངས་པ་དང་། (1–3–

543 དཀྱིལ་

544 སྐྱོལ་

545 བཙུགས་

546 བརྒྱ་

547 རྣམ་

548 གཙོན་

549 སྒོམ་

550 ?

551 གྱི་

552 དགུང་

553 གྲོ་བཞིན་ ?

554 ཀྱི་

2–5) དབུ་རྩེ་རིན་པོ་ཆེ་ལ་ཐོག་གང་གིས་བསྐལ[555]བ་དང་། (1–3–2–6) དེ་ཐམས་ཅད་ཀྱི་ཁྱམས་དང་དབུ་རྩེ་ཕྱི་མ་གསུམ་ལ་སྐོར་ [18a6] བ་དང་། སྦྱིན་བདག་གང་གིས་མཛད་པའི་ལོ་རྒྱུས་སོ།།

(1–3–2–1) དང་པོ་ཀ་གཉིས་མའི་ཁྱམས་སྣང་ (ཁྱིམ་སྣང་) གང་གིས་ +བཞེངས་པའི་ ལོ་རྒྱུས་ལ། དེ་ལྟར་དགེ་བཤེས་སྟོན་པ་སྐུ་གཤེགས་ནས། རྣལ་འབྱོར་པ་ཆེན་པོ་གདན་སར་བྱོན་ནས་གདན་ས་ལོ་ [18a7] བཅུ་གསུམ་མཛད། དེའི་དུས་སུ་ཞང་འཕྲང་ཁ་བེར་ཆུང་གི་བུ། དགྲ་བཅོམ། དེའི་སྲས་དར་མ་ཡེ་ཤེས་བྱ་བ་གཅིག་གིས་ཀ་ +གཉིས་ མའི་ཁྱམས་སྣང་དང་། ཁྱམས་ཆུང་དང་། ནག་ཚང་དང་གསུམ་མཛད་དེ་དེ་དག་ལ་རབ་ཏུ་གནས་ [18a8] པ་ནི། རྣལ་འབྱོར་པ་ཆེན་པོའི[556]བཞུགས: རྣལ་འབྱོར་པ་ཆེན་པོ་གདན་ས་མཛད་པའི་རིང་ལ། དགོན་བ[557]གོང་མ་ནས་མར་བྱོན་ད་ལྟ་དབུ་རྩེ་ཀ་བ་བཅུ་དྲུག་མ་ཅན་དེར་གཟིམས[558]ཁང་མཛད: དབུས་ཀྱི་རྒྱལ་ཁམས་ [18b1] འདིའི་བརྟེན[559]དང་། གཙུག་ལག་ཁང་མང་པོའི་རབ་གནས་མཛད་ ཅིང་ ། རྣམ་སྣྲིང་བསྐྱངས་རི་ཐེལ་གསུམ་ལ་སོགས་པའི་བཏྲ[560]བཙུགས: [illegible: ཀྱལ་ཀྱ་བྲི་ illegible] སྟོད་ལུངས[561]པ་ཆེན་པོ་དང་། ལྷ་མི་དང་། ལོ་འཁ་རུབ་དང་: མང་ར་ལ་སོགས་ [18b2] པ་སློབ་མ་མང་པོ་སྨིན་ཅིང་གྲོལ་བར་མཛད་དེ: རྟ་ལོ་བདུན་བཅུ་ཐམ་པ་བཞེས་པའི་ཚེ། ཆུ་མོ་བྱའི་ལོ་ས་ག་ཟླ་བའི་ཚེས་བཅུ་ཤིང་མོ་ཡོས་བུ་ལོ་རྒྱལ་ཀྱི[562]ཟླ་བའི་ཚེས་བརྒྱད་ལ་སྐུ་གཤེགས:[563] [18b3] དེ་ནི་ཀ[564]གཉིས་མའི་ཁྱམས་སྣང་གང་གིས་བཞེངས་པའི་ལོ་རྒྱུས་སོ།།

(1–3–2–2) གཉིས་པ། ཀ་བ་བཅུ་དྲུག་མ་བཞེངས་པའི་ལོ་རྒྱུས་ལ་གཉིས་སྟེ། (1–3–2–2–1) ཀ་བ་བཅུ་དྲུག་ (བཙུག་) མ་ [blank] བཞེངས་པའི་ལོ་རྒྱུས་དང་། (1–3–2–2–2) བཞེངས་པའི་ཚུལ་དངོས་སོ:

555 བཀབ་

556 པོས་

557 པ་

558 གཟིམ་

559 རྟེན་

560 པ་ཏྲ་ ?

561 ལུང་

562 གྱི་

563 Cf. *Gsal ba'i sgron me*: 113a2: རྟ་ལོ་ལ་རྣལ་འབྱོར་པ་གཤེགས་པའི་ལོ་དེ་ཉིད་

564 ཀ་

[18b4] (1–3–2–2–1) དང་པོ་ནི། དེ་ལྟར་རྣལ་འབྱོར་པ་ཆེན་པོ་སྐུ་གཤེགས་ནས། རྣལ་འབྱོར་ཀྱི་[565]དབང་ཕྱུག་དཔལ་ལྡན་དགོན་[566]བས་ལོ་བདུན་མཛད་དེ། དགོན་པ་གོང་མ་ཉིད་དུ་བཞུགས་ནས། རིན་པོ་ཆེ་སྣེ་ཟུར་བ་དང་། ཀ་མ་བ་དང་། ཞ་བོ་ [18b5] སྣང་པ་དང་། སྣ་མོ་བ་དང་། ཆུ་འཚུར་བ་དང་: མངའ་རིས་པ་ལ་སོགས་པ་མང་པོ་སྨིན་ཅིང་གྲོལ་བར་མཛད་ནས། འབྲུག་ལོ་བ་དྲུག་བཅུ་རྩ་དྲུག་བཞེས་པའི་ཚེ་ཆུ་མོ་བྱའི་ལོ་ས་ག་ཟླ་བའི་ཚེས་ [18b6] བཅུ་བདུན་ལ་སྐུ་གཤེགས་སྐད། དེ་ནས་དགེ་བཤེས་པུ་ཏོ་བས་གདན་ས་མཛད་པའི་སྐབས་སུ: དཔོན་ཆོས་ཀྱི་རྒྱལ་པོ་ལ་སོགས་པའི་ཁམས་པ་མ་རུངས་[567]པ་འགའ་ཞིག་གིས་བཞུགས་དབང་མ་བྱུང་བས། ལོ་གཅིག་ལས་ [18b7] མ་བཞུགས་སོ: དེ་ནས་དགེ་བཤེས་པུ་ཏོ་བ་དེ་དཀར་ཐུབ་ཀྱི་ནགས་ཁྲོད་དུ་དྲང་སྲོང་གི་སྤྱོད་ཚུལ་མཛད་པའི་སྐབས་དེར། རྟས་སྒྲིང་གི་གདན་ས་ལ་སྐྱེད་ཅག་བྱུང་སྟེ: དགོན་པ་གོང་མ་རུ་རུ་ཚང་འཆ་[568]ཡིན་ [18b8] བྱུང་། བླ་ཡེ་ཐང་སྐོག་[569]དུ་ཐགས་ར་བྲེད་པ་གཅིག་བྱུང་: དེ་ནས་དགེ་བཤེས་པུ་ཏོ་བ་འདས་ནས། ལོ་གཅིག་གཉིས་ལོན་པའི་སྐབས་དེར་རྟས་སྒྲིང་གི་གདན་ས་ལ་དགེ་བའི་བཤེས་གཉེན་མཐའ་བཞི་བསྒོམ་པ་སྐད་པ་དེ་ [19a1] དགེ་བཤེས་སྟོན་པ་ལ་ཡང་སློབ་པ: སྐུ་མཆེད་གསུམ་ཀའི་སློབ་མ་ཡིན་པ་ཡི་དམ་ཀྱི་[570]ལྷ་དུ་མའི་ཞལ་གཟིགས་པ། གཞན་དོན་མཛད་པའི་འཕྲིན་ལས་ལ་དབང་འབྱོར་པ་གཅིག་ཡོད་པ་དེས། བླ་མའི་ [19a2] གདན་ས་དགོས་[571]ནས་ཡོད་དོ་ཞེས་པའི་གཏམ་གསན་པས། རྟས་སྒྲིང་དུ་བྱོན་པས། བུད་མེད་ (བྱིད) རྣམས་མོ་ཁྲོམ་ཐབ་[572]སེ་བྱས་པའི་རྩ་ན་ཁྱི་ཐུ་མོ་མང་པོ་ཉལ་ནས་འདུག། བུད་མེད་རྣམས་ན་རེ། ཇོ་བོ་བ་ཁྱིས་སྐྱུག་གོ་ (སྐྱུགོ) [19a3] ཟེར། ང་བླ་མའི་གདན་ས་ཉུལ་དུ་འོངས་པ་ལ་ཁྱིས་སྐྱུག་པ་དང་། ཁ་སྤྱང་མ་དམ་སྲི་མ་འདི་རྣམས་ཁྱེད་རྣམས་འདིར་སྡོད་པ་ལ་ཨ་གསུངས་པས། ཁྱི་རྣམས་ཀྱི་[573]གཞུག་རིལ་དང་། གཞལ་ལེ་ (གཞལེ་)[574]བྱས་སྐད། [19a4] དེ་ནས་དགེ་བཤེས་འཐ་[575]བཞི་དེས། དགེ་བཤེས་ཤར་བ་བཞོའི་ཁང་པ་གནས་ན་བཞུགས་པ་དང་། ཀ་མ་བ་དང་། སྟེང་[576]པ་[577]བ་དང་། བྱ་ཡུལ་བ་དང་། དགེ་བཤེས་གླང་རི་ཐང་པ་རྣམས་ཀྱི་སྤྱན་མངར་[578]བྱོན་ནས། ཁྱེད་ [19a5] རྣམས་བླ་མའི་གདན་ས་ལ་ཕྱི་མིག་ཨེ་ལྟ། ལྟ་ན་དུས་ད་ལ་བབ་ནས་

565 ཀྱི་

566 + པ་

567 རུང་

568 འཆར་

569 སྐོག་

570 ཀྱི་

571 འཁྱོག་

572 ཐིབས་

573 ཀྱིས་

574 same as ཞལ་ལེ་ཞོལ་ལེ་

575 མཐའ་

576 སྟེངས་

577 པོ་

578 སྔར་

འདུག་གོ་གསུང་ (འདུགོ་སུང་) ¦ ཁོང་རྣམས་པ་དེ་རྣམས་ཀྱིས་ཀྱང་འབུལ་བ་ལ་སོགས་པ་ མང་པོ་ མཛད་དོ: པ་ཏྲ་ལ་སོགས་མང་པོ་ཡང་བཙུགས། ། [19a6] བུད་མེད་དང་¦ ར་ལུག་རྣམས་ཕུད་¦ དགེ་འདུན་པ་མང་པོ་ཡང་བཞུགས་པར་མཛད [illegible: ¦] དགེ་བཤེས་འཐའ་[579]བཞིས་ལོ་ཤས་སུ་ཚོགས་དཔོན་མཛད¦ ཁྱད་པར་དུ་དགེ་བཤེས་ཤར་བ་བས¦ དབུ་རྩེ་ཀ་བ་བཅུ་དྲུག་མ་ཅན་ [19a7] དང་¦ དབུ་རྩེ་ཀ་བ་དགུ་མ་གཅིག་མཛད: དེ་རྣམས་ནི་ཀ་བ་བཅུ་དྲུག་མ་མ་བཞེངས་པར་གྱི་ལོ་རྒྱུས་སོ།།

(1–3–2–2–2) གཉིས་པ། བཞེངས་པའི་ཚུལ་དངོས་ནི¦ དཔོན་གྱུད་པ་བྱ་བ་དང་¦ ཟེར་ཁྱུ་ཚོས་ [19a8] ཀྱི་གྲགས་པ་བྱ་བ་དང་¦ ཁོང་དེ་གཉིས་ཀྱི་གཙོ་བོ་བྱས་པའི་བཟང་འདུས་བཅུ་དྲུག་བྱ་བས་བདག་རྐྱེན་བྱས་ནས¦ [illegible] ཀ་གཉིས་མ་བཞེངས་ནས་བརྒྱད་སོང་བ་འབྲུག་གི་ལོ་ དབུ་རྩེ་ཀ་གཉིས་མའི་ནུབ་ཕྱོགས་སུ། དབུ་རྩེ་ཀ་བ་བཅུ་དྲུག་ཡོད་པ¦ [19b1] རྒྱལ་སྒོ་ལྷོ་ཕྱོགས་སུ་བསྟན་པ¦ ཉིས་ཐོག་བྱས་པའི་སྟེང་ན་གསེར་གྱི་[580]གླ་ལྷི་ར་[581]དང་། དེ་ལ་གསེར་གྱི་[582]རྨ་བྱ་གཉིས་ཁ་བལྟ་བས་མཛེས་པར་བྱས་པ¦ བསྐོར་[583]ཁང་དང་བཅས་པ་བཞེངས་སོ (བཞེངསྒོལ?) ། [illegible] དེའི་ཐོག་[584]ཁང་དང་རྟོག་[585]ནི་སུམ་པ་ཤེས་བློ་གྲོས་ཀྱིས་[586]བྱས་ དེའི་ཁྲམས་སྣད་སྣང་ [19b2] ཕྱུག་པོ་མ་བྱ་བས་བཞེངས¦ དེ་ནི་བཞེངས་པའི་ཚུལ་དངོས་སོ། །དེ་དག་ནི་དབུ་རྩེ་ཀ་བ་བཅུ་དྲུག་མ་བཞེངས་པའི་ལོ་རྒྱུས་སོ།།

(1–3–2–3) དབུ་རྩེ་ཀ་བ་ཉི་ཤུ་རྩ་བཞི་མ་བཞེངས་པའི་ལོ་རྒྱུས་ལ་གསུམ་སྟེ¦ (1–3–2–3–1) ལོ་ཚིགས་ [19b3] གང་ཡིན་པ་དང་¦ (1–3–2–3–2) བཞེངས་མཁན་གང་ཡིན་པ་དང་¦ (1–3–2–3–3) རབ་གནས་གང་གི་[587]བཞུགས་པའོ།།

579 མཐའ་

580 གྱི་

581 གན་ཛི་ར་ or གཉྫི་ར་

582 གྱི་

583 སྐོར་

584 Cf. *Dge bshes ston pa'i rnam thar*: 197b5: ཐིགས་

585 Cf. *Dge bshes ston pa'i rnam thar*: 197b5: ཐོག་

586 ཀྱིས་

587 གིས་

(1–3–2–3–1) དང་པོ་ལོ་ཚིགས་གང་ཡིན་པ་ནི། ཀ་གཉིས་མ་བཞེངས་ནས་ལོ་དགུ་བཅུ་རྩ་གསུམ་ལོན་པ་ན་དགེ་བའི་བཤེས་གཉེན་ཞང་ [19b4] འོད་འཇོ་བས་རྣམ་སྣྲིང་གི་གདན་ས་ལ་བྱོན་སྟེ[588]། རྣམ་སྣྲིང་དང་འོད་འཇོ་གཉིས་ལོ་བཅུ་གཉིས་སུ་སྐྱངས[589]། དེ་ཡན་ཆད་ལ་ཕྱུ་ཧོ་བ་བཞུད་ཧྲིང[590]ཕྱིན་ཆད་དེར་ལོ་དྲུག་བཅུ་རྩ་ལྔའི་བར་དེར་གདན་ས་བ་ལ་སོགས་པ་གཏན་ཐེབས་པ་ [19b5] མེད། མཐའ་བཞི་ལ་སོགས་པ་དང་། བགྲེས་པོ་འདྲ་བས་གྲལ་མགོ་འབྱེད་ཡིན། ཆོས་ཀྱི་ཉན་བཤད་ཡང་བཤ[591]མ་མེད་པ་དེ་འདྲ་བྱུང་སྐད། སྐབས་ཅིག་ཇོག་བློ་ལྡན་ཤེས་རབ་ལ་ཕྱུལ་བས། ཁོང་གིས་ [19b6] ཆོས་དཔོན་ལོ་ཁ་ཡར་ མཛད ། ཉུབ་མོ་མི་བུས་པའི་ཐལ་ཕྱུང་གི་སྟེང་ན། ལྕགས་ ཀྱི་ ཁྲིའུ་ +ཤིང་ བཙུགས་ཡིན་གླ་བ་རེ་རེ་ (རི་) གཉིས་གཉིས་བཞུགས་པ་གཅིག་མཛད། དེ་ནས་ཞང་འོད་འཇོ་བ་བཞུགས་པའི་དུས་དེ་ན། མི་[592]ཉག་གི་ [19b7] ○རྒྱལ་པོ་མངའ་དར་བའི་དུས་དེ་ལེགས་པར་གདའ་བས། ○རྒྱལ་པོའི་བླ་མཆོད་ལ་ཞང་འོད་འཇོ་བའི་སློབ་མ་དགེ་བཤེས་གདུགས་ཕུབ་པ་རང་ལ་ཉི་ཤུ་རྩ་ལྔ་ཙམ་ཡོད་པར་གདའ། དེའི་དུས་ན་མི་[593]ཉག་རྒྱལ་པོས་དབུས་བྱུས་པ་མདོ་སྨད། ཙོང་[594]དབུས་ཐམས་ཅད་ཀྱི་ཆོས་ [19b8] ཀྱི་འབུལ་པ། ནོར་ཀྱི་[595]འབུལ་པ། སློབ་གཉེར་ཀྱི[596]་བྱེད་པ: ཡང་དག་པ་གཅིག་བྱུང་། ཀུན་གྱིས་བསྐུར་[597]བའི་གནས་གཅིག་བྱུང་: ཐ་ན་གནས་དེར་ཚོང་དུ་ཡང་དག་པ་གཅིག་ ཡང་ བྱུང་། དེའི་དུས་ན་དགེ་ [20a1] འདུན་ལ་ལོངས་སྤྱོད་མངའ་ཐང་བསམ་གྱིས་མི་ཁྱབ་པ་ཡོད་སྐད། ཞང་འོད་འཇོ་བ་གདན་སར་བྱོན་སྟེ་[598]ལོ་ [illegible དྲུག] བཅུ་ཐམ་པ་ལོན། ཀ་གཉིས་མ་བཞེངས་ནས་ལོ་སྐོར་བཅུ་གཉིས་སོང་ནས་རྟ་ལོར་ ས་ཕོ་འབྲུག་གི་ (འབྲུགི་) ལོ་ལ་རྨང་བརྩལ་[599]པར་གདའ: དེ་ནི་ལོ་ཚིགས་གང་ [20a2] ཡིན་པའོ:

588 ཏེ་

589 བསྐྱངས་

590 དེང་

591 གཤའ་

592 ཉི་

593 ཉི་

594 གཙང་

595 ཀྱི་

596 ཀྱི་

597 བཀུར་

598 ཏེ་

599 བརྩམས་

(1–3–2–3–2) གཉིས་པ་བཞེངས་མཁན་གང་ཡིན་པ་ནི། ཞང་འབྲ་[600]ཀ་བེར་ཆུང་གི་སྲས། ཆོས་གྲགས། དགྲ་བཅོམ། ཤཱཀྱ་[601] གྲགས་[602]ལྔུན་པོའོ། །ལྔུན་པོའི་སྲས་སྤྱན་རས་སྐྱབས: ཤཱཀྱ་[603]སྐྱབས། [20a3] ཡེ་ཤེས་སྐྱབས། པདྨ་སྐྱབས། དང་བཞིའོ (ངོ) | | པདྨ་སྐྱབས་ཀྱི་སྲས། རྡོ་མོས་རྡོ་རྒྱལ་གི་[604]གཉིས (གིཉིས) | |[605]རྡོ་མོས་ཀྱི་སྲས་བཞི་ཡོད་པའི་གཅིག་ཡེ་པའོ། །ཡེ་པའི་སྲས་དཔོན་སེ་པོ་བཙོན་[606]རྩོལ་ [20a4] དང་། ཐང་པོ་དང་། ཁམ་པ་གྲགས་ལགས་སྐད། དེའི་ནང་ནས་དཔོན་སེ་པོ་བཙོན་[607]རྩོལ་དེས། སྤྱིར་ཡང་རྣམ་སྒྲིང་སྐོར་དུ་ཞབས་སྟོག་[608]དཔག་ཏུ་མེད་པ་མཛད། ཁྱད་པར་ཏུ་[609]དབུ་རྩེ་ཀ་བ་ཉི [20a5] ཤུ་རྩ་བཞི་མ་བཞེངས་པ་ལགས་ཏེ། དེའི་ཤིང་རྣམས་ནི་དཔོན་གྱི་གཅེན་པོ་བེར་རྒྱུད་ཐང་པོ་མང་རྗེས་གསད་པས་དེའི་བཏང་[610]ལ་མང་རྗེའི་ཡུལ་ནགས་ཤོད་ཀ་རོང་ནས་དྲངས་པ་ལགས་སྐད། [20a6] དེ་ཀ་གཉིས་མའི་ཤར་དུ་བཞེངས་དགོངས་པ་ལ། རིན་ཆེན་སྣང་[611]པ་སངས་རྒྱས་དཔོན་གྱི་ཞལ་ནས། ཤར་ནུབ་ནས་རྡོ་གཉིས་ཁྱེར་ལས་[612]ཤོག་གསུང་རྟག་[613]པ་གཅིག་བྱའི། རྡོ་གཉིས་ཁྱེར་བྱོན་པས་ཤར་ཕྱོགས་སུ་ [20a7] བཞེངས་ན་ཀླུའི་རྒྱལ་པོའི་པོ་[614]བྲང་ལ་གནོད་པར་འདུག་པས་ནུབ་ཕྱོགས་སུ་གྱིས་གསུང་སྐད། དེར་ནུབ་ཕྱོགས་སུ་བྲང་ཁང་ གཡས་གཡོན་དུ་ མང་པོ་སྤྱིས། རྨང་དུ་ས་སྡིང་[615]རིང་བྲུས་ཏེ། གྲམ་པ་སྡོ་སི་ལེ་ [20a8] བ་གཅིག་གི་སྟེང་ན་མར་བྲུས་ནས་རྨང་གཏད་[616]ནས་ཡོད་སྐད། [illegible] རྩ་སྡོ་སི་ལེ་འདི་བབ་ན[illegible] དེའི་ས་ཚོག་ནི་ཞང་འོད་འཇོ་བས་མཛད་དོ། །དེ་ནས་ལོ་གཉིས་ལོན་པ་ན་ཞང་འོད་འཇོ་བ་དེའི་ལྕགས་པོ་[617]རྟའི་ལོ་ལ་ [20b1] གུང་[618]ལོ་བདུན་བཅུ་རྩ་

---

600 འབྲང་

601 ཤཱཀྱ་

602 + །

603 ཤཱཀྱ་

604 གྱི་

605 - །

606 གཙོན་

607 གཙོན་

608 ཏོག་

609 དུ་

610 སྟེང་

611 སྣང་

612 ལ་

613 བརྟག་

614 ཕོ་

615 གཏིང་

616 བཏང་

617 ཕོ་

618 དགུང་

གསུམ་གྱི་སྟེང་དུ༑ ཛའི་619ཟླ་བའི་ཆོས་བཅོ་ལྔའི་ཕོ་རངས་སྐུ་གཤེགས། དེའི་གདན་ས་དགོན་འོད་འཛོམ་བ་ལ་གཏད་པས་ལོ་ཉི་ཤུར་ཙ་620དགུའི་བར་དུ་གདན་ས་མ་ཕུལ་སྐད། ། [20b2] དེའི་སྐབས་སུ་དགེ་བཤེས་སྒང་ཐང་དཀར་བས་ཐང་དཀར་དང་༑ རྣས་སྒྲིང་གཉིས་སྤྲུལ་ནས་ལོ་ཉི་ཤུ་ཙ་621དགུ་མཛད། དཔོན་སེ་བོས་དབུ་རྩེ་ཀ་བ་ཉི་ཤུ་ཙ་622བཞི་ཡོད་པ་ཉིས་ཐོག་པ་བསྐོར་623ཁང་དང་བཅས་པ་ [20b3] བཞེངས༑ གསེར་གྱི་གླ་ལྷི་རས་མཛེས་པར་བྱས་པ: སྤྱིན་བདད་དང་བཅས་པ [illegible: ¦] སྒོ་ལྷོ་ཕྱོགས་སུ་བསྟན་པ་དབུ་རྩེ་གཞན་རྣམས་ལས་འཕོ་624བ༑ ཁྱད་པར་དུ་འཕགས་པ་གཅིག་བཞེངས་སོ། །དེའི་ཁྲིམས་ [20b4] སྐད་ཅོང་ཁ་བ་ཤག་འབྱུང་གིས་བཞེང་625པ་ལགས། [illegible] པའི་ [illegible] ཤཀྱ་626འབུམ་གྱིས་ དེ་དག་ནི་བཞེངས་མཁན་གང་ཡིན་པའོ།།

(1–3–2–3–3) གསུམ་པ་རབ་གནས་གང་གི་627བཞུགས་པ་ནི། །བྱང་ཆུབ་སེམས་དཔའི་རྒྱུད་དུ་སྐུ་འཁྲུངས་ཤིང་༑ [20b5] སྐྱེ་བ་དཔག་ཏུ་མེད་པ་ནས་གཞན་དོན་ལ་ཐུགས་སྦྱངས་པ༑ འཕགས་པ་སྤྱ་628རས་གཟིགས་ཀྱི་སྤྲུལ་པ་ཡོངས་སུ་གྲགས་པ་རིན་ཆེན་སྣང་པ་སངས་རྒྱས་དགོན་ཀྱི་629བཞུགས་སོ། །དེ་དག་ནི་རབ་གནས་གང་གི་ [20b6] བཞུགས་པའོ། །དེ་ལྟར་དཔོན་སེ་བོ་བཙོན་630ཚུལ་དེས་དབུ་རྩེ་ཀ་བ་ཉི་ཤུ་ཙ་བཞི་མ་དང་༑ གསེར་ཀྱི་631མདོང་རྒྱུས་པ༑ འདུལ་བ་ལུང་ལ་སོགས་པ་དང་༑ སྦྲ་མོ་ཆེ་དང་༑ ཁྲིམས་ཆུང་བསྐྱེད་པ་དང་༑ [20b7] སྒོམ་སྡེ་སྡེ་ལ་སོགས་ཕྱག་རྗེས་མང་དུ་མཛད་པ་ཡིན་སྐད། དེ་དག་ནི་དབུ་རྩེ་བག་632བ་ཉི་ཤུ་ཙ་633བཞི་མ་བཞེངས་པའི་ལོ་རྒྱུས་ཟུར་ཙམ་མོ།།

---

619 བྱའི་

620 ཛ་

621 ཛ་

622 ཛ་

623 སྐོར་

624 མཐོ་

625 བཞེངས་

626 ཤཱཀྱ་

627 གིས་

628 སྤྱན་

629 གྱིས་

630 གཙོན་

631 གྱི་

632 ཀ་

633 ཛ་

(1–3–2–4) བཞི་པ་དབུ་རྩེ་ཀ་བཞི་མ་གང་གིས་བཞེངས་པའི་ [20b8] ལོ་རྒྱུས་ནི། དེ་ལྟར་དགེ་བཤེས་ཐང་ཀར་ +བས་ གདན་ས་ལོ་ཉི་ཤུ་རྩ་དགུ་མཛད་ནས་རྒྱུ་མོ་ [illegible: བྱའི་?] ལོ་ལ་སྐུ་གཤེགས། །དེའི་རྗེས་ལ་དགོན་འོད་འཛོ་བས་གདན་ས་ལོ་དྲུག་མཛད་ནས་སྐྱུང་[634] [illegible] [21a1] ལགས་པར་གདའ། ^ལོ་སློར་ [illegible] ཤིང་ཕོ་ལོར་^ དེ་དང་པོ་ཡོན་བཙུན་བརྩོན་འགྲུས་རྡོ་རྗེ་བྱ་བ་ཞང་འོད་འཛོ་བའི་སློབ་མ་ཡིན་པ། འབྱོར་པ་ཕུན་སུམ་འཚོགས་[635]པ་མངའ་བ་གཅིག་གིས། དབུ་རྩེ་ཀ་བཞི་མ་དེ་ཀ་ [21a2] གཉིས་མའི་རྒྱབ་དུ་[636]བཞེངས་པ་ལགས་སྐད། དེའི་རབ་གནས་དགོན་འོད་འཛོ་བས་མཛད་དོ། །དེ་དག་ནི་དབུ་རྩེ་ཀ་བཞི་མ་བཞེངས་པའི་ལོ་རྒྱུས་ཟུར་ཙམ་མོ།།

(1–3–2–5) ལྔ་པ་དབུ་རྩེ་རིན་པོ་ཆེ་ལ་གསེར་ཐོག་ [21a3] གང་གིས་མཛད་པའི་ལོ་རྒྱུས་ནི། །དགོན་འོད་འཛོ་བ་གདན་ས་མཛད་པའི་དུས་དེར། དཔོན་སེ་བོ་བཙོན་[637]ཚུལ་ཀྱི་[638]དབོན་པོ་ (དབོན་) སློབ་དཔོན་བཙོན་[639]ནུ་སེང་གེ་བྱ་བ་བྱུང་སྟེ། དེའི་དུས་སུ་དགོན་འོད་འཛོ་བ་དང་། [21a4] དཔོན་གཉིས་བཀའ་གྲོས་བྱས་ཏེ། སྔོན་གྱི་[640]སླམ་ནོར་རྙིང་པ་དང་: ཕྱོགས་ཕྱོགས་ཀྱི་བུ་སློབ་རྣམས་ཀྱི་འབུལ་བ་བསམ་གྱིས་མི་ཁྱབ་པ་བྱུང་བ་རྣམས་ལ་བརྟེན་ཏེ: བལ་པོའི་ལྷ་བཟོའ་རྣམས་དང་། [21a5] དབུས་པའི་ལྷ་བཟོ་བ་རྣམས་ཀྱི་[641]མཁན་པོ་བྱས་ཏེ། དབུ་རྩེ་རིན་པོ་ཆེའི་སྟེང་དུ་གསེར་ཐོག་[642]ཁམས་གསུམ་ཟིལ་གནོན་བཞེངས་སུ་ (བཞེངས྄ུ་) གསོལ་སྟེ། །དེ་ཡང་དབུ་རྩེའི་ +ཀ་བ་འོག་མ་སྟོབ་[643]ཀྱི་སྟེང་དུ་བྱས་ +ཀ་ཐོག་ཀ་གཞག་[644]བྱས་པའི་ཀ་ [21a6] བ་བཅུ་བཞི། ཀ་ཐུན་གྲངས་མེད་པའི་སྟེང་དུ་སྤུབ་[645]ལེབ: དེའི་སྟེང་དུ་ཟངས་ལ་ཆ་གཟེར་བྱས་པའི་རྣམ་པས་ཐམས་ཅད་ཁེབས་ +པར་ གཡོགས་ཏེ (གཡོགས་སྟེ?) | །སྟོལ་མཚམས་སུ་ (མཆོས྄ུ་) ལྕགས་གཟེར་གྱིས་བཏབ་ཏེ[646]། [21a7] གླ་ལྤྱི་ར་[647]དང་། ནམ་མཁའ་ལྡིང་གིས་དབུ་བརྒྱན: ཆུ་སྲིན་དང་སེང་གེ་ལ་སོགས་པའི་པ་ཏྲ་དུ་མས་མཛེས་པར་བྱས་སྟེ། མདོར་ན་དེ་འདྲ་བ་

634 བསྐྱངས་

635 ཚོགས་

636 ཏུ་

637 གཙོན་

638 གྱི་

639 གཙོན་

640 གྱི་

641 ཀྱིས་

642 ཏོག་

643 སྟོབས་

644 བཞག་

645 པང་

646 སྟེ

647 གན་ཇི་ར་ or གཉྫི་ར་

དབུས་ཀྱི་རྒྱལ་ཁམས་ན་མེད་པ་ལགས་སྟེ[648]། [21a8] དེ་ལ་རབ་ཏུ་གནས་པ་ནི་དགོན་འོད་འཇོ་པའི[649]སྤུར་གོང་ནས་ལན་མང་དུ་མཛད། ཕྱིས་ཡོངས་སུ་སྡོགས[650]བར་གྲུབ་པའི་སྐབས་སུ་ནི། བཀའ་བསྡོམས[651]པའི་དགེ་བའི་བཤེས་གཉེན་མང་པོ་གདན་དྲངས [21b1] ཏེ: དེ་རྣམས་ཀྱི་གཙོ་བོ་རིན་ཆེན་སྣང་བ་སངས་རྒྱས་དབོན་ཀྱི[652]དབོན་པོ། དཔལ་ཕྱུག་ན་རྡོ་རྗེའི་སྤྲུལ་པར་གྲགས་པ་སངས་རྒྱས་ཡོན་ཏན་ཀྱིས[653]གཙོ་བོ་མཛད་ནས་དགེ་བའི་བཤེས་གཉེན་མང་པོས་མཛད་དེ། དེའི་དུས་སུ་འདུ་ ×འབུལ་ བ་བསམ་ [21b2] གྱིས་མི་ཁྱབ་པ་<u>བྱུས་སྐད</u> (བྱེ་སྐད): དེ་དག་ནི་གསེར་ཐོག[654]ཇི་ལྟར་མཛད་པའི་ལོ་རྒྱུས་སོ།།

(1-3-2-6) རྡུག་པ་སྤྱིན་བདད་དང་། སྐྱིད་བདེ་ཇི་ལྟར་མཛད་པའི་ལོ་རྒྱུས་ནི། །དེ་ལྟར་དགོན་འོད་འཇོ་བས་གདན་ས་ [21b3] ལོ་བཅུ་དྲུག་མཛད་ནས་ཇ་མོ[655] རྒྱ བ[656] བཅུ་རྩ་བཞི་བཞེས་པའི་ཚེ། ས་མོ་གླང་གི་ལོ་ཕྲའི[657]ཟླ་བའི་ཚེས་ཉི་ཤུ་ལ་སྐུ་གཤེགས། དེའི་རྗེས་ལ་རྒྱུ་འདུལ་བ་འཛིན་པས་ལོ་གཅིག་མཛད: དེའི་རྗེས་ལ་ [21b4] སློབ་དཔོན་ཇོ་གདན་རྩང[658]པས་ལོ་ལྔ་མཛད: དེའི་རྗེས་ལ་སློབ་དཔོན་ཀོ་ཁྱིམ་པས་ལོ་གསུམ་མཛད། དེའི་རྗེས་ལ་སློབ་དཔོན་སྣ་རབས་ལོ་བཅུ་བཞི་མཛད། དེའི་དུས་སུ་བདུད[659]ཀྱིས་དགེ་འདུན་མང་པོ་སྐྱོངས[660]། [21b5] སློབ་དཔོན་སྣ་རབ་ཆུ་མོ་གླང་གི་ ཚ་ སྐུ་གཤེགས: དེ་ནས་སློབ་དཔོན་གྲུར་སྟོན་གདན་སར་བྱོན་ཏེ་གདན་ས་ལོ་བཅོ་ལྔ་སྐྱངས[661]། །ཁྱད་པར་དུ་དབུ་རྩེའི་སྐོར་རྣམས་སྤྱི་རིམས[662]ཀྱི[663]བཞེངས་པར་སོང་བས། [21b6] ཁྱམས་སྟོད་རྣམས་ལ་ལ་སྣ[664]། ལ་ལ་འཐོ[665]བ་དེ་ལྟ་བུ་ཡོད་པ་ལ།

---

648 ཏེ་

649 པས་

650 རྫོགས་

651 གདམས་

652 གྱི་

653 གྱིས་

654 ཏོག་

655 དགུང་ལོ་

656 བརྒྱད་

657 དབོ་

658 ཚོགས་ ?

659 ?

660 བཀྲོངས

661 བསྐྱངས

662 རིམ་

663 གྱིས་

664 དམའ་

665 མཐོ་

ཨ་རབ་དང༌། ཤིང་བཟོ་བ་མངའ་བོ་གདན་དྲངས། ས་རྫོ་དང༌། ཤིང་ལ་སོགས་པའི་རྒྱུ་རྣམས་ཚོགས་མཛད་དེ། །[666]དམའ་བ་རྣམས་འཕངས་ [21b7] སྟོད: མཐོ་བ་རྣམས་ཀྱི་སྙིང[667]པ་རྣམས་རྫེས་[668]ཏེ་གྲལ་མཉམ་བྱས་ནས་ཁྲམས་དང་སྐོར་ཁང་མདུན་རྒྱབ་ཐམས་ཅད་དུ། སྐེད་བད་དང༌། སྤེན་བད་སོ་མ་རེ་བྱས། དབུ་རྩེ་ཀ་བཞི་མའི་ཐིགས་ཁང་འཕངས་ [21b8] སྟོད་གཞི་ནས་བཙོས། ཀ་བ་བཅུ་དྲུག་མ་དང༌། ×ཉི་ཤུ་རྩ་བཞི་མ་གཉིས་ལ་ཡང་སྤེན་བད་སོ་མ་རེ་བྱས་ཉི་ཤུ་རྩ་བཞི་མའི་ཀ་བ་དང་ཁྲམས་རྣམས་བཙོས་བཅུ་དྲུག་མའི་ཁྲམས [illegible] དབུ་རྩེ་ཀ་བ་བཅུ་དྲུག [illegible] ×ཉི་ཤུ་རྩ་བཞི་མའི་བར་ལག་གཅིག་ཡོད་པ་བཀག། དེ་ལ་སྒོ་གཅིག་བཙུགས། དེ་ལྟ་བུ་རྣམས་ཆུ་མོ་ཕག་གི་ (ཕགི་) ལོ་ལ་ཚར་བར་མཛད། །[669] [22a1] རབ་ཏུ་གནས་པ་ནི། ལྷ་གཡེལ་ (ཕྱེལ་) ཞུ་བ་དང། རིན་ཆེན་སྣང་བ་དང༌། བྱ་ཡུལ་བ་དང༌། ཀམ་ཀམ་པ་དང༌། སློབ་དཔོན་ཉིད་དང༌། དགོན་པ་གོང་མ་རྣམས་ཀྱིས་མཛད་དོ། །དེ་དག་ནི་སྤེན་བད་གང་གིས་མཛད་པའི་ [22a2] ལོ་རྒྱུས་སོ།།

དེ་ལ་སྤྱིར་གདོངས་[670]པས་དབུ་རྩེ་རྣམས་ཀྱི་སྟེང་འོག་རྣམས་ན་ཀ་བ་བརྒྱ་སུམ་བཅུ་སོ་དྲུག: སྟེང་འོག་ན་རྒྱལ་སྒོ་བདུན: དབུ་རྩེ་རྣམས་ཀྱི་སྤྱིའི་ཁྲམས་གཅིག་དུ་ཡོད: རྒྱ་འཕྱོངས་[671]གསུམ་ཡོད༌། ཁྲམས་ལ་ [22a3] ཀ་བ་བརྒྱ་རྩ་བརྒྱད་ཡོད། རྒྱལ་སྒོ་གསུམ་སྒྲོ་[672] [illegible: སྒོ་] གཉིས་དང་ལྔ་ཡོད: དབུ་རྩེ་རྣམས་ལ་སྐོར་ཁང་གཅིག་ཏུ་ཡོད: ཀ་གཉིས་མ་ ལ་ དགོས་སུ་ (དགོསུ་)[673]བསྐོར་[674]ཁང་གཅིག་ཡོད་པའོ། །དེ་ལྟར་དོན་དྲུག་གིས་ (དྲུགིས་) དེའི་རྫེས་སུ་ (རྫེསུ་) གང་ཟག་གང་དང་གང་གིས་ [22a4] དབུ་རྩེ་གཞན་རྣམས་བཞེངས་པའི་ལོ་རྒྱུས་སོ།།

སྐབས་འདིར་པ་ཏྲ་[675]རྣམས་ཀྱི་ལོ་རྒྱུས་ཅུང་ཟད་བརྗོད་ན། དཀོན་གཉེར་དང༌། ནགས་ཉེར་[676]དང: སྤྱི་ཁང་གཅིག་དང་རྣམས་དགེ་བཤེས་སྟོན་པས་བརྩུགས[677]། དགོན་པ་གོང་མའི་པ་ཏྲ་ [22a5] ནི། རྗེ་བོའི་བླ་མཆོད་རྣམས་ཀྱི་པ་ཏྲ་གཉེ་ཐང་ན་ཡོད་པ་གསེར་དུ་བཅོས་ནས། དེའི་

---

666 -།

667 སྙིང་

668 བརྫེས་

669 -།

670 བསྡོམས་

671 མཐོངས་

672 གློ་

673 སྒོས་སུ་

674 སྐོར་

675 Cf. Lhun grub chos 'phel (1994: 90):ས་ཏྲ་

676 གཉེར་

677 བཙུགས

གསེར་གྱིས་ཆོས་པའི་གསེར་ཞིང་ལ་སོགས་པ་རྣམས་ཡིན་ནོ། །ཛ་གཉེར་དགེ་བཤེས་ཁམ་པ་ལུང་པས་བརྩིགས[678]: ཟུར་གཉེར་གཡུ་ [22a6] བརྟན་གྱིས་བརྩིགས[679]། རྡོར[680]གཉེར་དགེ་བཤེས་གླང་རི་ཐང་པས་བརྩིགས[681]། ཞོ་གཉེར་དཔོན་རིན་ཆེན་འབུམ་གྱིས་བརྩིགས[682]། སྤྱི་ཁང་ཁྲལ་མི་འབྲེལ་[683]དགེ་སློན་[684]སྤྱི་པས་བརྩིགས: སྤྱི་ཁང་ པ་ཏ་ གཅིག་སྐོར་[685]པོ་གུགས་བྲིས་བརྩིགས[686]: [22a7] ཞིང་གཉེར་ཡང་དཔོན་ [illegible] གཞོན་ཚུལ་ རིན་ཆེན་འབུམ་གྱིས་བཙུགས[687]: [illegible] [illegible: ཨེད་ཤིན་མངའ་རིས་པ་] [illegible] ཤ་བཙུགས འབུམ་གཉེར་དགེ་འདུན་སྤྱི་པས་བརྩིགས[688]: དེ་རྣམས་ཀྱི་སོ་སོའི་ཐབ་གཉེར་ཇི་ལྟར་ཡོད་པ་རྣམས་ཡི་གེ་མངས་ཀྱིས་དོགས་པས་འདིར་མ་བྲིས་སོ། །དེ་རྣམས་ཀྱི་ [22a8] དཔལ་ཀྱི་[689]རྣམ་སྙིང་རྒྱལ་བའི་དབེན་གནས་ཇི་ལྟར་བཞེངས་པའི་ལོ་རྒྱུས་ཟུར་ཙམ་བསྟན་ཏོ།།

678 བཙུགས་

679 བཙུགས

680 རྡོ་

681 བཙུགས

682 བཙུགས

683 འཇལ་ ?

684 བསློན་

685 ཀོང་ ?

686 བཙུགས

687 བཙུགས

688 བཙུགས

689 གྱི་

(2) སྐུ་གསུང་ཐུགས་ཀྱི་རྟེན་རྣམས་ཀྱི་བཤད་པ།

གཉིས་པ་དེ་ན་བཞུགས་པའི་སྐུ་གསུང་ཐུགས་ཀྱི་རྟེན་རྣམས་ཀྱི་བཤད་པ་ལ་གཉིས་ཏེ། | (2–1) ཕྱི་ན་བཞུགས་ [22b1] པ་རྣམས་དང་;
(2–2) ནང་ན་བཞུགས་པ་རྣམས་ཀྱི་བཤད་པའོ།།

(2–1) ཕྱི་ན་བཞུགས་པ་རྣམས་ཀྱི་བཤད་པ།

དང་པོ་ཕྱི་ན་བཞུགས་པ་རྣམས་ཀྱི་བཤད་པ་ཡང་འདི་ལྟར་རིམས་[690]ཀྱིས་[691]ཞེས་པར་བྱའོ། །གཙུག་ལག་ཁང་ཆེན་པོ་ནས་ནུབ་བྱང་མཚམས་སུ་འཇལ་[692]བའི་ས་ན་ [22b2] དགོན་པ་གོང་མ་ཡོད་དེ། དེ་ན་དགོན་པ་བ་ཆེན་པོའི་ཐུགས་དམ; དམ་ཚིག་གསུམ་བཀོད་པའི་རྒྱལ་པོས་དབུ་མཛད་པའི་ཐང་སྐུ་ལྔ་བརྒྱ་ལྷག་ [693]བརྒྱ་དང་ལྔ་བཅུ ཙམ་བཞུགས། ལྷུགས་[694]མ་སུམ་བཅུ་རྩ་ཤས་བཞུགས; རྗེ་བོའི་གདུང་ཁང་ [22b3] དུ་ དཔལ་ལྡན་དགོན་པ་བས་བཞེངས་པའི་གསེར་ཆབ་ཅན་ཀྱིས་[695]དབུ་མཛད་པའི་གདུང་ཁང་རྒྱ་[696]བདུན་བཅུ་ཙམ་བཞུགས། རིན་པོ་ཆེའི་པོ་ཏི་སུམ་བཅུ[697]; ལྷག་ཙམ་ པོ་ཏི་དཀར་པོ་སུམ་བརྒྱ; བསྟན་ཆོས་ཀྱི་པོ་ཏི་མང་པོ་བཞུགས་སོ: [22b4] དེ་རྣམས་ལ་རེ་རེ་ནས་བཤད་པ་མང་དུ་ཡོད་མོད་ཀྱང་། མངས་ཀྱིས་དོགས་པས་འདིར་མ་བྲིས་སོ (བྲིསོ) | །ནུས་སྙིང་མཐོང་ནས་དགོན་ པ་ གོང་མ་ +མ་ མཐོང་ན; ཕྱེད་ [698]མ་ མཐོང་ཟེར་ཏེ; བདེན་པ་འདྲ་བའི་རྟེན་མང་པོ་བཞུགས་སོ། | [22b5] ས་བརྒྱན་བདུན་ཆ་བཅུ་བཞི་ཡོད། དེ་ན་གྲུབ་ཐོབ་མང་པོ་བྱོན་པའི་གནས་ ལགས་ སོ། | ཕྱིས་དེའི་གདན་སར་བྱོན་པའི་དགེ་བའི་བཤེས་གཉེན་ནི; དགེ་བཤེས་ཤར་བའི་སློབ་མ་དགོན་པ་བ་ཞི་བ་བླ་མ་བྱ་བ་བྱོན། དེའི་རྗེས་སུ་དགེ་བཤེས་ [22b6] འཁོམས་པ་བྱ་བ་བྱོན། དེའི་རྗེས་སུ་དགོན་པ་བ་དོར་རྗེ་ ཤེས་རབ་གསལ་ བྱ་བ་བྱོན། དེའི་རྗེས་སུ་དགོན་པ་སྐྱ་ཡལ་ [illegible] གཞོན་ [illegible] ཡལ་དེ་དེ་བྱོན་པ་ལགས་པར་གདའ། ནང་གི་འཁར་ལན་གྱི་བཀོད་པ་རྣམས་སྔར་ཀྱི་[699]དུས་ལས་བསྒྱུར་ནས་ཡོད་དོ། |

---

690 རིམ་

691 ཀྱིས་

692 མཇལ་

693 dot-line annotation mark

694 ཀླུགས་

695 ཀྱིས་

696 བརྒྱ་

697 རྩ

698 dot-line annotation mark

699 ཀྱི་

ཀ་གཉིས་ [22b7] མའི་ནུབ་ཕྱོགས་དགོན་པ་གོང་མའི་རྒྱུད་ཁྲིད་པ་ན་ནུབ་གླིང་ཡོད་དེ། བྲང་ཁང་རེ་རེ་ནས་ཡང་སྐུ་གསུང་ཐུགས་ཀྱི་རྟེན་མང་པོ་བཞུགས་སོ། །དབུ་རྩེའི་བྱང་ནས་དགོན་པ་གོང་མའི་ཐད་གྲང[700]ན་སློམ་སྡེའི་ས་ཡོད་དེ། [22b8] དེ་ན་དགེ་སློང་བཞི་སྡེ་རྒྱུན་མ་ཆད་པར་བཞུགས་པ་ཡིན། གདན་ས་བ་བཞི་ལ་མི་བཞུགས་དུས་སུ་ཚོགས་ཀྱི་གྲལ་མགོ་དང་གཏམ་ལན་ཡང་ཁོང་གིས་མཛད་པ་ཡིན། སློམ་སྡེ་ན། སྐུ་གསུང་ཐུགས་ཀྱི་རྟེན་ [23a1] མང་པོ་བཞུགས་སོ།[701] དེའི་ལྷོག་ན་མར་ལ་དགོན་རྒྱུད་བྱ་པའི[702]བྲང་ཁང་གེར་མ་རྣམས་ཡོད། ཀ་གཉིས་མའི་ཤར་ ཕྱོགས་ ན་བྱ་[703]ཁང་དང་།[704] ནག་ཚང་ཡོད། ཛ་ཁང་ན་དགེ་བཤེས་སྟོན་པའི་གཟིམས་[705]ཆུང་ཡོད། ཀ་གཉིས་མའི་ [23a2] ཤར་ལྷོ་མཚམས་སུ་ན། དགེ་འདུན་ཀྱི་[706]འདུ་ཁང་ཡོད། མིང་ཁྱམས་ཆུང་ཟེར། ཀ་བ་ཉི་ཤུ་རྩ་བཞི་ཡོད། རྒྱ་མཐོངས་གཉིས་ཡོད་པའི་གོང་མའི་ཐད་ན་ཟངས་ཐེར་པོ་ཆེན་པོ་ གཅིག་ ཡོད་དོ། གླང[707]ང་ཆེན་མོ་ལྔ་ཡོད། མངས་[708]སྐྱོལ་དང་སྟོན་ [23a3] མོ་བྱེད་པའི་བྱ[709]ཚོ་སྐྱོལ་བའི་སྟོད་ལགས། དེ་ནས་ཁྱམས་ཆུང་ལ་བཏགས་པ་ངོས་ན། ཤར་གླིང་ཡོད། གླིང་སྟོད་ན་དཔོན་སེ་པོ་མན་ཆད་ཀྱི་གཟིམས་[710]ཁང་སྟེང་ཁང་ཆེན་མོ་གཅིག་ཡོད། དེ་རྣམས་ན་ཡང་སྐུ་གསུང་ཐུགས་ཀྱི་ [23a4] རྟེན་མང་པོ་བཞུགས་སོ། དབུ་རྩེ་ནས་ནུབ་ཕྱོགས་སུ་གླན་པ་ན་དཀོན་གཉེར་ཀྱི་[711]ཁང་པ་ཡང་དག་པ་གཅིག་ཡོད། དེའི་ནུབ་ཕྱོགས་གླིང་ན་སྨྲུན་སྦྲ་རིན་པོ་ཆེའི་གཟིམས་[712]ཁང་ཡིན་ཟེར་བ་དང་། ཀ་མ་བ་དང་། འགོང་སྡེ་སློམ་པ་དང་ [illegible: ¦] [23a5] འཐ་[713]བཞི་དང་། སྡིང་[714] པ་[715] བ་ དང་། ཆུ་བཙུར་གཉིས་ལ་སོགས་པ་རྣམས་ཀྱི་གཟིམས་[716]ཁང་

700 དྲང་

701 ||

702 བའི་

703 ཛ་

704 : ?

705 གཟིམ་

706 གྱི་

707 སླ་

708 མང་

709 ཛ་

710 གཟིམ་

711 གྱི་

712 གཟིམ་

713 མཐའ་

714 སྡིངས་

715 ཕོ་

716 གཟིམ་

ཡིན་ཟེར་བ་རྣམས་ཡོད། ཤར་གླིང་ན་ཁམས་པ་ལུང་པའི་གཟིམས[717]ཁང་དང་། ཕུ་ཚུང་བ་ལ་སོགས་རྣམས་ཀྱི་གཟིམས[718]ཁང་ཡིན་ཟེར་བ་རྣམས་ཡོད། ། [23a6] སྤྱིར་བྲང་ཁང་རྒྱ[719]རྩ་བཅུ་ཙམ་ཡོད་དོ། །དེ་ནས་དབུ་རྩེ་ནས་ (བྱང་ཕྱོགས་) མདའ་རྒྱང་གང་ཙམ་ཀྱི[720]ས་ན། ཕར་ལ་དགེ་བཤེས་སྟོན་པའི་ཐུགས་དམ་མཆོད་བརྟེན་བརྒྱ་རྩ་བརྒྱད་ཡོད་དོ། །དེ་རྣམས་ལ་རབ་གནས་མཛད་པའི་དུས་རྒྱལ་ཀྱི[721]ཟླ་བ་ [23a7] ལ་བྲུམ་པའི་ཁ་བརྒྱན[722]ལ་མེ་ཏོག་འཁྲུངས་སྐད། །རབ་གནས་ཀྱི་དཀྱིལ་འཁོར་བཞེངས་པའི་ས་ན། མཆོད་བརྟེན[723]ཆེ་བ་ཅིག་ཡོད། མཆོད་རྟེན་རྒྱ[724]རྩ་བརྒྱད་ཀྱི་སྟེ་མོ་ཤར་ཕྱོགས་ན། དགེ་བཤེས་སྣང་དང་། དགོན་པ་བ་དོར་ཛེ་ [23a8] དང་། དགོན་པ་བ་སྐྱ་ཡལ་གསུམ་ཀྱི[725]མཆོད་རྟེན་བདད་གཅིག་མ་ཆེ་བ་གསུམ་བཞུགས། ཀ་གཉིས་མའི་ཤར་ཕྱོགས་མདའ་རྒྱང་གང་ (ཡོད་མེད་) ཙམ་གྱི་ས་ན། མཆོད་བརྟེན[726]རྩེ་ལྔ་པ་གཅིག་ཡོད། དེ་ལ་སྐུ་རྒྱབ་བཏད[727]ནས་དགེ་བཤེས་སྟོན་པས་ [23a9] ཆོས་གསུངས་པ་ཡིན། དེའི་གོང་རྡོ་རྒྱང་གང་ཙམ་ན། རྣལ་འབྱོར་གཡུ་རྡུང་རྒྱལ་མཚན་བྱ་བ་ཅན་པོས་ཀྱི་ཡོན་ཏན་མ་ལུས་པ་རྒྱུད་ལ་སྐྱེས་པ་གཅིག་གི་སྤུར་བཞུགས་ས་ཡིན་ཟེར་བའི་ས་སྣ་བག་ཙམ་འབུར་ (བ་) གཅིག་ཡོད། [23b1] ཀ་གཉིས་མའི་ནུབ་བྱང་མཚམས་སློ་འབེན་གང་ཙམ་ན། དགེ་བཤེས་ཕུ་ཏོ་བའི་སྐུ་འབུམ་བར་གསུམ་མ་མཐོའ་བ་ཅིག་ཡོད། དེའི་ནང་ན་ཕུ་ཏོ་བའི་གཟིམས[728]སྐྱོར་ཡོད་ཟེར་བྱིན་བརླབས[729]ཅན་དུ་བྱེད། དབུ་རྩེ་ནས་ནུབ་བྱང་ (ནུབྱང་) མཚམས་སུ་ [23b2] འཇལ[730]བའི་ས་མདའ་རྒྱང་གང་ཙམ་ན་ནུབ་གླིང་གི་མགོ་ན། མཆོད་རྟེན་བདད་གཉིས་མ་ཆེ་བ་གསུམ་གྲལ་བྱས་ (པའི་) ལོ་རྒྱུས་ནི། དེ་ནས་ཚུར་ལ་ཙན[731]གྱི་རྒྱུན་སྲུང་ཡོད་པ་ལ་ (དགེ་འདུན་པ་ཞིག་དང་) རྣལ་འབྱོར་པ་རྣམས་ཀྱི་ཐུགས་ (ལ་) གནོད་པ་བག་རེ་སྐྱལ་ [23b3] བས། དེར་རྣལ་འབྱོར་ཆེན་པོས་མཐོ[732]གཅིག་བསྒིགས[733]། དེ་ལ་བཙན་གྱི་རྟ་པ་རྣམས་འཚོམས་པས་ཕྱིད་དེ་ཉིན་པར་རྣལ་འབྱོར་པའི་གསུང་ནས་ད་འདིར་མཆོད་ (རྟེན་)

---

717 གཟིམ་

718 གཟིམ་

719 བརྒྱ་

720 གྱི་

721 གྱི་

722 རྒྱན་

723 རྟེན་

724 བརྒྱ་

725 གྱི་

726 རྟེན་

727 གཏད་

728 གཟིམ་

729 རླབས་

730 མཇལ་

731 བཙན་

732 ཐོ་

733 བརྩིགས

གཅིག་ བསྒྲིགས་པས་ས་རྡོ་རྡུགས་མཚན་ཅན་ཅིག་མ་བྱུང་བར་དུ་སྐོས་ཅིག སྡིང་[734]རིང་དུ་ [23b4] སྐོས་པས་ཕོ་[735]ཕྱོང་[736]རྡིད་པ་ཞོ་ལེ་ བ་ ཆེན་པོ་གཅིག་འདུག དེ་ལ་རྨང་གཏིང་[737]མཆོད་རྟེན་དབུས་མ་དེ་བཞེངས༑ དེའི་ནང་སྦྱོངས་སུ་ (སྦྱོངསུ་)[738] བྲམ་ཟེའི་ཕོད་སྐུ་གཅིག་དང༔ རྗེ་བོའི་གདུང་ཐལ་དང༑ སྐུ་རགས་གཅིག༑ དེ་བཞིན་གཤེགས་ (པིཞེཏ་) པའི་རིང་བསྲེལ་ཡང་བཞུགས། ། [23b5] དེ་ཤིན་ཏུ་བྱིན་བརླབས་[739]ཆེ་བར་བྱུང་ནས། དེའི་གཡས་གཡོན་གཉིས་སུ་དེ་དང་མཉམ་པ་རི་བཞེངས་ཏེ་བཀྲ་ཤིས་སྤུན་གསུམ་ཟེར་ནས་བྱིན་བརླབས་[740]ཅན་དུ་བྱེད༑ དེའི་བྱང་ཕྱོགས་ [illegible] མདོམ་[741]བཞི་ཙམ་གྱི་ས་ན༑ མཆོད་རྟེན་ [23b6] བད་གསུམ་མ་འཐོན་[742]པོ་གཅིག་བཞུགས་སྐྱེ༑ དེ་ནི་རྣལ་འབྱོར་ཀྱི་[743]དབང་ཕྱུག་དཔལ་ལྡན་དགོན་པ་བའི་སྐུ་འབུམ་ལགས༑ དེའི་ཤར་ཕྱོགས་མདོམ་འ[744]དོ་ཙམ་ཀྱི་[745]ས་ན་མཆོད་རྟེན་ (མཆིན་) བད་གཅིག་མ་མི་ལངས་པ་ཙམ་གཅིག་ཡོད་པ་དེ་ནི༑ དགེ་བཤེས་སྟོན་ཙ་ [23b7] ཟུར་བའི་ལགས་ཏེ་ཁོང་གི་ཞལ་ནས༔ ངའི་རུས་པ་རྣམས་རུས་སྒྲིང་གི་བླ་མའི་སྐུ་འབུམ་ཀྱི་[746]ཙ་[747]དེར་མཆོད་རྟེན་ཆུང་ཆུང་གཅིག་གིས་གསུང་བ་ལགས། དེ་གཉིས་བྱིན་བརླབས་[748]ཅན་ཡིན་པར་གདའ། དེའི་ནུབ་ཕྱོགས་ [23b8] མདོམ་[749]བཅུ་ ཙམ་ གྱི་ས་ན༑ དགེ་བཤེས་མཐའ་བཞིའི་སྐུ་འབུམ་བད་གཅིག་མ་ཆེ་བ་ཅིག་བཞུགས། །དགོན་པ་གོང་མའི་ནུབ་ན་དཔལ་ལྡན་དགོན་པ་བའི་ཆོས་ཁྲི་ཡོད༑ དེའི་འོག་ན་མར་དགོན་པ་བ་ [illegible] [illegible] དགོན་པའི་བྱང་ཤར་ན་དགོན་པ་བ་ཕྱི་མ་རྣམས་ཀྱི་ [24a1] ཕྱི་མ་ཀུན་གྱི་[750]ཆོས་ཁྲི་ཡོད། [751]ཙ་བརྒྱད་སྣེ་ན་དེ་ཚོག[illegible] ×དབུ་རྩེ་རྣམས་ཀྱི་བྱང་ན། ཞིངས་[752]ཟེར་བའི་

---

734 གཉིང་

735 ཕ་

736 ཕོང་

737 གཏད་

738 ལྦྱོངས་སུ་

739 རླབས་

740 རླབས་

741 འདོམ་

742 མཐོན་

743 གྱི་

744 འདོམ་

745 གྱི་

746 གྱི་

747 རྩ་

748 རླབས་

749 འདོམ་

750 གྱི་

751 no annotation mark

752 ཞིང་

ཞིང་ཆེན་པོ་གཉིས་ཡོད། དེའི་ཞིང་མགོ་ན། འོད་འཛོ་བའི་ཆོས་ཁྲི་ཡོད། སྣང་ཐང་དཀར་བའི་ཆོས་ཁྲི་གཅིག་དང་གཉིས་བཞིབས་ཡོད། དེ་རྣམས་ཐམས་ཅད་ཕྱི་ [24a2] མོའི་ནང་དུ་ཚུད་པ་སྟེ། ཕྱི་སྐོར་ལན་གཅིག་དང་: རྒྱས་པ་ཚར་གཅིག་གླགས[753]པ་བྱིན་བརླབས[754]མཉམ་པར་བྱེད། དབུ་རྩེ་ནས་ནུབ་ཕྱོགས་སུ་མདའ་རྒྱང་གང་ཙམ་གྱི་ས་ན། དགེ་བཤེས་སྟོན་པའི་སྤྱུར་སྤྲུངས་ས་ན། སྐུ་འབུམ་བད་གསུམ་མ་བ[755] [24a3] བ་གཅིག་བཞུགས། བྱིན་བརླབས[756]ཅན་དུ་བྱེད། དེ་ནས་བྱང་ཕྱོགས་མདའ་རྒྱང་གང་ཙམ་ཀྱི[757]ས་ན། གཙང་པ་ཇོ་ཕགས[758]ཅེས[759]བྱ་བའི་སྒྲུབ་པ་པོ་གཅིག་ [illegible] ཡི་དམ་ཞལ་གཟིགས་པ་ གི་མཆོད་རྟེན་བད་གཅིག་མ་ཆེབ་གཅིག་བཞུགས། དེའི་བྱང་གློ་འབེན་གང་ཙམ་ཀྱི[760]ས་ན་ཀླུ[761] [24a4] མཆོད་རྟེན་མི་ལངས་པ་ཙམ་གཅིག་ཡོད། དབུ་རྩེ་ནས་ལྷོ་ནུབ་མཚམས་སུ་མདའ་རྒྱང་འབྲིང་པོ་གསུམ་གྱིས། ཤུག་པའི་ནགས་ཕྱིར་སྒྲལ་བ་ན། མཆོད་རྟེན་བད་བཞི་མ་མཐོ་བ་གཅིག་བཞུགས་ཏེ། དེའི་ལོ་རྒྱུས་ནི། རྣལ་འབྱོར་པ་ཆེན་པོའི་ [24a5] གསུང་ནས། ངའི་སྤྱུར་འདི་དྲི་ཙ་འདི ལ་ ཁོལ། འདིགར་ཞལ་པར་མཆོད་བརྟེན་གཅིག་བརྩིགས་དང་། རྣམས་སྐྲིང་ལ་ཕན་ཐོགས་པ་ཅིག་འོང་གསུང་། དེ་ལྟར་བྱས་ཏེ། མ་འདས་པའི་གོང་ནས། དེ་ན་མི་མ་ཡིན་གྱི་ཁྲོམ་ཆེན་པོ་འདུག་པ་ [24a6] ཀ་མ་བས་གཟིགས། དཔྲ་ཡང་ཤིན་ཏུ་བྱིན་བརླབས[762]ཆེ། འདི་གདོན་ཀྱི[763]རྩེར[764]བ་རྣམས་དེ་ལ་སྐོར་བ་བྱེད་པ་རྒྱུན་མ་ཆད་པ་འོང་: དེའི་ནུབ་ཕྱོགས་གློ་དབེན་གང་ཙམ་ཀྱི[765]ས་ན། མཆོད་རྟེན་བད་གཅིག་མ་མཐོ་བ་ [24a7] གཅིག་བཞུགས་ཏེ། དེ་ནི་སྐལ་པ་ཇོ་ལྷོད་བྱ་བའི་སྒྲུབ་པ་པོ་གཅིག་གི་ཡིན་ཏེ། འད[766]ཁའི་དུས་སུ་ལྷའི་བུས་བདུད་རྩི་འདྲེན་པ་གཅིག་བྱུང་། དེའི་མཆོད་རྟེན་ཡིན: དེ་ནས་ནུབ་ཕྱོགས་ན་ཇོ[767]རྒྱང་གང་ཙམ་ན་མཆོད་རྟེན་པད[768]གཅིག་མ་གཅིག་བཞུགས་ཏེ།

753 བགླགས་

754 རླབས་

755 བྱ་

756 རླབས་

757 གྱི་

758 འཕགས་

759 ཞེས་

760 གྱི་

761 ?

762 རླབས་

763 ཀྱིས་

764 གཙོ་

765 གྱི་

766 འདའ་

767 མདའ་

768 བད་

[24a8] དེ་ནི་རྣལ་འབྱོར་པ་ཆེན་པོས་བྱིབས་769ལ་འཚམས་770པའི་ས་ལགས། མཆོད་རྟེན་ཕྱི་མ་གསུམ་པོ་དེ་ཤུག་པའི་ནགས་ཚལ་ཆེན་པོའི་ཕྱི་རོལ་ན་ཡོད་ལགས། གཞན་རྣམས་ནི་ཤུག་པའི་ནགས་ཚལ་ཆེན་པོའི་བསེབ་771ན་ཡོད་དོ།772 གཞན་ཡང་ཤུག་ [24b1] པའི་ནགས་ཚལ་ཆེན་པོའི་གསེབ་རྣམས་ན་ཚ་ཚའི་773ཕུང་པོ་རི་རྒྱུད་ཙམ་པ་རྣམས་སྔོན་གྱི་སྐྱབ་པ་པོ་རྣམས་ཀྱིས་བཏབ་པ་བསམ་གྱིས་མི་ཁྱབ་པ་བཞུགས་སོ། ། དེ་རྣམས་ཕྱི་ན་བཞུགས་པ་རྣམས་ཀྱི་བཤད་པར་ ཟུར་ཙམ་མོ ||

(2–2) ནང་ན་བཞུགས་པ་རྣམས་ཀྱི་བཤད་པ།

གཉིས་པ་ ནང་གི་ རྟེན་རྣམས་ཀྱི་ [24b2] གཤད་774པ་ལ་གསུམ་775ཏེ776; (2–2–1) སྐུའི་རྟེན་དང་; (2–2–2) གསུང་གི་རྟེན་དང་། (2–2–3) ཐུགས་ཀྱི་རྟེན་དང་: (2–2–4) མཆོད་སྡུས་777ཀྱི་<u>གྲངས་སོ</u> (གྲངསོ) །

(2–2–1) དང་པོ་སྐུའི་རྟེན་ལ་ལུགས་སུ་བླུག་པ་དང་; <u>རིས་སུ</u> (རིསུ་)778 བྲིས་པའོ། དང་པོ་ལུགས་སུ་བླུགས་པ་ལ; [24b3] ཇོ་བོ་འཇམ་དཔལ་རྡོ་རྗེ་ལུགས་མ་ཞལ་གསུམ་ཕྱག་དྲུག་པ་པདྨའི་གདན་ལ་བཞུགས་པ་; ཁྲུ་གང་ཙམ་གཅིག་བཞུགས་པ་དེའི་ལོ་རྒྱུས་ནི; དང་པོ་ལྷི་779 [illegible: རྒྱལ་] པོ་གཅིག་གི་ཐུགས་དམ; དེ་ནས་གཅིག་ནས་གཉིས་སུ་རྒྱུད་780པས་ཇོ་བོའི་ཕྱག་ཏུ་781བྱོན་ [24b4] ཇོ་བོས་བཤེས་གཉེན་སྟོན་པ་782གནང་། སློབ་མ་གཞན་རྣམས་ཀྱིས་ཕྱག་དོག་བྱས་ཀྱི་དོགས་ནས་ནུ་783བཟའ་མང་པོས་གྲིལ་784ནས་ར་ཕགས་དུ་བཞུགས་

769 ཆིབས་
770 བཅིབ་
771 གསེབ་
772 ||
773 ཚྭ་ཚྭའི་
774 བཤད་
775 བཞི་
776 སྟེ་
777 རྫས་
778 རས་སུ་
779 ལྷིའི་
780 བརྒྱུད་
781 ཏུ་
782 པར་
783 ན་
784 དྲིལ་

ཡིན་གདན་འདྲེན། ཕྱིས་བསམ་ཡས་ནས་རྣམ་སྣང་དུ་བྱོན་ཏེ་སྣང་བ་དག་པ་ལ་ཆོས་ [24b5] གསུང་པ་ཡིན་སྐད། རྣམ་སྣང་དུ་བྱོན་པའི་རྟེན་ཀྱི་[785]སྔ་ཤོས་ལགས། དེའི་གཡོན་ན་བསྟན་པའི་བདག་པོ་སྐུ་གདན་ཁྲི་མཐོ་གང་ཙམ་པ་གཙོ་འཁོར་དུ་བཞུགས་པའི་བསྟན་པའི་བདག་པོ་དེ། བླ་མ་གསེར་གླི་[786] [24b6] པ་བྱིས་པའི་དུས་སུ་གསེར་གླིང་བྱེ་མའི་བསེབ་[787]ནས་རྙེད། གསེར་གླིང་ཐམས་ཅད་འོད་ཀྱིས་ཁེངས། ཕྱིས་གསེར་གླིང་པས་ཇོ་བོ་ལ་གནང་། ཇོ་བོས་དགེ་བཤེས་སྟོན་པ་ལ་གནང་། དེའི་གཡས་ཀྱི་ཁང་[788]སར་[789]པ་[790]ནི་[791]སོར་བཞི་ཙམ་ [24b7] ཇོ་བོས་རྣལ་འབྱོར་པ་ཤེས་རབ་རྡོ་རྗེ་ ལ་ གནང་། གཡོན་ཀྱི་[792]སྒྲོལ་མ་སོར་བཞི་ཙམ་པ་དེ།[793] ཇོ་བོས་རྣལ་འབྱོར་པ་ཕྱག་ཁྲི་མཆོག་ལ་གནང་། གཙོ་འཁོར་དུ་དཔོན་ཆོས་ཀྱི་རྒྱལ་པོས་སྤེབས་པ་ལགས་སོ། །གཡོན་ཀྱི་[794]ཇོ་བོ་ཁང་[795]སར་[796]པ་ཆེ་[797]གདན་ [24b8] ཁྲི་ བག་ཙམ། མཐོ་བ་རྒྱབ་ཡོལ་ཅན་ཅག་[798]གྲུ་གང་པ་ཙམ་གཅིག་བཞུགས་པ་དེ། སོག་པོ་དཔལ་འཁོར་བྱ་བས་བཞེངས་ནས་དགེ་བཤེས་སྟོན་པ་ལ་ཐམས་ཅད་དུ་ཕུལ་བ་ལགས། །རབ་ཏུ་གནས་པ་སྟོན་ [illegible: པ་] ཉིད་ཀྱི་བཞུགས། [25a1] དེའི་གཡོན་ན་རྒྱལ་བ་འོད་[799]མེད་འགྲེད་[800]ཁྱུད་[801]གང་ཙམ་ཅིག་བཞུགས་པ་བསྟན་པ་སྔ་མའི་ལྷ་ཡིན། རབ་ཏུ་གནས་པ་སངས་རྒྱས་འོད་བསྲུངས་[802]ཀྱི་བཞུགས། ཕྱིས་ལྷ་ལུང་དཔལ་ཀྱི་[803]རྡོ་རྗེའི་ཕྱག་ཏུ་ [illegible: བྱོན།] [25a2] ཁོང་གི་ཐུགས་དམ་དུ་བསྒྲང་བ་ལགས། དེའི་གཡོན་ན་བྱམས་པ་བཞེངས་ཁ་མ་གདན་

785 གྱི་

786 གླིང་

787 གསེབ་

788 ཁ་

789 སརྡ་

790 - པ་

791 ཆེ་

792 གྱི་

793 ¦?

794 གྱི་

795 ཁ་

796 སརྡ་

797 ཆེ་

798 ཕྱག་

799 + དཔག་

800 - འགྲེད་

801 མཁྱུད་ or འཁྱིད་

802 སྲུངས་

803 གྱི་

ཁྲི་རྒྱབ་ཡོལ་དང་བཅས་པ་མཐོ་གང་ལྷག་པ་གཅིག་བཞུགས། [804]རབ་ཏུ་གནས་པ་ཀླུ་སྒྲུབ་ཀྱི་བཞུགས་ ×དགེ་བཤེས་སྣིང་པའི་ཕྱག་དུ་བྱོན་[805]ཕོང་གི་ཐུགས་དམ་དུ་བཟུང: དེའི་གཡོན་ན་ [illegible][806] [25a3] ཐུག་མ་མཐོ་གང་ཙམ་གཅིག་བཞུགས་པ་དེ། སྟོད་ལུངས་[807]ཀྱི་བསྒོམ་པ་དམར་བསྒོམ་[808]བྱ་བ་ལ་གསུང་ཕྱུང་ནས་ཆོས་གསུངས་པ་ཡིན། སྒོམ་པ་དམར་སྒོམ་ཀྱི་[809]གསུང་འབྱིན་མ་བྱ་བ་ལགས་སྐད། དེའི་གཡོན་ཕྱོགས་ [25a4] པད་སྤྱུངས་ཁ་ཡར་སྒྲལ་བའིས་ན་སྒྲོལ་མ་ཕྱག་བརྒྱད་མ་གཅིག་བཞུགས་པ་དེ། ཁྲ་ཕུ་བ་ཕྲན་ཀྱི་[810]ཐུགས་དམ: དེའི་ནང་ན་དེ་[811]སིའི་རིང་སྲེལ་ཆེ་ལུ་གང་ཙམ་བཞུགས། དེའི་གཡོན་ན་མཆོད་རྟེན་ཕྲེ་[812]བ་རྣམས་ཀྱི་གྲལ་ [25a5] དེ་ལ་པ་ཏྲ་ལ་བརྟེན་པའི་གཙོ་འཁོར་དགུ་པ་ཅིག་ཡོད་པ་དེ། རྣལ་འབྱོར་ པ་ ཆེན་པོའི་ཐུགས་དམ་མཐོང་བ་དོན་ཡོད་ཀྱང་ཟེར། ཟངས་ཀྱི་མི་བོ་ཆེ་ཡང་ཟེར། བྱིན་བརླབས་[813]ཅན་དུ་བྱེད། །དེའི་རྩའི་ཐབ་ པ་ ལོངས་སྤྱོད་རྫོགས་སྐུ་ཆེ་ [25a6] གསེར་མ་བྱིས་པ་ལོ་བཅུ་བ་ཙམ་ཅིག་བཞུགས་ཡོད་དེ། དཔོན་ཆོས་ཀྱི་རྒྱལ་པོས་ཇོ་བོའི་སྐུ་ཚབ་དུ་[814]བཞེངས་པ་ལགས། །ཀ་བ་གཡས་མའི་སྟོང་[815]དེ་ལ། ཇོ་བོ་ཐུགས་རྗེ་ཆེན་པོ་ཞལ་བཅུ་གཅིག་པ་བཞུགས་པ་དེ: བཙུ [illegible] [25a7] རྡོ་རྗེ་འོད་ཀྱི་ཐུགས་དམ། དེའི་འོག་ན་སྒྲོལ་མ་བཞེངས་སྐུ་རྒྱབ་ཡོལ་ཅན་ཁྲུ་གང་ཙམ་གཅིག་བཞུགས་པ་དེ། སློབ་དཔོན་འཕགས་པ་ཀླུ་གྲུབ་[816]ཀྱི་ཐུགས་དམ་ལགས། [817]གསུང་འབྱོན་མ་རྗེས་ཆེ་ཤོས་ལགས།། ཀ་བ་ཤར་མའི་སྟོང་[818]ལ་ཡི་གེ་ཐུག་མ་གཙོ་འཁོར་གསུམ་བཞུ[illegible གས་] [25a8] པ་དེ། དཔོན་དབང་སེང་གི་ཐུགས་དམ (ཐུཾ) । རབ་ཏུ་གནས་པ་དགོན་འོད་འབྱོ་[819]བའི་བཞུགས། དེའི་འོག་ན་སྐུ་འབག་མཐོ་གང་ཙམ་གཅིག་བཞུགས་པ་དེ། དགོན་འོད་འཇོ་བའི་གདུང་ཁང་དུ་དཔོན་བཞོན་[820]ནུ་སེང་གེས་ (སེངེས་) བཞེངས [illegible: །] [25b1] དབུ་རྩེ་ཀ་བ་བཅུ་ཐུག་མ་ +ནི་ ཡང་སོ་ས་བས་བཞེངས་པའི་ཇོ་བོའི་སྐུ་ཚབ་གཅིག་དང་།

[804] no annotation mark

[805] + །

[806] ཡི་གེ་ ?

[807] ལུང་

[808] སྒོམ་

[809] ཀྱི་

[810] ཀྱི་

[811] ཏེ་

[812] ཁྲི་

[813] རླབས་

[814] ཏུ་

[815] གདོང་

[816] སྒྲུབ་

[817] with dot-line annotation mark

[818] གདོང་

[819] འཇོ་

[820] གཞོན་

རིན་ཆེན་དཔོན་ཀྱིས[821]ཡོན་བདག་བྱས་པའི་བཅུ་གཅིག་ (བཅིག་) ཞལ་དང་། རྒྱལ་བ་རིགས་ལྔ་མང་པོ་དང་། ཉི་ཤུ་རྩ་བཞི་མ་ན་ཡང་མང་པོ་བཞུགས་སོ། ། [25b2] སྤྱིར་ལུགས[822]མ་སུམ་བརྒྱ་ལྷག་ཙམ་བཞུགས་སོ། །གཞན་ཡང་སྔགས་ཀྱི་བུམ་སྐུ་དང་། ཚ་ཚའི་སྐོར[823]ཕོར་དང་། སློ་རྡེབས་མང་པོ་བཞུགས་སོ། །དེ་རྣམས་ཀྱིས་ལུགས་མ་བསྟན་ནས (བསྟནས་) ། དཔྱིས་སུ་ཕྱིས་པ་རྣམས་བརྗོད་པར་བྱའོ།།

དང་པོ་ [25b3] ཇོ་བོའི་ཐུགས་དམ་བཞི། དགེ་བཤེས་སྟོན་པའི་ཐུགས་དམ་བཅོ་ལྔ: རྣལ་འབྱོར་པ་ཆེན་པོའི་ཐུགས་དམ་བཞི། དཔལ་ལྡན་ དགོན་པ་བའི་ཐུགས་དམ་མང་རབ་གཅིག སྐུ[824]མཆེད་གསུམ་ཀྱི[825]ཐུགས་དམ་དུ་མ་བཞུགས་པ་ལས། དང་པོ་ཡི་གེ་དྲུག་མ་དེ་རྣལ་འབྱོར་པ་མེ་ཏ[826] [25b4] ཐུགས་དམ་དུ་ [illegible བཞེངས།] རབ་ཏུ་གནས་པ་སློབ་དཔོན་པདྨ་སཾ་བྷ་ བའི་ བཞུགས། དེ་ནས་གཅིག་ནས་གཉིས་སུ་རྒྱུད[827]ཇོ་བོའི་ཕྱག་ཏུ[828]བྱོན: ཇོ་བོས་རྣལ་འབྱོར་པ་ཤེས་རབ་རྡོ་རྗེ་ལ་གནང་། རྣལ་འབྱོར་མ་མེ་ཏན་མན་ཆད་ནས་གསང་ཕུ་བ་ཡན་ཆོད་དུ་ [illegible: རྣལ་འབྱོར] [25b5] པ་བཅུ་གསུམ་གྱིས་ཞལ་གཟིགས་པ་ལགས། །དེའི་ཞལ་ཐེངས་གཅིག་མཐོང་བས་ངན་སོང་གསུམ་དུ་ལྷུང་ཡང་མི་སྐྱེ་གསུང་སྐད། ཇོ་བོ་བྱང་ཆུབ་ཆེན་པོ་དང་། སེང་ལྡེང་ནགས་ཀྱི་སྒྲོལ་མ་གཉིས། རལ་བ་མཐོ་བཞི་མ་ ཇོ་བོའི་ཡབ་ [25b6] རྒྱལ་པོ་དགེ་བ་དཔལ་དང་། ཡུམ་པདྨོ་འོད་ཟེར་ཅན་གཉིས་ཀྱི་ཐུགས་དམ། བུ་མོ་ལོ་བརྒྱད་མས་རས་ཏགས[829]། ཁྱེའུ་ལོ་བརྒྱད་སྐུ་རིས་བཏབ་མཆེན[830]སྐྱིས[831]། རབ་ཏུ་གནས་ས་བླ་མ་གསེར་གླིང་པའི་བཞུགས: ཇོ་བོས་ [illegible: འཇིགས་] [25b7] པ་བརྒྱད་བསྐྱབ[832]དེ། ཇོ་བོས་རྣལ་འབྱོར་པོ[833]རྒྱ་གར་དུ་བཞེངས་སུ་བཏང་ཏེ[834]། ཤར་ཕྱོགས་པ་སེམས་དཔའ་ལ་མཁས་པས་ཆོས་སྒྲོལ་མཛད་དང་། དཔལ་ན་ལེན་ཏྲ་ན་སྒྲོལ་མ་རང་བྱོན་གསུམ་ (༣) བཞུགས་པས་སྒྲོལ་མ་དང་། མ་ག་ [illegible: དྷེ] [25b8] ན་བྱང་ཆུབ་ཆེན་པོ་བཞུགས་པས་མཆོད

821 གྲིས་

822 ལྷུགས་

823 བསྐོས་

824 སྐུ་

825 གྲི་

826 ཏན་ Cf. Lhun grub chos 'phel (1994: 125): མེ་ཏ་ར

827 བརྒྱུད་

828 ཏུ་

829 གཏགས

830 ཆོན་

831 བཀྲིས

832 སྐྱོབ་

833 པ་

834 སྟེ་

ཧེན་བརྒྱད་པ་དང་བཞེངས་སྟེ། ཚུར་བྱོན་གཉེ[835]ཐང་ན་རབ་གནས་བརྒྱ་རྩ་བརྒྱད་མཛད། ཆོས་སྐྱོལ་མཛད་གཉེ[836]ཐང་རང་དུ་བཞུགས༔ མཆོད་ཧེན་བརྒྱད་པ་གསང་ཕུ་ན་བཞུགས་སོ། ། [26a1] སྐྱོལ་མ་འདིས་ཇོ་བོ་ལ་ཆོས་གསུངས་པ་ལགས་སྐད༔ ཕྱིས་དགེ་བཤེས་སྟོན་པ་ལ་གནང་ནས་ [illegible: འདིལ་] གསོལ་བ་ཐོབ་དང་ཕྱོད་ཀྱི་དོན་གྲུབ་ནས་འོང་གི་གསུང་ (གིསུང་)༔

དགེ་བཤེས་སྟོན་པའི་ཐུགས་དམ་བཅོལ་[837]ཞིང་། །[838]གསེར་ [illegible] [26a2] པོ་འདི་དབུ་རྩེ་རིན་པོ་ཆེའི་ནང་སྤྱོངས་[839]སུ་བཞེངས། བཅོམ་ལྡན་འདས་ཤཀྱ་[840]ཐུབ་པ༔ རྣམ་པར་སྣང་མཛད་གང་[841]ཆེན་[842]མཚོ༔ སྣང་བ་མཐའ་ཡས༔ བྱམས་པ་མངོན་པར་བྱང་ཆུབ་པ།[843] སངས་རྒྱས་སྨན་པོའི་[844]རྒྱལ་པོ་ ངང་ ལྷོའི་ (རྒྱལ་ཕྱོ) ། དེ་དག་གི་ལྷ་བཞིའ་ [26a3] རྒྱ་ཙག་གེས་ (ཙགེས་)[845]དང་། དོམ་སྟོན་སྐྱིད་[illegible: པ་] ལགས་སོ། ། སྐུ་ཐམས་ཅད་ནི་གསེར་ལས་བྱས་པ། ཆེ་ཆུང་ནི་མཐོ་བཅུ་གཉིས་ལྷག་པ་ཙམ་མོ༔ ཕྱག་ན་རྡུལ་[846]ཀྱི་དངོས་པོ་ཡོད་པ་རྣམས་ལྷ་བཞིའ་ལ་སྤྱོང་དག་གི་ཚུལ་དུ་ཕུལ། གསེར་ལྷ་[847] [26a4] མ་རབ་གནས་མཛད་ནས། ངའི་གསེར་ལྷ་ལྷ་པོ་འདིའི་ཞལ་ལན་ཅིག་མཐོང་བས་ངན་སོང་གསུམ་དུ་ཕུལ་ཡང་མི་སྐྱེ་གསུང༔ འདིའི་སེར་བུ་ཐོག་པས་ཀྱང་ [illegible] གྲོལ་ འཁོར་བ་ནས་ཐར་ནས་འགྲོ་གསུང་ (འགྲོསུང་) ༑། དེ་ནས་ཇོ་བོའི་སྐུ་འ[illegible: བག་] [26a5] ཨུ་[848]ཡོན་མ་དེ་དགེ་བཤེས་སྟོན་པས་བཞེངས་ནས་ཇོ་བོ་ལ་རབ་གནས་ཞུས་པས། ཨ་རེ་ཁོ་བོ་འདི་ལྟ་བུ་གཅིག་ཡོད་དམ་ཨང་གསུང་མཉེས་སྐད༔ ཇོ་བོ་དངོས་[849]བྱང་ཆུབ་ཀྱི་ཐུགས་སྦྱོང་བའི་འདྲ་འབག་ལགས་ གསུང་། ×དགེ་བཤེས་གླང་རི་ཐང་པའི་ཞལ་ནས། བྱང་རྣམ་སྒྲིང་གི་ཧེན་དེ་རྣམས་ལས་འདམ་བཅུག་ན་ཇོ་བོའི་སྐུ་འབག་ཨུ་[850]ཡོན་མ་ཆེབ་དེ་འདམ༔ དེའི་ཕྱིར་ན༔ ཇོ་བོ་དངོས་[851]བྱང་ཆུབ་ཀྱི་ཐུགས་

835 སྙེ་

836 སྙེ་

837 བཅོལྟ་ ?

838 - །

839 ལྟོངས་

840 ཤཱཀྱ་

841 གངས་ ?

842 ཅན་ ?

843 : ?

844 པའི་

845 ?

846 རྡུས་

847 ལྷག་

848 དབུ་

849 + ཀྱིས་

850 དབུ་

851 + ཀྱིས་

སྒྲུབ་པ་དང་ཕྲད་མེད་གསུང་:॥ དེའི་གཡོན་ན་འཇམ་དཔལ་ [26a6] བསྟན་[852]པའི་འཁོར་ལོ་དང་། འཇམ་[853]གཡོ་བའི་འཁོར་ལོ་གཉིས་བཞུགས་པ་དེ་དགེ་བཤེས་ [illegible] སྟོན་ [illegible] གྱི་ སློབ་མ་འབྲོམ་ཉ་པ་དབང་ཕྱུག་མགོན་བྱ་བ། གྲོང་སར་ [illegible] ཀུན་དགའ་ར་བ་བཞེངས་མཁན་དེས་བཞེངས་ནས་དགེ་བཤེས་སྟོན་པ་ལ་ཕུལ་[854]རབ་གནས་ [26a7] ལོ་ཉིད་ཀྱི་བཞུགས། ཁོང་རང་དང་སྐུ་མཆེད་གསུམ་ཀྱི་[855]ཞལ་གཟིགས་པ་ལགས། དེའི་གཡོན་ཀྱི་[856]ཇོ་མོ་ཙུན་རྡེ་དཀར་མོ་དེ: ཇོ་བོ་སེ་བཙུན་དབང་ཕྱུག་གཞོན་ནུའི་ཐུགས་དམ་ཡིན། ཇོ་བོ་སེ་བཙུན་ལྷ་འདི་ལ་ [26a8] བརྟེན་ནས་མཐུ་དང་ནུས་པ་ཆེན་པོ་ཡང་དག་པ་མངའ་བ་ལགས། ཁོང་གིས་དགེ་བཤེས་སྟོན་པ་ལ་གནང་བ་ལགས། དེའི་གཡོན་ན་སྒྲོལ་མ་དཀར་སྔོན་གཉིས་བཞུགས་པ་དེ། ཇོ་བོས་དངུལ་གདུགས་ [26b1] ཅན་ཀྱི་[857]དངུལ་ [blank] འདོན་པ་ལ། རྣལ་འབྱོར་ པ ཕྱག་ཁྲི་མཆོག་གིས་བྱོན། དངུལ་འགྲུབས་[858]ནས་ཚུར་བྱོན་པའི་དུས་སུ། རྗེ་བཙུན་མ་སྒྲོལ་མ་རྣམ[859]ལམ་དུ་བྱོན་ནས་སང་ཕྱེ་ཝུ་རས་འཚོང་བ་ཅིག་འོང་: དེ་ཚོས་ལ་དེད་ལ་ཕུ[illegible: ལ་] [26b2] དང་། ཕྱེད་ཀྱི་བར་ཆད་ཐམས་ཅད་དས་བསྲུང་བ་ཡིན་གྱི་གསུང་། ནང་པར་ཕྱེ་ཝུ་རས་འཚོང་བ་གཅིག་བྱུང་བས་རས་ཉོས་སྟེ[860]། ཇོ་བོ་ལ་ཕུལ་ནས་ཚོང་པ་ཚན་གཅིག་ དད་ འགྲོགས་ནས་དཔལ་མོ་དཔལ་ཐང་ལ་བྱོན་པའི་དུས་སུ། [26b3] བྱག་[861]པ་བྱུང་ནས་ཚོང་པ་རྣམས་བཅོམ། ཁོང་གིས་དངུལ་ཀྱི་[862]ལྷུང་[863]པ་ཀ་བ་[864]ལིག་[865]གི་[866]དབྱིབས་སུ་བྱས་ཡོད་པས། གད་སྐྱིབས་གཅིག་ལ་བཞག་ཡོད་པས། བྱག་[867]པ་རྣམས་དེ་ལ་འགོངས་[868]ནས་སོང་སྐད། ཕྱིས་རྣས་སྒྲིང་སླེབ[869] [26b4] སྟོན་པའི་སྔན་དུ་ལོ་རྒྱུས་རྣམས་ཞུས་པ་ལ། སྒྲོལ་མ་དཀར་མོར་སྣང་ངམ། སྔོན་མོར་སྣང་གསུང་། དཀར་སྔོན་གང་ཡིན་ཡིད་ལ་མ་ཟིན་སྟེ། ཇོ་བོས་དངོས་སུ་

852 བརྟན་
853 + དཔལ་
854 །
855 གྱི་
856 གྱི་
857 གྱི་
858 གྲུབ་
859 རྨི
860 ཏེ་
861 ཇག་
862 གྱི་
863 ཧྲང་
864 ལྟ་
865 ལའི་
866 - གི་
867 ཇག་
868 བགོམས་
869 སླེབས་

སྐྱབས་ཞུས་པས། རས་དེ་ལ་སྒྲོལ་མ་དཀར་སྤོ་[870] [26b5] གཉིས་ཀ་བཞེངས་སོ། དགེ་བཤེས་ཤར་བའི་གསུང་ནས། རི་མོ་དང་རྣམ་པ་འདྲ་ཙམ་ཡིན་ཏེ (ཡིནྟེ) ¦ སྤྲུལ་པའི་སྐུ་དངོས་དང་ཁྱད་མེད་གསུང་། །དེ་ནས་མཆོད་རྟེན་བརྒྱད་པ་དེ། དགེ་བཤེས་སྟོན་པས་ཁ་ཆེ་གསེར་ཁར་བྱོན་པའི་དུས་སུ། [26b6] ཨ་ཙ་ར་ཅིག་གིས་བྲམ་ཟེའི་ཐོད་སྐུ་གཅིག་དང་ལྷ་འདི་དགེ་བཤེས་སྟོན་པ་ལ་ཕུལ་བས། དགེ་བཤེས་སྟོན་པས་ཀུང་ཕྱག་ན་དངོས་པོ་ (དངོས་) ཡོད་པ་རྣམས་ཨ་ཙ་ར་དེ་ལ་བྱིན་སྟེ[871]། འདི་ལ་རྒྱ་གར་ཕན་ཆོད་ཀྱི་རབ་གནས་དཔག་ཏུ་ [illegible: མེད་] [26b7] པ་བཞུགས། འཇམ་དཔལ་རྡོ་རྗེ་གསེར་ལྷ་ཆུང་ཆུང་དེ། དགེ་བཤེས་སྟོན་པས་ཇོ་བོ་འཇམ་དཔལ་རྡོ་རྗེའི་སྐུ་ཚབ་ཏུ་འབྲལ་བའི་བསྲུང་བའི་རྟེན་དུ་བཞེངས། གཤིན་རྗེ་གཤེད་དེའི་ (གཤིནྡེའི་) དབང་དུ་བྱས་ན། ཇོ་བོས་དགེ་བཤེས་སྟོན་པ་ལ་སྒྲུབ་ཐབས་ [26b8] གནང་ནས། ལྷ་འདི་ཡང་གྲུས་[872]བྱེད་པ་ཅིག་ཡིན། ངའི་བླ་མ་གཤིན་རྗེ་གཤེད་ཀྱི་རྣལ་འབྱོར་པས་ཞལ་གཟིགས: ངས་མ་འཐོང་[873]ཁྱོད་ཀྱིས་སྒྲུབས་དང་མཐོང་ནས་འོང་གིས་གསུང: སྒྲུབ་པ་མཛད་པས་རིང་པོར་མ་ལོན་ [26b9] ཞལ་གཟིགས་པ་ལགས། བྱིན་བརླབས་ཅན་དུ་བྱེད: དཔལ་ཚོགས་ཀྱི་བདག་པོ་དེ: དགེ་བཤེས་སྟོན་པས་ཇོ་བོ་ལ་ཕུལ་བ་མཛད་པའི་དུས་སུ་སྒྲུབ་པ་ཅིག་མཛད་པས་དངོས་སུ་ཞལ་གཟིགས་པ་ལགས། ། [27a1][874] ད་ལྟ་ཡང་དགེ་སློང་བཞི་སྡེ་རེས་གསོལ་བ་བཏབ་ན་བྱིན་བརླབས་[875]དངོས་སུ་ཡོད་པ་ལགས། དེ་རྣམས་ [illegible] དགེ་བཤེས་སྟོན་པའི་ཐུགས་དམ་བཅོ་ལྔའོ།།

རྣལ་འབྱོར་པ་ཆེན་པོའི་ཐུགས་དམ་བཞི་ནི། ཇོ་བོ་དམ་ཚིག་གསུམ་བཀོད་པའི་ [illegible: རྒྱལ་པོ་] [27a2] གཙོ་འཁོར་ལྔ་པོ་དེའི་སྒྲུབ་ཐབས་ཇོ་བོས་སྣང་[876]། རྣལ་འབྱོར་པ་ཆེན་པོས་བཟླས་པ་སྟོང་ཕྲག་བརྒྱད་བསྐྱལ་བ་དང་ཞལ་གཟིགས་ [illegible: པ་] ལགས་སྐད། ཡི་གེ་དྲུག་མ་གཙོ་འཁོར་གསུམ་པོ། དབུ་རྩེ་ཀ་བ་བཅུ་དྲུག་མ་ན་གཟིམས་ [27a3] མཛད་ནས། ར་[877]སྒྲིང་གོང་གི་གདན་ས་མཛད་དུ ས་ ཞལ་གཟིགས། དང་པོ་བོ་དྷི་ཙི་ཏའི་ཕྲེང་བ་རྒྱ་[878]རྩ་བརྒྱད་པ་ཅིག་ [illegible] ཡོད་པ་དེ་ཕྱག་ཏུ་[879]ཕུལ [illegible: །] དེ་ནས་ཆོས་[880]རྒྱ་

870 སྤྱོན་

871 ཏེ་

872 གྲོས་ ?

873 མཐོང་

874 The folio 27a has a damage in the center part.

875 རླབས་

876 གནང་ ?

877 རྭ་

878 བརྒྱ་

879 ཏུ་

880 + ཆོས་གོས་

གར་མ་དེ་ཕྱུལ་བས་དེ་རྣམས་དར[881]གཅིག་ཕྱག་དུ་བསྣམས་ [27a4] ནས་བཞུགས༏ བྱ་འདབ་འོག་མའི་དབྱངས་རྟ་དེ་ཡང་དེ་དུས་མཛད་པའོ། །ཇོ་བོ་མི་གཡོ་བ་དེའི་སྐུ་རིས་འདེབས་མ[illegible: ཁ]ན་ཇོ་བོས་མཛད༏ སྣང[882]བསྣབས[883]གཅིག་ཀྱང་མཛད་ནས་དྲང་སོང[884]འཁྲོས་པའི་ཆབྱུད་ཅན་འདི་ [illegible: ལྷ་བུ] [27a5] གཅིག་འཚལ་བ་ཡིན་གསུང༏ རབ་གནས་ཇོ་བོ་ཉིད་ ཀྱི་ བཞུགས༏ རྣལ་འབྱོར་པ་ཆེན་པོའི་ཐུགས་དམ་བྱང་རྣམས་སྐྱིད་གི་མི་གཡོ་མེ་རི་སེ[illegible: ར] པོ་ཅན་བྱ་བར་གྲགས། བྱིན་བརླབས[885]ཤིན་ཏུ་ཆེ་བ་ལགས། ཇོ་བོའི་སྐུ་འབག་དེ་ལ་ཇོ་བོ་ [illegible: ཉིད་] [27a6] ཀྱི་རབ་གནས་དཔག་ཏུ་མེད་པར་བཞུགས། རྣལ་འབྱོར་པ་ཆེན་པོའི་ཐུགས་དམ་འབྲལ་བ་བསྲུང་བ་ལགས་སྐད༔ རྣལ་འབྱོར་བའི་ཐུ[illegible: གས་དམ་] བཞིའོ། །གསེར་ལྷ་ཆེན་པོ་དེ་དགེ་བསྙེན་བཞིས་བཞེངས་ནས་དཔལ་ལྡན་དགོན་པ་ལ་ཕུལ་ [27a7] བས་དགོན་བ[886]བའི་འོད་མི་འབྲུག[887]པ་བྱ་བ་ལགས་སོ། །དེ་ནས་ཡིང་ཙེ[888]བཞི་པོ་དེ༏ མཁན་པོ་ཡེ་རྒྱལ་གྱི[illegible: ས] དགེ་བཤེས་སྟོན་པ་ལ་སྐུ་འབག་བཞེངས་པར་ཞུ་བ་ཕུལ་བས༏ མིའི་གཟུགས་བྲིས་ནས་ཅི་བྱེད༏ [illegible: དེ] [27a8] བཞིན་གཤེགས་པའི་སྐུ་ཅིག་བཞེངས་གསུང༏ ཡང་དང་ཡང་དུ་ཞུ་བ་ཕུལ་བས༏ དེ་འོན་མིའི་ [illegible: གཟུ]གས་ལ་ལྷའི་ ཆ བྱད་ཐོན་པ་གཅིག་བྱེད་གསུང་ནས། དབུ་སྐྲ་ཚབ་ཀྱིས་བསིལ་ནབ[889]བཟའ་ [27b1] གཡང་དཀར་གསོལ༏ ཐྲམ་ཟེའི་གདན་ལ་ ཉིམ་ལ་ བཞུགས་ནས་ལྷ་བཟོས་སྐུ་རིས་བཏབ་པ་ལགས༔ བྱང་རྣམས་སྐྱིད་གི་མ[illegible: ཁ]ན་པོ་ཡེ་རྒྱལ་པ་བྱ་བ་དགེ་བཤེས་སྟོན་པ་དངོས་དང་ཁྱད་མེད་པར་བྱེད་པ་ལགས། དེ་ལ་བཏ[illegible: གས་] [27b2] པའི་ཇོ་བོ་ཐུགས་རྗེ་ཆེན་པོ་བཅུ་གཅིག་ཞལ་དེ༏ རྒྱལ་པོ་སྔེ[890]སྒྱོད་བཟང་པོའི་ཐུགས་དམ༏ རབ་ཏུ་གནས་པ་འཕགས་པ་ཀླུ་སྒྲུབ[891]ཀྱི་བཞུགས༏ ཇོ་མོ་དཀར་ཆུང་མ་དེ༏ དཔལ་ན་རོ་པའི་ཐུགས་དམ་ཞལ་གཟིགས་བྱིན་བརླབས[892]ཅན་ལ[illegible: གས་] [27b3] གཤེད་དམར་མ་རྟེ་ལ་བཅིབས་པ་དེ༏ ཇོ་བོའི་བླ་མ་གཤིན་རྗེ་གཤེད་ཀྱི་རྣལ་

---

881 དལ་

882 སྣངས་

883 སྣབས་

884 སྲོང་

885 རླབས་

886 པ་

887 འབྲུགས་

888 ཚེ།

889 ན་

890 Cf. Lhun grub chos 'phel (1994: 130): བདེ

891 སྒྲུབ་

892 རླབས་

འགྲོར་པའི་ཐུགས་དམ་ལགས: མ་ག་[893]ཧར་[894]ཧུར་ཧུ (ཧུཧུ) ཀའི་དམག་བྱུང་བའི་དུས་སུ། བླ་མ་དེས་ལྷ་འདི་དབུ་བསྐུས་[895] (དབུསྐུས་) ན་བཀྲམ་ནས་ [illegible] ཚོས་ [illegible] བཞུགས་པས་བག་ཟན་ [illegible: ལ་] [27b4] བྱ་རོག་གི་ (རོགི་) གཟུགས་བྱས་ནས་དམིགས་པས་ནམ་མཁའ་ཁྱིངས་པ་གཅིག་ཏུ་སྤྲུལ་ནས། བྱ་རོག་གི་ས་དམག་ཐམས་ཅད་གསོག་པས་བསྡུས་ནས་ཆུ་བོ་གླ་[896]གླ་[897]སྤྲུལ་ནས་བཏང་སྐད། དེའི་དུས་མ་ཏེ་འདིའི་ཐལ་ཅག་[898]གིས་ (ཅགིས་) རྗེས་པས་མ་ [illegible] [27b5] རྩོར་རྩོར་[899]བྱུང་སྐད། དབུ་ཐལ་ལྷུག་གིས་ (ཐལྷུགིས་) རྗེས་ཕ་ལེ་ཡོད། དེ་ནི་ཇོ་བོའི་བླ་མ་གཤེན་རྗེ་གཤེད་རྣལ་འབྱོར་པས། ཇོ་བོ་ལ་གནང་། ཇོ་བོས་དགེ་བཤེས་ཁུ་ལ་གནང་། ཁུའི་དཔོན་པོ་གཅིག་གིས་དགེ་བཤེས་ཤར་བ་ལ་གནང་། ཤར་བ་ནས་ [27b6] རུས་སྲིད་དུ་ཕྱུལ་ཏེ་ཁོང་གི་ཐུགས་དམ་དུ་བཀྲང་། བཅོམ་ལྡན་འདས་ཤཀྱ་[900]ཐུབ་པའི་སྐུ་དེ: པོ་ཏོ་བ་འབྲུལ་བ་བསྲུང་བའི་ལགས། ཇོ་བོ་སེང་ལྡེང་ནགས་ཀྱི་སྒྲོལ་མ་ ཆུང་ཆུང་ དེ། ཇོ་བོས་དགོན་པ་བ་ལ་གནང་། དེ་སྔེ་ཟུར་བ་ལ་[illegible] [27b7] དེ་ནས་གཅིག་ནས་གཉིས་སུ་རྒྱུད་[901]ཞང་འོད་འཇོ་བའི་ཕྱག་ཏུ་[902]བྱོན་ཏེ་ཁོང་ཐུགས་དམ་དུ་བཀྲང་། བསྟན་པའི་བདག་པོ་དང་། ཟཇོ་མོ་སྒྲོལ་མ་གཉིས། ཇོ་མོ་སྟོན་པོ་གཉིས་པོ་དེ་སྨན་སྟུའི་ཐུགས་དམ་སྨན་སྟུའི་རབ་གནས་ [illegible: བརྒྱ་རྩ་] བཞུགས། ཟདགེ་བཤེས་པོ་[903]ཆུང་བའི་ཐུགས་དམ་ཞལ་གཟིགས། ལྷ་མོ་འོད་ཟེར་ཅན་དེ་སྨྲུན་མདའ་[904]རིན་པོ་ཆེའི་ཐུགས་དམ། སྨྲ[illegible: ན]་ [27b8] མདའ་[905]རིན་པོ་ཆེའི་རབ་གནས་ [906]ལན་བརྒྱ་རྩ་བརྒྱད་ བཞུགས: ཡང་ཇོ་བོ་སྒྲོལ་མ་དེ་རོང་པོ་རྡོ་རྗེའི་ཐུགས་དམ། སྨྲུན་མདའ་[907]རིན་པོ་ཆེའི་རབ་གནས་བརྒྱ་རྩ་བརྒྱད་བཞུགས། ཇོ་བོ་ཡི་གེ་དྲུག་པ་བཅུ་གཅིག་ [illegible: ཞལ་ཏེ]། རྒྱལ་པོ་ཁྲི་སྲོང་ལྡེ་བཙན་ཀྱི་[908]ཐུགས་དམ་

893 ཀླ་
894 ཏྲར་
895 སྐུས་
896 གཏྲ
897 - ཀླ་
898 ལྷུག་
899 ?
900 ཤཱཀྱ་
901 བརྒྱུད་
902 དུ་
903 ཕུ་
904 སྨྲ་
905 སྨྲ་
906 dot-line annotation mark
907 སྨྲ་
908 ཀྱི་

[27b9] ཏུ་[909]གནས་པ་སློབ་དཔོན་པདྨ་སམ་བྷ་བའི་བཞུགས། ཕྱིས་སྲིད་[910] [illegible: པ་[911]] པའི་[912]ཕྱག་དུ་བྱོན་ཁོང་གི་ཐུགས་དམ་དུ་བསྒྲང་། ཡང་ཡི་གེ་དྲུག་པ་གཙོ་འཁོར་གསུམ་པོ་དེ: ལོ་ཚ་བ་ནག་ཚོ་ཚུལ་ཁྲིམས་རྒྱལ་བའི་ཐུ་གས་ [illegible: དམ་] [28a1] ལགས། བསྟན་པའི་བདག་པོ་དང་། རྡོ་བོ་མི་གཡོ་གཉིས་མཐའ་བཞིའི་ཐུགས་དམ། སྤྱན་རས་གཟགས་[913]གར་ཀྱི་[914]དབང་པོ་[illegible]ས་ཚོན་མ་དེ། མཁའ་ཏུ་བའི་ཐུགས་དམ་རབ་ཏུ་གནས་པ་རྒྱ་གར་ཕན་ཆད་ཀྱི་དཔག་ [28a2] ཏུ་མེད་པ་བཞུགས། རྡོ་མོ་ཀུ་རུ་ཀུ་ལེ་དེ་ཡང་འཐ་[915]བཞིའི་ཐུགས་དམ: ཐུགས་རྗེ་ཆེན་པོ་དེ་དགེ་བཤེས་ཕྱག་དར་ཀྱི་[916]ཐུགས་དམ། མི་གཡོ་བ་དེ་བྲ་ཡུལ་བའི་ཐུགས་དམ། ཕྱག་ན་རྡོ་རྗེ་དེ་དགེ་བཤེས་སྟོན་པའི་བླ་སྨན་ཨ་མི་སྨན་ཐན་གྱིས་ [illegible] [28a3] བཞེངས། དགེ་བཤེས་སྟོན་པའི་ཕྱག་ནས་བཞུགས། དཔོན་ཆོས་ཀྱི་རྒྱལ་པོས་རྡོ་བོའི་སྐུ་ཚབ་ཏུ་བཞེངས་པའི་སྐུ་འབག་ལ་སོགས་པའི་ཐང་སྐུ་བཅོ་ལྔ། སྟབས་བཞོན་ནུ [illegible] དབང་ཕྱུག་[917] འོད་ཀྱི་ཐུགས་དམ་དགེ་བཤེས་སྟོན་པའི་སྐུ་འབག [28a4] རྣལ་འབྱོར་ པ་ ཕྱག་ཁྲི་མཆོག་གི་ཐུགས་དམ། རྡོ་མོ་རྡོ་རྗེ་སྒྲོལ་མ་ཞལ་གཟིགས། དགེ་བཤེས་ཀོ་ཁྲིམ་བྲག་རྩ་བའི་ཐུགས་དམ། མི་གཡོ་བ་ཞལ་གཟིགས། ཀ་མ་བའི་ཐུགས་དམ། རྡོ་བོ་ཡི་གེ་དྲུག་པ། ཆོས་སྐྱོང་ (ཆོ་སྐྱོང་) མགོན་པོ་ཞལ་གཟིགས། [28a5] བཙུན་པ་རྡོ་རྗེ་བོད་[918]ཀྱི་ཐུགས་དམ: སྟོན་པའི་སྐུ་འབག། ཤར་བའི་ཐུགས་དམ་རྡོ་བོ་ཁང་[919]པར་[920]ས་[921]ནིས་[922]དབུ་མཛད་པ་ བརྒྱ་ བཅུ་བ[illegible: དཀྱུན། དགེ་འདུན་སྒྲི་པའི་ཐུགས་དམ་རྡོ་བོའི་ཆོས་གྲ[923] ཁམས་པ་ལུང་པའི་སྐུ་འབག། ཀ་མ་བའི་ [28a6] སྐུ་འབག་[924]གསེར། སྲིད་པའི་[925]སྐུ་ ཞབག་འཛམ་དཔལ་དཔའ་བོ་ལ་སོགས་པ་མང་དུ་བཞུགས་སོ། །དོལ་ པ་ ཡོན་ཏན་

---

909 ཏུ་
910 སྲིདས་
911 པོ་
912 བའི་
913 གཟིགས་
914 གྱི་
915 མཐའ་
916 གྱི་
917 ?
918 ?
919 ཁ་
920 སརྫ་
921 _ ས་
922 ཉིས་
923 གོས་
924 + །
925 པོ་བའི་ ?

སེང་གེའི་ཐུགས་དམ[926]རིན་ཆེན་སྣང་བའི་སྐུ་འབབ། ཡོང་ཉིད་ཀྱི་རབ་གནས་རྒྱ[927]རྩ་བརྒྱད་བཞུགས། སྟོད་ལུངས་པའི་ཐུགས་དམ། [28a7] རྣམ་པར་སྣང་མཛད་གདངས་ཅན་མཚོ་ལ་སྤྱན་མངའི[928]རབ་གནས་རྒྱ[929]རྩ་བརྒྱད་བཞུགས། རབ་གནས་ཕྱི་མའི་དབུ་སྤྱན་མངའ[930]བ་ལ་ཆོས་གསུངས་པ་ལགས། སངས་རྒྱས་མ་ཆགས་པད་མའི་སྤྱན། དྲི་མེད་ [28a8] ནམ་མཁའ་དཔལ། དཔལ་ཀྱི[931]སྙིང་རྣམ་པར་བརྩེགས་པ་སྣྲགས་པའི་རྒྱལ་པོ། བྱམས་པ་མངོན་པར་བྱང་ཆུབ་པ: སངས་རྒྱས་སྨན་པའི་རྒྱལ་པོའོ། །རྒྱལ་བ་ཤཱཀྱ་ཐུབ་པ། དེ་རྣམས་ཀྱི་ལྷ་བཟོ་དམ་གསེར་གཟུངས། སྤྱན་མངའི[932]རབ་ [28a9] གནས་བཞུགས་སོ། །ཞང་འོད་འཇོ་བའི་ཐུགས་དམ་རྗེ་བོའི་ཆོས་གྲུས་དབུ་མཛད་པ་བཅུ་ཐམ་པ། སྟབས་ཁ[933]བའི་ཐུགས་དམ་བྱང་ཆུབ་ཆེན་པོ། རྗེ་བོ་བཅུ་གཅིག་ཞལ་ཡོང་རང་གི་ཞལ་གཟིགས། རབ་གནས་ཡང་ཡོང་རང་བཞུགས། । [28b1] དགོན་འོད་འཇོ་བའི་ཐུགས་དམ་བཅུ་གཅིག ལྷ་རྗེ་ཟེར[934]སྨན་ཀྱི[935]ཐུགས་དམ་བཅུ། སུམ་པ་སྙེད་ ཤེས་རབ་བློ་གྲོས་ཡང་ཟེར། ཉག་པའི་ཐུགས་དམ་སྐུ་འབབ་ཆེན་པོ། རྗེ་གདན་དབོན་པོའི་ཐུགས་དམ། དགོན་འོད་འཇོ་བའི་སྐུ་ ཆེན་པོ་ གཅིག། རིགས་ལྔ་ཕྱོགས་མཚོན་སྤྲུལ་སྐུ་ [28b2] ཀ་མ་བའི་རབ་གནས་བཞུགས། བེར་རྒྱུད་དར་མ་ཡེ་ཤེས་ཀྱི་ཐུགས[936]མི་གཡོ་བ། བྱམས[937]ཀྱི[938]རྗེ་བོ་ཡབ་སྲས། སློབ་དཔོན་སྣ་ར་བའི་ཐུགས་དམ་རྗེ་བོ་ལྷ་ས་མས་དབུ་མཛད་བཅུ་ཐམ་པ། མར་པ་དགེ་བསྙེན་ (དགེན་) ཀྱི[939]སངས་རྒྱས་སྟོང་རྩ་གཉིས་ [28b3] རྗེ་བཙུན་མར་ཡུག་གི་ (ཡུགི་) སྨན་ལྷ[940]བདུན། སྤྱི་སྟོན་ཀྱི[941]མཛད་པ་བཅུ་གཉིས། བྱང་ཆུབ་གྲགས་ཀྱི་ལྷ་མོ་ཆེ་བདུན་ གསུམ ། སྤྲུལ་ནས་བྱོན་པའི་རིགས་ལྔ་སེར་འཇམ་ཀྱི[942]ལྷ་མོ་ལྔ་། སློབ་དཔོན་གུར་སྟོན་ཀྱི[943]ཐུགས་དམ་དགུ། [28b4] གཞན་ཡང་བྲིས་སྐུ་ངོ་མཚར་ཅན་བསམ་

---

926 + །

927 བརྒྱ་

928 སྤྱི་

929 བརྒྱ་

930 སྤྱ་

931 གྱི་

932 སྤྱི་

933 ཀ་

934 ཟུར་ ?

935 གྱི་

936 དམ་

937 འགྲོམ་

938 གྱི་

939 གྱི་

940 བླ་

941 གྱི་

942 གྱི་

943 གྱི་

གྱིས་མི་ཁྱབ་པ་བཞུགས་ཏེ། སྤྱིར་ཐང་སྐུ་སྟོང་ཕྲག་སུམ་ (ཕྲག་སུཾ་) དང་དྲུག་བརྒྱ་ལྔག་པ་གཅིག་བཞུགས་ཏེ། བྱིན་བརླབས་'944ཅན་ཤ་སྟག་ཡིན་ནོ། །དེ་རྣམས་ཀྱི་སྐུའི་རྟེན་རྣམས་ཀྱི་ [28b5] བཤད་པ་ཟུར་ཙམ་མོ།།

(2–2–2) གཉིས་ པ་ གསུང་གི་རྟེན་རྣམས་ཀྱི་བཤད་པ་ནི། ཇོ་བོའི་ཕྱག་དཔེའ་དང་། པོ་ཏི་ལྔ་བཅུ་ལྷག་ཙམ་ [illegible] དགེ་བཤེས་སྟོན་པའི་ཐུགས་དམ་ཕྱི་མོ། པོ་ཏི་གསུམ་བཅུ་རྩ་ལྔག་ གསེར་ཀྱི་'945གླེགས་བམ། རྣལ་འབྱོར་པ་ཆེན་པོའི་ཐུགས་དམ་སྤུར་ཁབས་'946ཅན། དགེ་བཤེས་སྟོད་'947 [28b6] པའི་ཐུགས་དམ་སྤུར་ཁབས་'948ཅན། མཁན་པོ་གུག་'949ཤྲིའི་'950 ཐུགས་དམ་ མཚན་མདངས།། དག་'951ནི་གསེར་ཀྱི་'952གླེགས་བམ་ལ་སེང་ལྡེང་གི་གླེགས་ཤིང་ལ་དངུལ་ཀྱི་'953སྤུར་ཁབས་'954འབུར་དུ་དོད་པ། རིན་པོ་ཆེའི་ཕྲ་དུ་མས་མཛེས་ [28b7] པར་བྱས་པ། དར་ཟར་'955གྱི་ནའུ་'956སྦྲགས་མ་ ×སུམ་བཅུ་ཙམ་ཀྱིས་'957 ×མཛེས་པར་བྱས་པ་ ཡིན ¦ དེ་དག་ལ་གསུང་རབས་སྤུར་ཁབས་'958ཅན་ཞེས་གྲགས་སོ། །དེ་རྣམས་ ཀྱི་ དབུ་མཛད་པའི་པོ་ཏི་སྐྱ་བོའོ་959དང་སྟོན་པོ་འདི་རྣམས་བཞུགས་ཏེ། གསེར་གྱི་ [28b8] མདོ་མངས་ཚར་བརྒྱད། མདོ་མངས་དཀར་པོ་ཚར་ ཀྱིས་ བཅུ་གཉིས། སྟོན་ར་960སྙིང་སྤྱི་པས་བྲིས་པ། ལྔ་བཅུ་རྩ་བཞི་ཟེར་བ་ཡང་འདུག གསེར་འབུམ་ཚར་དྲུག་བཅུ་རྩ་གཉིས: [illegible]ས་པ་དཀར་པོ་སྟོང་སུམ་

---

944 ཀླབས་
945 ཀྱི་
946 ཁབ་
947 སྟོན་ ?
948 ཁབ་
949 གུ་ ?
950 ཤྲཱིའི་ or ཤིའི་ ?
951 དེ་དག་
952 ཀྱི་
953 ཀྱི་
954 ཁབ་
955 ཟབ་
956 ན་བཟའ་
957 ཀྱིས་
958 ཁབ་
959 བོ་
960 རྔ་

བརྒྱ། རིན་པོ་ཆེའི་ཡུམ་བར་མ་ཚར་དགུ་བཅུ། བརྒྱད་[961]བརྩ་[962]བརྒྱད་ཡང་ཟེར། ཉི་ཁྲི་ དཀར་པོ་ཚར་རྒྱ་[963]ཉི་ཤུ། རིན་པོ་ཆེའི་ [illegible གླི་[964]]
[29a1] བམ་ གསུམ་ བརྒྱ་ [illegible] རྒྱ་[965]བཅུ། བརྒྱད་སྟོང་པ་སྐྱ་བའོ་[966]ཉི་[967]སྟོང་དང་བདུན་བཅུ་རྩ་ལྔ་ལྷག་པ་དང་། རིན་པོ་ཆེའི་ལ་བ་
ལུང་བདུན། སངས་རྒྱས་ཕལ་པོ་ཆེ། དཀོན་རྩེགས[968]། ཤེས་རབ་ཁྲི་པ། [969]གསུམ་ཡང་ཟེར། ཁྲི་བརྒྱད་སྟོང་པ། ཤེས་རབ་སྣ་ཚོགས་ [illegible]
[29a2] གསེར་གྱི་ལགས: དཀར་པོ་ [illegible: ཐ་བས་སྤྱན་] ཚར་ཉིས་བརྒྱ་བཞུགས། གསེར་བསྡུད་ཕྱེ་[970]དང་ལྔ་བརྒྱ་བཞུགས: དཔལ་གསང་
བ་འདུས་པ་ལ་སོགས་པ་རྒྱུད་ཀྱི་པོ་ཏི་སུམ་བརྒྱ་བསྟན་ཆོས་ཀྱི་པོ་ཏི་སུམ་སྟོང་སུམ་ [29a3] བཅུ་པ་[971]ཐམ་པ་བཞུགས། ཕྱིར་[972]
སྟོངས་[973]པས་པོ་ཏི་<u>སྟོན་པོ་</u> (སྔོན་) དང་<u>སྐྱ་བོར་</u> (སྐྱོར་)[974]ཆེ་ཆུང་: ས་ཡ་ཕྲག་བཅུ་བཞུགས་ཟེར། ལ་ལ་ན་ཁྲི་ཕྲག་གཉིས། བརྒྱ་ཕྲག་
གཉིས། སྟོང་ཕྲག་བརྒྱད། བཅུ་ཕྲག་བདུན། དྲུག་ཕྲག་ཅིག་བཞུགས་ [29a4] [975][illegible] བརྒྱད་བསྒོམས་པས་ [illegible][976] ×ཟེར་སྟེ[977]།
མདོར་ ན་ བསམ་གྱིས་མི་ཁྱབ་པ་བཞུགས་སོ། །དེས་གསུང་གི་རྟེན་རྣམས་ཀྱི་བཤད་པའོ།།

(2–2–3) ཐུགས་ཀྱི་རྟེན།

གསུམ་པ། ཐུགས་ཀྱི་རྟེན་རྣམས་ཀྱི་བཤད་ པ་ཡང་ སེམས་ཀྱི་བཤད་པའོ། །དངུལ་གདུགས་ཅན་ཆུང་བ་འདིའི་དབང་དུ་བྱས་ན་ [29a5] རྡོ་པོ་རྗེ་
ལྷ་ཅིག་གི་བླ་མ་གསེར་གླིང་པའི་གདུང་ཁང་དུ་བཞུགས། ཆེ་ཆུང་གི་ཚད་ནི་སྦྱིར་ཁྲུ་གང་ཡོད་པ། དངོས་[978]བཞི་ལ་མཐོ་གང་ཡོད་པ། དེ་ལ་དངུལ་

961 བརྒྱ་
962 རྩ་
963 བརྒྱ་ ?
964 གླིགས་
965 བརྒྱད
966 སྐྱ་བོ་
967 ཉིས་
968 བརྩེགས་
969 dot-line annotation mark
970 ཕྱེད
971 - པ་
972 སྦྱིར་
973 བསྒོམས་
974 སྐྱ་བོ་
975 no annotation mark, upper the first line
976 This line is unclear on the photograph of the manuscript.
977 ཏེ་
978 དོས་

གྱི་[979]གདུགས་ཉིས་རྟེགས་ཡོད་པ། སྟེང་ལ་བྱ་ཁྱུང་ལ་སོགས་པའི་བཟོ་ཕྲ་མོ་ [29a6] བསམ་གྱིས་མི་ཁྱབ་པ་ཡོད་པ། ནང་སྦྱོངས་[980]སུ། དེ་བཞིན་གཤེགས་པའི་རིང་སྲེལ་བརྒྱ་རྩ་བརྒྱད། བླ་མ་གསེར་གླིང་པ་ལ་སོགས་པའི་བླ་མ་བརྒྱ་ལྔ་བཅུའི་གདུང་རིང་སྲེལ་སོགས་པ་མང་པོ་བཞུགས། རབ་གནས་ཇོ་བོ་ཉིད་ཀྱི་བཞུགས། ཕྱ[illegible] [29a7] འདི་དང་ཤིང་གི་མཆོད་རྟེན་དང་། འབེན་ཚད་རེ་ལས་རིང་བར་མི་འབྲལ་བར་བཞུགས་པ་ལགས་སྐད། །[981]མཆོད་རྟེན་ཆུང་ཆུང་གཅིག་ལ་བྱིན་བརླབས་[982]ཀྱང་འདི་ལས་ཆེ་མེད། གྲགས་པ་ཡང་འདི་ལས་ཆེ་བ་མེད། ། དེའི་རྩ་ [29a8] ན་ཐྱ་མ་[983]མེ་ལོང་གི་རྒྱབ་ཡོལ་ཅན་མཐོ་གང་ལྷག་པ་གཅིག་བཞུགས་པ་དེ། དཔལ་ལྡན་ན་རོ་པའི་ཐུགས་དམ་ [984]གདུང་ཁང་ ཡིན་[985]བྱིན་བརླབས་[986]ཤིན་ཏུ་ཆེ་བ་ལགས། དེ་ཇོ་བོ་དངུལ་གདུགས་ཅན་ཆེ་བ་དེ། ཇོ་བོ་ཛྲ་ལྷ་གཅིག་གི་གདུང་ཁང་དགེ་བཤེས་སྟོན་ [29a9] པས་བཞེང་[987]། འདིའི་ལྷ་བཟོ་ཨ་ཙ་རམ་ནུ་བྱ་བ་རྒྱ་གར་ཡུལ་བཞི་ན་མཁས་པ་གཅིག་སྤྱན་དྲངས། ལྷ་བཟོ་བྱོན་ནས་ [illegible] ། དགེ་བཤེས་སྟོན་པའི་ཞལ་ནས་དངུ་ཁུག་ཤས་སློལ་སོ་གསུང་། [29b1] དེ་ནས་ཉིན་གཅིག་འཆིང་དཀར་གཅིག་ལ་བརྒྱད་ལྟེབ་བྱས: དེ་ལ་མཚལ་དཀར་ཀྱི་[988]ཐིག་གདབ་ནས། ཁོ་བོའི་བླ་མ་ཨ་ཏི་ཤའི་གདུང་བཞུགས་ས་ལ། དེ་ལྟ་བུའི་སྐུ་ཚོས་ཀྱིས་མི་འོང་། རི་རབ་ཐེག་པ་ཆེན་པོའི་ཕ་རོལ་ཏུ་ཕྱིན་པའི་ལུགས་སུ་བྱས་ [29b2] ཕྱོགས་བཞི་ན་ལྷ་གཙོ་འཁོར་གསུམ་གསུམ་ཡོད་པ། བུམ་པ་ཐེག་པ་ཆེན་པོ་གསང་སྔགས་ཀྱི་ལུགས་སུ་བྱས་ནས། གསང་བ་འདུས་པ་ལྷ་ [illegible] དགྱུ་མ་ཕྱི་ནང་ ཏུ་ འབུར་དུ་དོད་པ། བཟོ་ཁྱད་འདི་ལྟ་བུ་གཅིག་བྱེད་འཚལ་གསུངས་པས། ལྷ་བཟོ་ [29b3] བཤུམས་ཏེ། བོད་བ་[989]གླང་དང་འདྲ་ཟེར་ཅན་བཟོ་བགྱིད་དཀའ་མོ་འདི་ལྟ་བུ་དགོས་ཨང་གསུང་། འོན་ཀྱང་ཇོ་བོ་ཡབ་སྲས་ཀྱི་ཐུགས་རྗེ་དང་། ལྷ་བཟོ་དེ་མཁས་པ་ལ་བརྟེན་ཏེ། དགེ་བཤེས་སྟོན་པ་ཉིད་ཇི་ལྟར་བཞེད་པ་བཞིན་བྱོན་ [29b4] དེ་ཡང་རི་རབ་ཕ་རོལ་ཏུ་ཕྱིན་པའི་ལུགས་སུ་བཞེངས་ཏེ། མདུན་ན་རྒྱལ་བ་ཤཀྱ་[990]ཐུབ་ པ་ <u>གཙོ་འཁོར་</u> (གཙོཾར) གསུམ: ནུབ་ཏུ་དམ་ཚིག་གསུམ་བཀོད་པའི་རྒྱལ་པོ་གཙོ་འཁོར་གསུམ: བྱང་ན་བྱམས་པ་མངོན་པར་བྱང་ཆུབ་གཙོ་འཁོར་གསུམ། ཤར་ན་སྨན་གྱི་ལྷ་ [29b5] གཙོ་འཁོར་གསུམ། དེ་དག་ལ་ཡང་སྒྱུ་རི་དང་རྒྱན་སྣ་བཞི་ལ་སོགས་པའི་བཟོ་ཁྱད་དུ་འཕགས་པ་ཡོད། བུམ་པ་ཐེག་པ་ཆེན་པོ་གསང་སྔགས་ཀྱི་ལུགས་སུ་བགྱིས་ཏེ། གསང་བ་འདུས་པ་

---

979 ཀྱི་

980 ལྡོངས་

981 - །

982 རླབས་

983 བ་

984 dot-line annotation mark

985 + །

986 རླབས་

987 བཞེངས་

988 ཀྱིས་

989 པ་

990 ཤཱཀྱ་

ལྷ་ཡབ་བཞི། ཕྱིའི་ཕྱོགས་བཞི་ན་འབྱུར་དུ་ [illegible: དོད་] [29b6] ×ཡུམ་བཞི་ནི་ཕྱིའི་མཚམས་བཞི་ན་འབྱུར་དུ་དོད། ×མཆོད་པའི་ལྷ་ [blank] མོ་དྲུག་ནང་དུ་གཏོད། མཐར་བྱེད་ཀྱི་ཁྲོ་བོ་ (ཁྲོ་) ཞལ་གསུམ་ཕྱག་དྲུག་པ་ནས་ཙམ་991དེ་ཡོད་པ། རི་རབ་ཀྱི་སྟེང་ན་མཆོད་རྟེན་ སོར་བཞི་ པ་ཙམ་པ་རིའི་ནང་ ན་ བཞུགས། དབུས་ཀྱི་གཙོ་བོ་འཇམ་དཔལ་རྡོ་རྗེ་ནི་ལུགས་མ་ [29b7] ཞལ་གསུམ་ཕྱག་དྲུག་པ་སོར་བཞི་ཙམ་པ་བྲེའི་གུལ་ (བྲེའི་གུལ་)992ན་བཞུགས་སོ། །དེ་ལ་འཁོར་ལོ་བཅུ་གསུམ། དེའི་སྟེང་ན་དངུལ་གྱིས་993གདུགས་ཁྲུ་གང་ཙམ་གཅིག་ཕུབ། དེའི་བཟོའི་རྣམ་པ་འདྲ་བ་བོད་ན་མེད་སྐད། ནང་སྦྱོངས་994སུ་རྗེ་ [29b8] ཤཀྱ་995ཐུབ་པའི་གདུང་ལུག་ཐོང་པའི་སེ་བ་ཏྲུས་996ཙམ་ཅིག། སངས་རྒྱས་མྱ་ངན་ལས་འདས་དུས་སུ་ཀུན་དགའ་བོས་ཚགས་མཛད།997 དེས་དགེ་སློང་ (དེསློང) ཟླ་འཆང་གཏད། དེས་སློབ་དཔོན་ཀླུ་སྒྲུབ998། དེས་ཟླ་བ་གྲགས་པ། དེས་རིག་ [29b9] པའི་ཁུ་བྱུག། དེས་ཇོ་བོ་ཨ་ཏི་ཤ་ལ་འབོ། དེས་དགེ་བཤེས་སྟོན་པ་ལ་གནང་གསེར་གྱི་གཙུའི་ནང་ ན་ : དེ་དངུལ་གྱི་གཙུ། དེ་རགན་གྱི་གཙུ། དེ་ཟངས་ཀྱི་གཙུའི་ནང་ན་བཞུགས་པ་ནི་བྲེའི་ནང་ན་བཞུགས་སོ། [illegible: །] [30a1] ཐུམ་སྟོད་ན་གདུང་ཐལ་ཆེབ་སའི་ཐྲུགས་སུ་ (སིཐྲུགསུ) བཞུགས་སོ། །དངུལ་ཀྱི་999ལྷུང་པ་ལ་བཟོ་རིས་སུ་བྱས་པའི་གཟུ་སྣ་ཐེམ་པ་བཞུགས་སོ། གྲོ་བ་དང་ཤོག་གུ་ (ཤོགུ) ལ་བྲིས་པ་མི་བཞུགས་སོ། རབ་ཏུ་གནས་པ་སྟོན་པ་རིན་པོ་ཆེ་ཉིད་ཀྱི་ལན་མང་ [30a2] དུ་བཞུགས།། བྱང་རྣམས་སྙིང་གི་ཇོ་བོ་དངུལ་གདུགས་ཅན་ཞེས་གྲགས་སོ། །དེའི་ཤར་ན་གདུང་ཁང་གསེར་ཆབ་ཅན་གཅིག་བཞུགས་པ་དེ། དགེ་བཤེས་སྟོན་པའི་གདུང་ཁང་དུ། རྒྱལ་འབྱོར་པ་རྣམས་ཀྱིས་བཞེངས། ལྷ་བཟོ་ཨ་ཙ་ར་མ་ནུས་ [30a3] བྱས། རབ་གནས་གསང་ཕུ་བའི་བཞུགས། དེའི་ཤར་ཀྱི་1000གསེར་ཆབ་ཅན་དེ། རྒྱལ་འབྱོར་པ་ཆེན་པོའི་གདུང་ཁང་དུ་ལྷ་ཙ་ཡི་དེས་བྱས། རབ་གནས་དགོན་པ་ཆེན་པོའི་བཞུགས། །དེའི་ཤར་ཀྱི་1001གསེར་ཆབ་ཅན་དེ། དགོན་1002 [30a4] ཆེན་པོའི་གདུང་ཁང་དུ། ལྷ་བཟོ་ཙ་ཡི་དོས་1003བྱས། རབ་གནས་སྐུ་མཆེད་གསུམ་ཀྱི་1004བཞུགས: དེའི་ཤར་

991 བརྩམས་

992 བྲེའུ་མགུལ་ ?

993 གྱི་

994 ལྷོངས་

995 ཤཱཀྱ་

996 སེའུ་ ?

997 : ?

998 སྒྲུབ་

999 གྱི་

1000 གྱི་

1001 གྱི་

1002 + པ་

1003 དེས་

1004 གྱི་

ཀྱི་[1005]དདུལ་གདུང་ཁང་དེ: དགེ་བཤེས་ཀ་མ་བའི་གདུང་ཁང་དུ: དགེ་འདུན་སྤྱི་པས་བཞེངས། །ལྷ་བཟོ་དམ་སྨོན་ [30a5] དར་ཀྱིས་བྱས། རབ་གནས་བྱ་ཡུལ་ཆེན་པོའི་བཞུགས། དེའི་ཤར་ཀྱི་[1006]དདུལ་ཀྱི་[1007]གདུང་ཁང་དེ། དགེ་བཤེས་སྒྲིང་[1008] པོ[1009]འི་གདུང་ཁང་། ལྷ་བཟོ་དམ་སྨོན་དར་ཡིན། རབ་གནས་ཀོ་ཁྲིམ་བྲག་རྩ་བའི་བཞུགས: དེའི་ཤར་གྱི་དདུལ་ [30a6] ཀྱི་[1010]གདུང་ཁང་དེ། དགེ་བཤེས་མཐའ་བཞི། རྒྱུའུ་རབ། ཀོ་ཁྲིམ་པ་གསུམ་ཀྱི་[1011]སྤྱིའི་གདུང་ཁང་དུ། དགེ་འདུན་སྤྱི་པས་བཞེངས། དེའི་ནང་ན་དེ་བཞིན་གཤེགས་པའི་རིང་སྲེལ་ཆེ་ལུ་གང་ཙམ་བཞུགས། བྲམ་ཟེའི་ཐོད་ [30a7] སྐུ་གཅིག: ཤ་རི་[1012]བུའི་ལྷུང་བཟེད: ཇོ་བོའི་ཡབ་རྒྱལ་པོ་དགེ་བ་དཔལ་གྱི་ཐུགས་དམ། དཔལ་དགྱེས་པ་རྡོ་རྗེའི་ཐང་སྐུ་གཅིག ཇོ་བོའི་ཐུགས་དམ་ཞལ་ཀྱི་[1013]ཕྲེང་བ་བརྒྱ་རྩ་བརྒྱད་པ་གཅིག རྣལ་འབྱོར་པ་ཆེན་པོས་ཇོ་བོ་ཡི་གེ་དྲུག་མ་ཞལ་གཟིགས་དུས་སུ་ [30a8] ཕྱུལ་བའི་བོ་དོ[1014]རྩེའི་[1015]ཕྲེང་བ་དང་། ཆོས་གོས་དང་། སྦྱིན་སྲེག་མཛད་པའི་བགང་[1016]བཟར་[1017]ཀླུག་ཟེར[1018]། སྟོན་པ་དང་: རྣལ་འབྱོར་པ་དང་། དགོན་བ་[1019]བ་དང་གསུམ་གྱི་སྤྱད་སྤྱུངས་མང་པོ་བཞེངས་སོ། རབ་གནས་བྱ་ཡུལ་ [30a9] བ་མཆོད་གནས་ཀྱི་བཞུགས། །དེའི་རྩའི་དེ་[1020]དཔོན་ཆོས་ཀྱི་རྒྱལ་པོའི་གདུང་ཁང་། ལྷ་བཟོ་མགོན་པོ་དར་ཀྱི་[1021]བྱས། རབ་གནས་གསང་ཕུ་བའི་བཞུགས། དེའི་རྩའི་ [1022]གདུང་ཁང་ དེའི་ཕྱུ་ཏོ་བའི་ཐུགས་གསུམ་བྱོན་པའི་གཅིག་བཞུགས། ། [30b1] མཐའ་བཞིས་བཞེངས། རབ་གནས་ཁམས་ལུང་པའི་བཞུགས། དེའི་རྩ་དེ་རྣལ་འབྱོར་པ་ཆེན་པོའི་གདུང་ཁང་དུ། སྟོད་ལུངས་པ་ཆེན་པོས་བཞེངས། རབ་གནས་སྤྱན་མངའི་ ཀྱ་[1023]རྩ་

1005 གྱི་

1006 གྱི་

1007 གྱི་

1008 སྒང་

1009 + པ་

1010 གྱི་

1011 གྱི་

1012 ཤཱ་རིའི་བུ་

1013 གྱི་

1014 དེ་

1015 ཙེའི

1016 དགང་

1017 གཟར་

1018 གཟར

1019 པ་

1020 དེའི་རྩར་

1021 གྱིས་

1022 dot-line annotation mark

1023 བརྒྱ་

བརྒྱད་ བཞུགས། དེའི་ལྷུང་1024ན་དགེ་བཤེས་སྟོན་པའི་སྐུ་རང་བྱོན་ [illegible] བཞུགས། རབ་གནས་བྲ་ཡུལ་རྩང་པས་ [illegible] དེའི་རྩ་དེ་སྣབས་ཁ་1025བའི་གདུང་ཁང་དུ་བཞེངས། ། རབ་གནས་སྟེང་1026པོ་བའི་བཞུགས། ། [30b2] དེ་ནས་དཔལ་གདུགས་ཅན་ཀྱི་1027ནུབ་ཕྱོགས་ན། ར་གན་ཀྱི་1028གདུང་ཁང་ཆེན་པོ་གཅིག་ཡོད་པ་དེ། རྣལ་འབྱོར་ཆེན་པོའི་གདུང་ཁང་དུ། སྟོད་ལུང་པས་1029ཆེན་པོས་བཞེངས། ལྷ་བཟོ་སྐལ་ལྡན་ (སྐན་ལ་) གྲགས་ཕྱུག་ཡིན། ། རབ་གནས་སྨྲུན་མངའི་1030 [30b3] ལན་བདུན་བཞུགས། །དེའི་རྩའི་དེ་ཁམ་1031པ་ལུང་པའི་གདུང་ཁང་དུ་དགེ་འདུན་སྒྲི་པའི་1032བཞེངས། །དེའི་རྩའི་དེ་དགེ་བཤེས་མཐའ་བཞིའི་གདུང་ཁང་དུ། བྲ་ནང་ཟུར་གསུམ་ཀྱིས་1033བཞེངས། རབ་གནས་ཀ་མ་བའི་བཞུགས། ། [30b4] དེའི་རྩའི་དེ་ཤར་བའི་གདུང་ཁང་དུ། རབ་གནས་ཀོ་ཁྲིམ་པའི་ [illegible] ཐག་རྩ་ [illegible] བཞུགས། དེའི་རྩའི་དེ་སྣབས་ཁ་1034བ་དང་། དགོན་པ་བ་སུམ་སློམ་གཉིས་ཀྱི་སྤྱིའི་གདུང་ཁང་། དེའི་རྩའི་དེ་ཞང་འོད་འཇོ་བའི་གདུང་ཁང་། རབ་གནས་རིན་ཆེན་སྣང་ [30b5] པ་སངས་རྒྱས་དཔོན་ཀྱི་1035བཞུགས་སོ། །དེའི་རྩའི་དེ་སྣང་ཐང་དཀར་ པའི་ གདུང་ཁང་། རབ་གནས་རིན་ཆེན་སྣང་པའི་བཞུགས་སོ། ། དེའི་རྩའི་དེ་དགོན་འོད་འབྱོ་1036བའི་གདུང་ཁང་དཔོན་བསོན་ནུ་སེང་གེས་བཞེངས [illegible: །] དེའི་རྩའི་གདུང་ཁང་དེའི་ནང་ན་དགེ་བཤེས་ [30b6] སྟོན་པའི་སྐུ་རང་བྱོན་ཡང་བཞུགས། རབ་གནས་བྲ་ཡུལ་བའི་བཞུགས། དེའི་རྩའི་.: .:དབུས་ཀྱི་1037གདུང་ཁང་ཆེན་པོ་དེ་ དེ་བླ་རྒྱུགས་ཕྲིའི་གདུང་ཁང་། རབ་གནས་སྤྱིལ་ཕུ་བའི་བཞུགས། དེའི་རྩའི་དེ་མངའ་རིས་པ་ཆམ་ཆོས་མེད་ཀྱི་གདུང་ཁང་། རབ་གནས་ [30b7] ཀ་མ་བའི་བཞུགས། དེའི་རྩའི་དེ་འཕྲང་ས་རྗེ་གདན་ཀྱི་1038གདུང་ཁང་། རབ་གནས་བྲ་ཡུལ་བ་སྣུབས་ཀྱི་བཞུགས། དེའི་རྩའི་དེ་དགེ་བཤེས་སྤྲང་སློ་བའི་

1024 སྟེང་
1025 ཀ་
1026 སྟེངས་
1027 ཀྱི་
1028 ཀྱི་
1029 པ་
1030 སྨྲའི་
1031 ཁམས་
1032 པས་
1033 ཀྱིས་
1034 ཀ་
1035 ཀྱི་
1036 འཇོ་
1037 ཀྱི་
1038 ཀྱི་

གདུང་ཁང་: རབ་གནས་འཁོར་ཐོག་པའི་བཞུགས། དེའི་རྩའི་དེ་ཞང་འོད་འཛེ་ [30b8] བའི་གདུང་ཁང་དུ། དགོན་འོད་འཛེ་བའི་བཞེངས། རབ་གནས་གླང་འདུད་པའི་བཞུགས། དེ་རྣམས་ཆེ་ཏིས་[1039]ཀྱི་བཤད་པ་ཟུར་[1040]སོ།།

ཚུང་བ་རྣམས་ལ་ཛོ་བོ་དངུལ་གདུགས་ཅན་གྱི་མདུན་ན་པད་སྤུངས་ཀང་[1041]གང་ [30b9] ཙམ་པ། དངུལ་ལས་བྱས་པ་དངུལ་ཀྱི་[1042]གདུགས་གཅིག ཡོད་པ་དེ་ [1043]ཛོ་བོ་ཡབ་སྲས་ཀྱི་གདུང་ཁང་དུ་དཔོན་ཆོས་ཀྱི་རྒྱལ་པོས་བཞེངས [illegible:]] ལྷ་བཞི་རྩ་ཡི་དེས་བྱས་རབ་གནས་གསང་ཕུ་བའི་བཞུགས [illegible:]] དེའི་རྩ་ན་པར་ལ་རྩ་ཡི་ཉོ་བཅུ་གསུམ་ཡོད་པ་དེ་རྣམས་ན་[1044] ཛོ་བོའི་གདུང་ལུག་ཐོང་པའི་སེ་བ་རས་[1045]ཙམ་པ་དེ་བཞུགས་སྐད། གཡས་ཕྱོགས་ཀྱི་མཆོད་རྟེན་ ཀྱི་[1046]ཐྲེའི་གཡུལ་[1047]ན་ལྷ་ཡོད་པ་དེ: རྣལ་འབྱོར་པ་ཆེན་པོས་ཛོ་བོ་ཡབ་སྲས་ [31a1] གདུང་དུ་བཞེངས: རྣལ་འབྱོར་པ་ཆེན་པོའི་ཨ་མི་དེ་བ་ཅན་བྱ་བ་བྱིན་བརླབས་[1048]ཅན་ཡིན: དེའི་རྩར་[1049]ད་[1050]མང་པོ་ཛོ་ལེགས་ཀྱིས། ཛོ་བོའི་གདུང་ཁང་དུ་བཞེངས། རབ་གནས་དགེ་བཤེས་སྟོན་པའི་བཞུགས། དེའི་ [31a2] གདུང་ཁང་དུ་སྟག་ར་གསང་གིས་བཞེངས། རབ་གནས་དགེ་བཤེས་སྟོན་པའི་བཞུགས། རབ་གནས་དགེ་བཤེས་སྟོན་པའི་བཞུགས།[1051] སེར་ཆབ་ཅན་ སྟག་ར་དང་དབང་གི་བཀྲ་ཤིས་སློ་མངས་བྱ་བར་གྲགས། དེའི་རྩའི་དེ་སྟོང་བརྩུན་ན་ [illegible: མགོ་བའི་?] [31a3] གདུང་ཁང་། རབ་གནས་དགེ་བཤེས་སྟོན་པའི་བཞུགས། སྟོང་བརྩུན་ན་མགོ་བའི་པད་མ་ཁ་སྦྱོར་དུ་གྲགས། དེའི་རྩའི་དེ་སྤྱན་མངའ་[1052]རིན་པོ་ཆེའི་གདུང་ཁང་དུ་སློབ་མ་གཉིས་ཀྱིས་བཞེངས། རབ་གནས་ཀ་མ་པའི་བཞུགས། [31a4] དེའི་རྩའི་དེའི་[1053]སྣེ་ཟུར་བའི་གདུང་ཁང་། སྤྱན་ཡ་གཅིག་ ངང་ | ལྷགས་བཞུགས། རབ་གནས་ཀ་མ་པའི་[1054]བཞུགས། བྱིན་བརླབས་[1055]མཛོན་

1039 གྲས་
1040 + ཙམ་
1041 བང་ ?
1042 གྱི་
1043 dot-line annotation mark
1044 ནི་
1045 སེའུ་རུས་
1046 གྱི་
1047 མགུལ་
1048 རླབས་
1049 རྩའི་
1050 དེ་
1051 duplication
1052 སྔ་
1053 དེ་
1054 བའི་
1055 རླབས་

རྒྱུགས་སུ་ཡོད། དེའི་རྩའི་དེ་དཔྱལ་གྱི་གདུང་ཁང་དེ། བྲོ་ཡུལ་པ་1056སངས་རྒྱས་སྒོམ་པའི་གདུང་ [illegible: ཁང་?] [31a5] རབ་
གནས་ཟེམ་རིན་པོ་ཆེའི་བཞུགས། དེའི་རྩའི་ ཇེ་ བྲོ་ཡུལ་བའི་གདུང་ཁང་། དེའི་རྩའི་དེ་འོད་འཇོ་བའི་གདུང་ཁང་། དེའི་ [illegible: རྩ] འི་དེ་རིན་
ཆེན་སྣང་པ་དཀྱེད་ཚོ་དེའི་གདུང་ཁང་། །ཤར་ཕྱོགས་ཀྱི་ཆུང་བ་རྣམས་ལ། པད་སྤྱུངས་ [31a6] གདན་ཁྲི་ཅན་གཉིས་པོ་དེ: ཡུང་བའི་མེ་ཏོག་ཟླ་
མཛེས་སྤྱུན་གཉིས་ཀྱིས་ཇོ་བོ་ཡབ་སྲས་ཀྱི་གདུང་ཁང་དུ་བཞེངས། རབ་གནས་རྣལ་འབྱོར་བ་ཆེན་པོའི་བཞུགས། །དེའི་རྩའི་དེ་འཆད་ཁ་
པའི་1057གདུང་ཁང་། ○འདིའི་ནང་ན་ཆད་ ○ཚོངས་པའི་ [31a7] གནས་ནས་བྱོན་པའི་རྣལ་འབྱོར་མའི་སྐུ་རང་བྱོན་གཅིག་བཞུགས། རབ་གནས་སྤྱི
ལ་ བུ་1058བའི་བཞུགས། དེའི་རྩའི་དེ་བྲོ་ཡུལ་བས་1059གདུང་ཁང་དུ་ བཞུགས། རབ་གནས་བྲོ་ཡུལ་བ་ཆེན་པོའི་བཞུགས། །1060དེའི་རྩའི་དེ་བྲག་
དཀར་བ་སྟོན་1061མའི་གདུང་ [31a8] ཁང་། བྲག་དཀར་བ་ཕྱི་མའི་ +རབ་གནས་ བཞུགས། །དེའི་རྩའི་དེ་དགེ་བཤེས་དོན་མོ་རི་པའི་གདུང་ཁང་།
སྤྱན་སྔ་ དོན་མོ་རི་པ་ཕྱི་མའི་རབ་གནས་བཞུགས: དེའི་རྩའི་དེ་རིན་ཆེན་སྣང་པ་སངས་རྒྱས་དཔོན་1062གྱི་གདུང་ཁང་ [illegible] དེ་ནས་ དེའི་རྩའི་དེ་སྟྭབས་ཁ་1063
པའི་1064གདུང་ཁང་: རབ་གནས་སྙིང་པོ་བའི་ [31b1] བཞུགས: དེ་རྣམས་ཀྱི་གཙོ་མཛད་པའི་ སྤྱིར་ གདུང་ཁང་ཆེ་ཆུང་གདོངས་1065པ་ལ་
བདུན་བརྒྱ་དང་སུམ་བཅུ་རྩ་ལྔ་ཙམ་བཞུགས། །ད྄ི་1066འདི་རྣམས་ངོ་མཚར་ཅན་འདི་ལྟ་བུ་ཡིན་པས། བྱང་རྣམས་སྒྲིང་དུ་གདན་དྲོངས་ཅིག་ཟེར་བའི་
རྩིས་ཅན་ཤ་སྟག: [31b2] དེ་རྣམས་ཀྱིས་ཐུགས་ཀྱི་ བརྟེན་1067ཀྱི་1068 བཤད་པ་ཙམ་བསྟན་ཟིན་ཏོ།།

1056 བ་

1057 བའི་

1058 ཕུ་

1059 བའི་

1060 _།

1061 སྟོན་

1062 དཔོན་

1063 ཀ་

1064 བའི་

1065 བསྒོམས་

1066 རྟེན་

1067 རྟེན་

1068 རྟེན་གྱི་

(2–2–4) དེ་དག་གི་མཆོད་རྫས་ཀྱི་གྲངས།

བཞི་པ་དེ་དག་གི་མཆོད་སྟེས་[1069]ཀྱི་གྲངས་ནི། གསེར་དངུལ་ཀྱི་[1070]གདུགས་དྲུག །རྨ་བྱའི་གདུགས་དང་གཞན་ཡང་གོས་དར་ཀྱི་[1071] གདུགས་ ཉི་ཤུ་རྩ་གཉིས། ཟ་འོག་གི་བླ་རེ་[1072] [31b3] སུམ་བཅུ་རྩ་གཉིས། དར་ཟབ་ཀྱི་གདན་ཁྲི་སུམ་བཅུ་རྩ་གྲངས་ཡོད། །འཆར་དར་བཞི་བཅུ་ཐམ་པ། འཕྱེད་དར་རིང་པོ་ལེགས་པ་ གཅིག གདུང་གཡོགས་ཉི་ཤུ་[1073]བཅུ་རྩ་གསུམ། དངུལ་ཀྱི་[1074]མཧྚལ་ཆེན་པོ་གཉིས། མེ་ལོང་གི་ མཏྟན་[1075] [31b4] བཅུ་གཅིག། དུང་དཀར་བདུན། རག་དུང་བཞི། ཆ་ལང་བཅོ་བརྒྱད། འཁར་རྔ་ཉི་ཤུ་ཐམ་པ། ཕེབ་གསུམ། ཕྱེ་མ་ཕུར་མ་ བརྒྱ་བཅུ། རྔ་ཡབ་ཉི་ཤུ། མན་ཏིང་བདུན་ཆ་ཉི་ཤུ་རྩ་གཅིག ཀ་ཏོར་བརྒྱ་བཞི་བཅུ [31b5] པ་ཡོད། པད་[1076]ཞོང་སུམ་བཅུ། རིན་པོ་ཆེ་སུམ་ བཅུ་སོ་ལྔ། གསེར་བུམ་གཅིག རིན་ཆེན་གསལ་བྱེད་ཀྱི་བུམ་པ་གཅིག གོང་[1077]བ་[1078]དྲུག་བརྒྱ་ལྷག་པ་ཡོད། དེ་རྣམས་ཀྱི་མཆོད་ སྟེས་[1079]ཀྱི་གྲངས་སོ།།

འོན་དེ་ལྟ་བུའི་གཙུག་ [31b6] ལག་ཁང་དེའི་ཆོས་སྐྱོང་གང་ཡིན་ཟེར་ན། སྤྱིའི་ཆོས་སྐྱོང་ནི་དཔལ་མགོན་པོ་ལྕམ་དྲལ་ཡིན། དགོས་[1080]སུ་ནི་ འགྲོག་གནས་མཆེད་ལྔ་། དགེ་བཤེས་སྟོན་པ་ལ་རང་བབས་སུ་བྱོན་པའི་དྲང་སྲོང་ཉ་མིག་མ་པ[illegible] [31b7] ལྷོ་ནུབ་མཚམས་ན་ གཏེར་མར་བཞུགས་སོ། །རྗེ་བོའི་དམ་ཅན་ཤ་ཟ་མ་མཆེད་ནི། རྗེ་བོའི་ཕྱུག་དཔེའ་དང་། བརྟེན་[1081]མཆོད་བསྲུང་བའི་ཆོས་སྐྱོང་ཡིན། སྤྱིར་ ×བདུད་དང རྒྱལ་པོ་དང་། བཙན་མ་ལ་སོགས་ [illegible] [31b8] པས་ཤིན་ཏུ་ཉམས་དགའ་ཞིང་། ཐུགས་དམ་པ་རྣམས་རྫོགས་པ་དང་དགེ་སྦྱོར་ འཕེལ་བར་བྱེད་པ་ཡིན། །དེ་ན་བཞུགས་པའི་རྟེན་རྣམས་ཀྱི་བཤད་པ་ཟུར་བ་ཆེ་ལོང་བརྗོད་པ་ཡིན་ནོ། །རྒྱས་པར་ཆེ [illegible] [32a1] ཅིང་[1082]བརྗོད་ཀྱིས་མི་ལང་ངོ།།

1069 རྫས་

1070 ཀྱི་

1071 ཀྱི་

1072 བྲེ།

1073 or སུམ་ཅུ་?

1074 ཀྱི་

1075 མཧྚལ་

1076 སྤོས་

1077 ཀོང་

1078 བུ་

1079 རྫས་

1080 སྲོས་

1081 རྟེན་

1082 ཞིང་

དེ་ལྟར་དོན་གཉིས་ཀྱི་གཙུག་ལག་ ཁང་ ཆེན། རྣམ་སྣྲིང་ཞེས་ཡོངས་[1083]གྲགས་པའི། རྒྱལ་པའི་དབེན་གནས་རིན་པོ་ཆེ་དེའི་ལོ་རྒྱུས་ཅུང་ཟད་
ཅིག་བརྗོད་ཟིན་ཏོ།།

དམ་བས་[1084]བསྔགས་པའི་དབེན་གནས་ [32a2] དེའི་[1085]
བཞེངས་ཚུལ་ལོ་རྒྱུས་སྔར་ཡང་མང་སྣང་མོད།།
འདོན་ཀྱང་དེ་དག་དབང་དོན་ཕྱི་ཐག །
འགོ་བར་དཀའ་ཞིང་མ་འབྲེལ་མ་འགྲིབས་[1086]པར།།
ཕྱོགས་སུ་བསྡེབས་ལ་གོ་བར་སླ་བ་གཅིག །
བདག་ལ་གྱིས་ཅེས་[1087]མཁས་པའི་སྐྱེ་བོ་དང་།།
དད་ལྡན་ [32a3] སྐྱེ་བུས་བསྐུལ་བར་གྱུར་བས་ན།།
སྔོན་གྱི་[1088]ཡི་གེ་རྙིང་པོའི་གསུང་རྣམས་དང་།།
རང་གི་[1089]མཐོང་དང་ཐོས་ཚོད་ལ་<u>བརྟེན་ནས</u> (བརྟེནས) །།
གཞོན་ནུ་མིང་ཅན་དགེ་སློང་རྣམ་སྣྲིང་པས།།
ཡི་གེར་བཀོད་ཀྱི་འགལ་འཁྲུལ་ མཆིས་ སྲིད་ན།།
[32a4] རྗེ་བོ་ཡབ་སྲས་བླ་མ་བརྒྱུད་[1090]པ་དང་།།
ཡི་དམ་ལྷ་དང་ཆོས་སྐྱོང་བསྲུང་མར་བཅས།།
མཁས་པའི་ཚོགས་ལ་བཟོ་བ་མཛད་པར་རིགས།།
གཞན་གྱིས་བསྐུལ་ནས་བདག་གིས་བྲིས་ པ་ ཡིས།།

1083 སུ་

1084 པས་

1085 + །།

1086 བསྒྲིབ་

1087 ཞེས་

1088 གྲི་

1089 གིས་

1090 བརྒྱུད་

བསོད་ནམས་དེ་ཡིས་སྐྱེ་བ་ཐམས་ཅད་དུ།།
[32a5] ཇོ་བོ་ཡབ་སྲས་ཆོས་ལ་ལོངས་སྤྱོད་ཅིང་།།
འགྲོ་དོན་ ལྷུན་གྲུབ་ བྱང་ཆུབ་ཐོབ་པར་ཤོག[1091]

རྒྱལ་བའི་དབེན་གནས་རྣམ་སྣང་གླིང་གི་བཤད་པ་ཉི་མའི་འོད་ཟེར་ཅེས་བྱ་བ་འདི་ནི། །རྒྱལ་བའི་དབེན་གནས་དེ་ཉིད་བཞེངས་ནས། ལོ་ཉིས་ [32a6] བརྒྱ་དང་བཞི་བཅུ་རྩ་གཉིས་ལོན་པའི་ཚེ། ཡོངས་ཀྱི་དགེ་བའི་བཤེས་གཉེན་ཆེན་པོ་རྣལ་འབྱོར་བྱང་སེང་གི་གདན་སར། དད་པ་དང་ཤེས་རབ་ཕུན་སུམ་ཚོགས་པ་དང་ལྡན་པའི་དགེ་སློང་དགེ་འདུན་དབང་ཕྱུག་ལ་སོགས་པ་འགའ་[1092]ཞིག་གིས་བསྐུལ་ [32a7] ནས: ཞིང་མོ་ཕག་གི་ལོ་ལ་འབྲོམ་ཤེས་རབ་མེ་ལྷེ་བྱ་བས་ཡི་གེར་བཀོད་པའོ། །སྫོགས་[1093]སྷོ། །འདི་བྲིས་ [illegible] དགེ་བས་བདེ་གཤེགས་ཤེས་རབ་ཐོབ་པར་ཤོག །ཤུ[1094]། ། མཾ་[1095]གཾ་[1096]ལཾ: ། ། [32a8] ཨོཾ་[1097]སྭ་སྟི། མ་[1098]ག་[1099]ལཾ། དུས་གསུམ་རྒྱལ་བ་སྲས་བཅས་འཁྲིན་ལན་[1100] ཀྱི་གདུལ་བྱ་གང་ལ་སྤྲུལ་པ་དེ་ལྟ་བུས། གདུལ་བའི་སྤྲུལ་པའི་སྐུར་སྟོན་པའི་དཔལ་ལྡན་ཇོ་བོ་ཡབ་སྲས་ལ་ཕྱག་འཚལ་ལོ། །ཤུ[1101]། ། མཾ་[1102]གཾ་[1103]ལཾ། བཾང་གཾ་བོང་།།

1091 + །
1092 འགའ་
1093 རྫོགས་
1094 ཤུ་བྷཾ
1095 མངྒ་
1096 - གཾ་
1097 ཨོཾ
1098 མངྒ་
1099 - ག་
1100 ལས་
1101 ཤུ་བྷཾ
1102 མངྒ་
1103 - གཾ་

Index

1) Persons

2) Places

3) Texts

4) Expressions

1) Persons

ང

ཅ

ཆ

ཇ

ཉ

ཏ

ཐ

ད

ཧ

ཨ

2) Places

ཨ

3) Texts

4) Expressions

ཆ

ཇ

ཏ

ཐ

ད

ན

པ

ཕ

བ

ར

ལ

ཤ

ས

ཧ

ཨ

FACSIMILE OF THE *RGYAL BA'I DBEN GNAS RWA SGRENG GI BSHAD PA NYI MA'I 'OD ZER* MANUSCRIPT

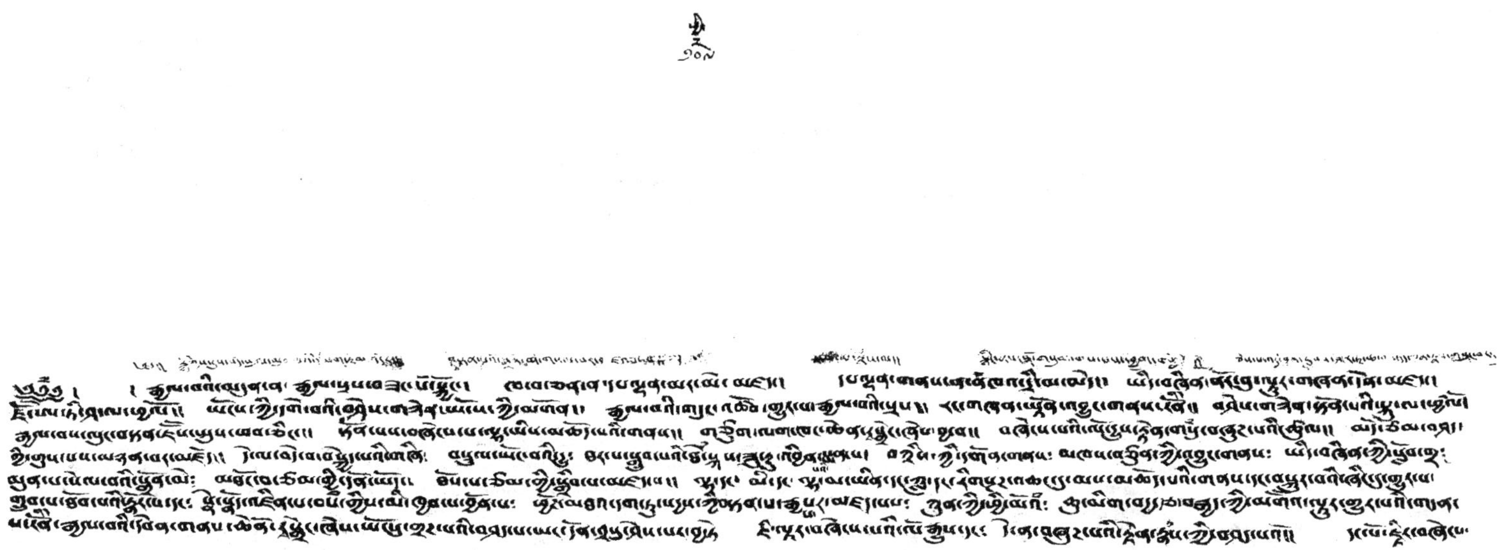

fol. 1

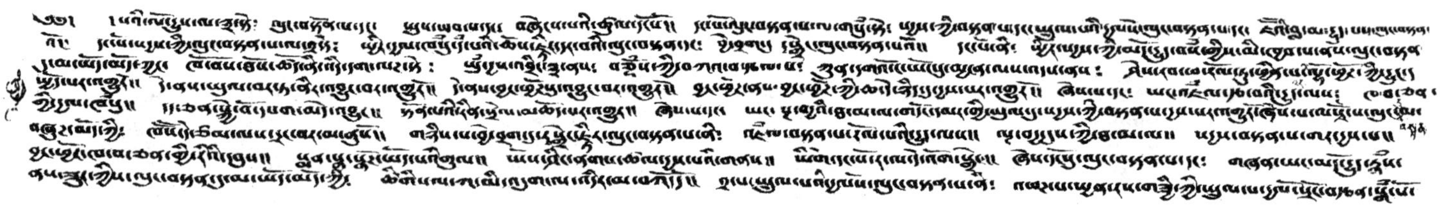

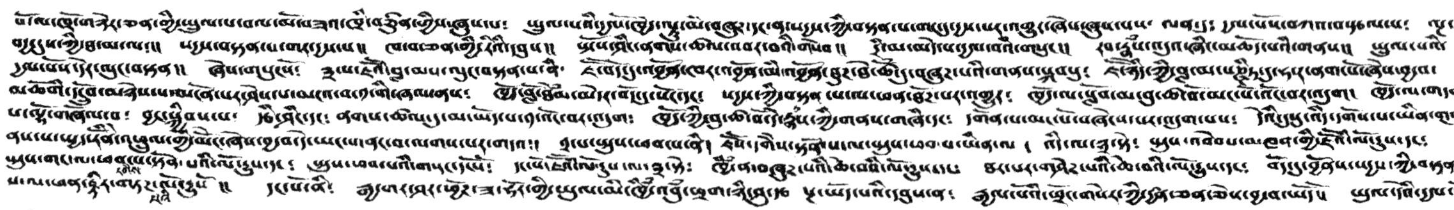

fol. 2

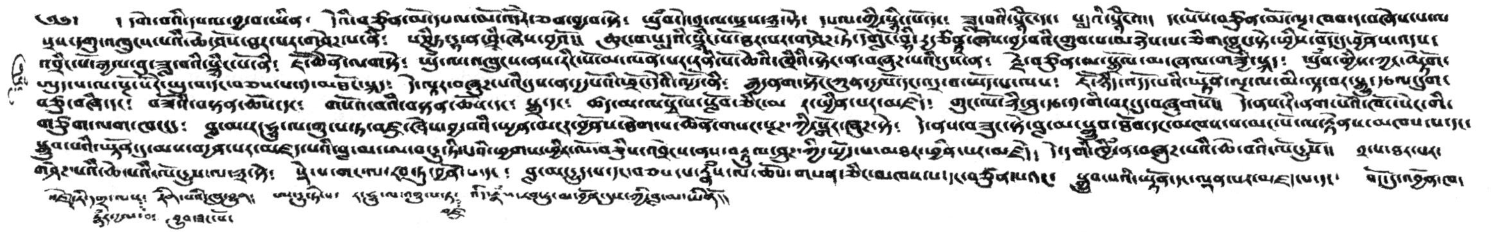

fol. 3

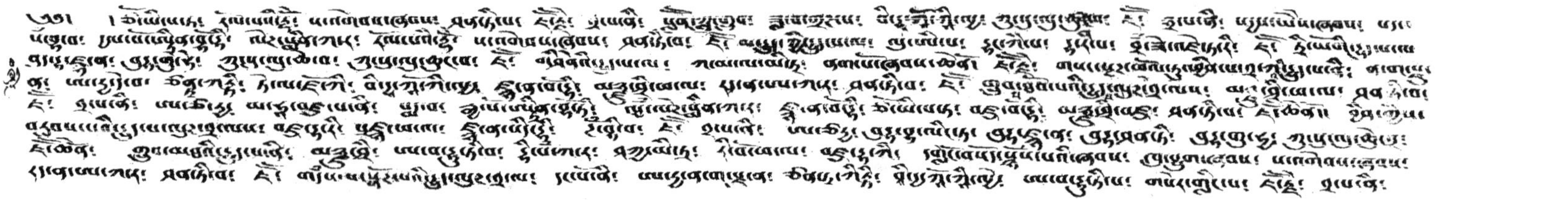

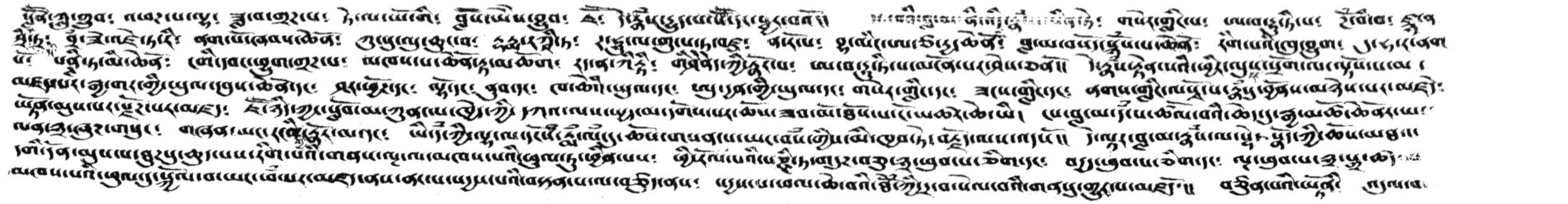

fol. 4

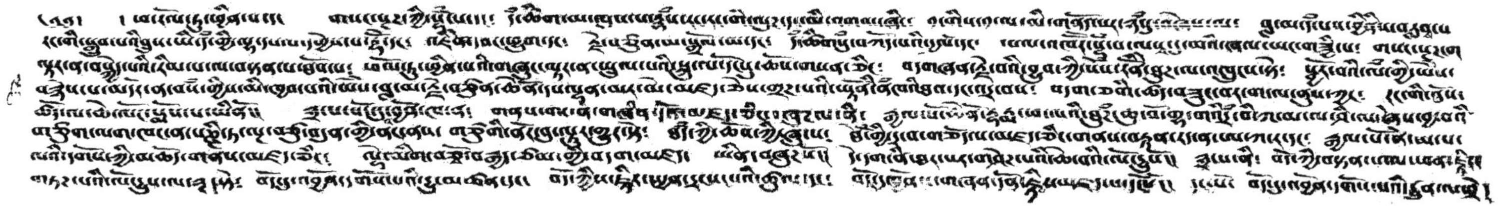

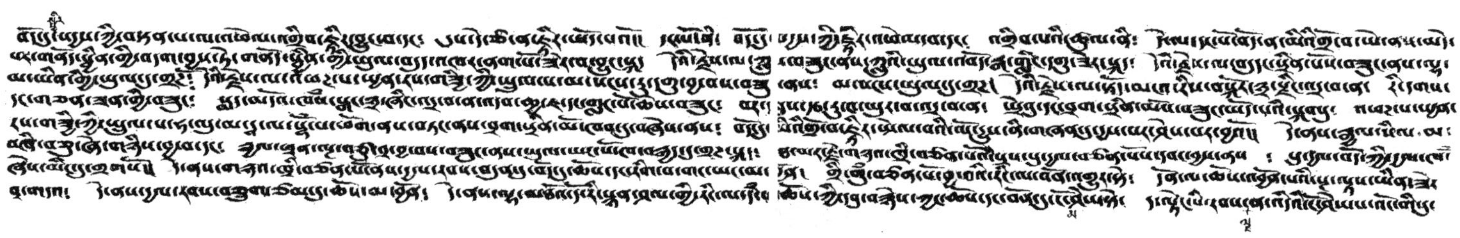

fol. 5

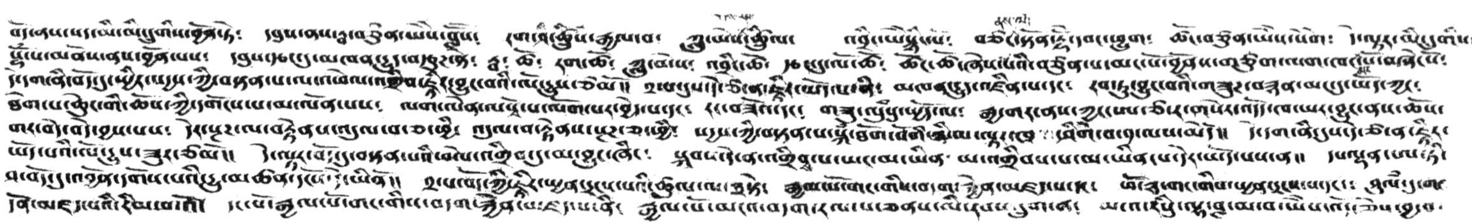

fol. 6

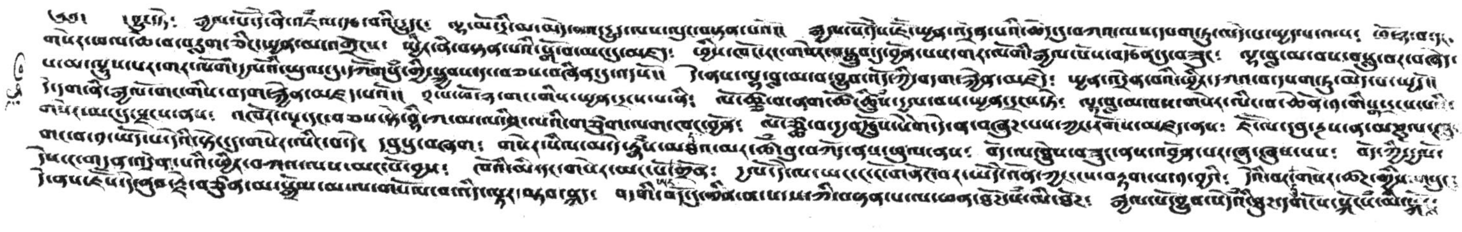

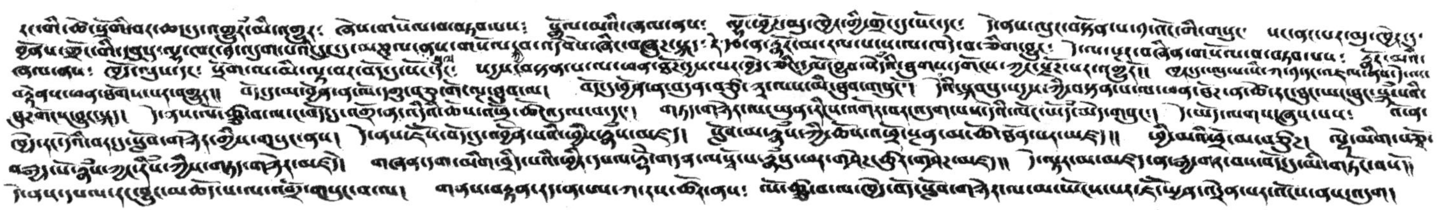

fol. 7

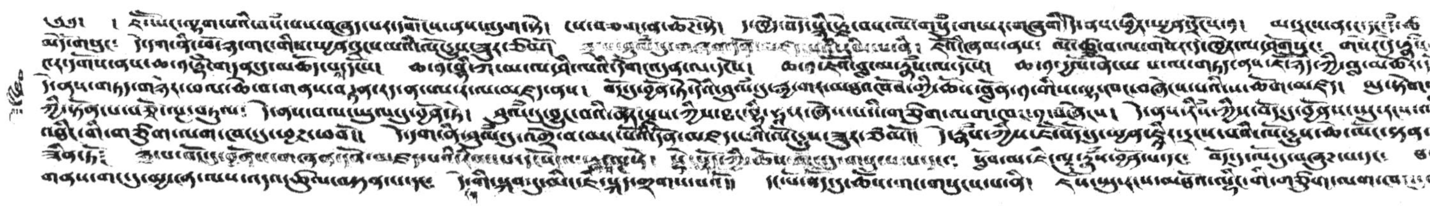

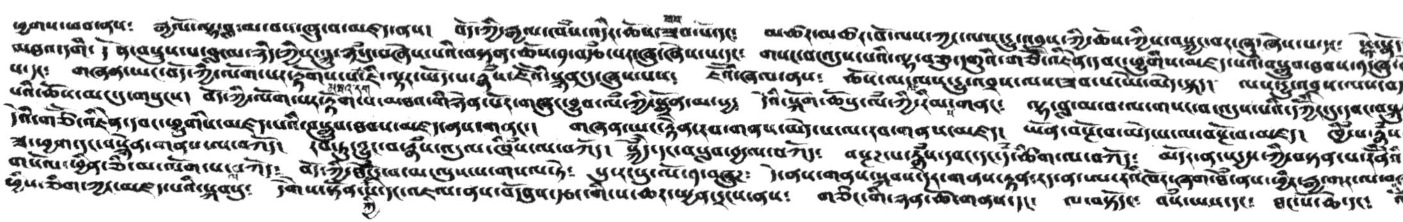

fol. 8

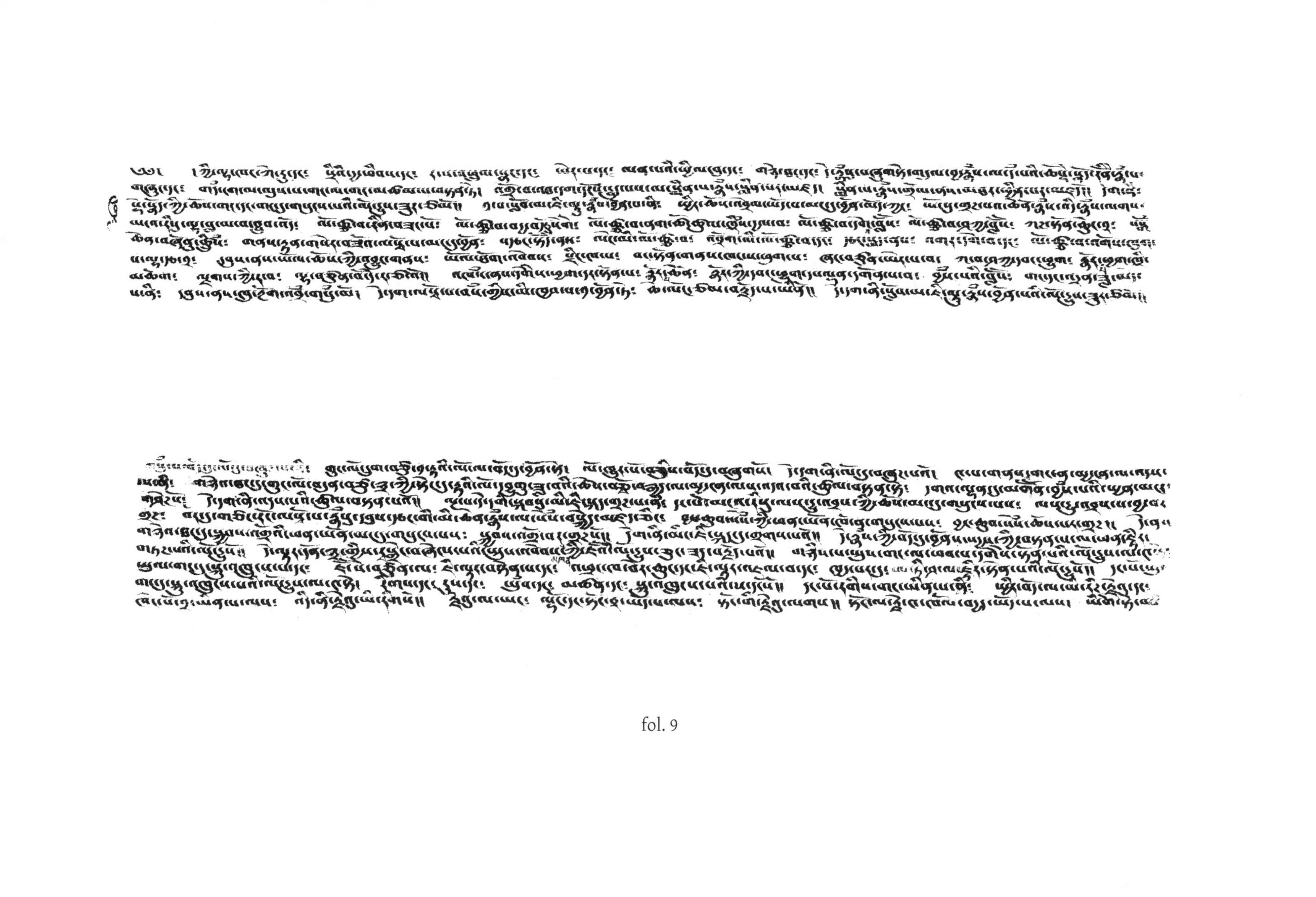

fol. 9

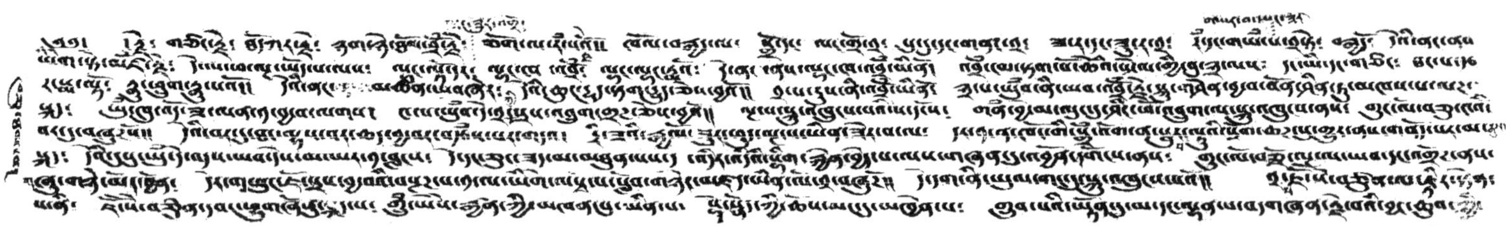

fol. 10

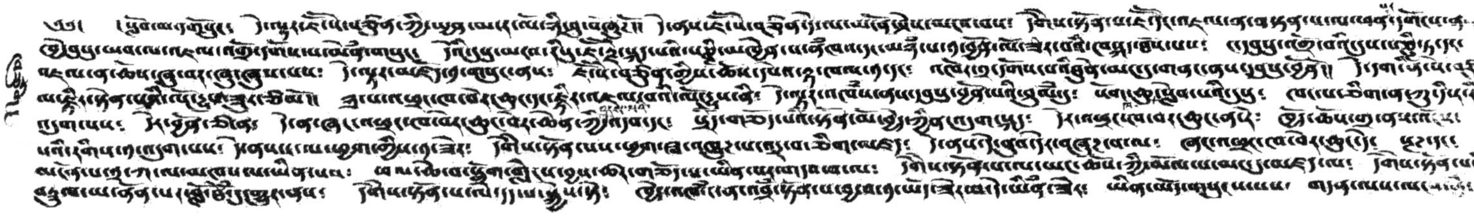

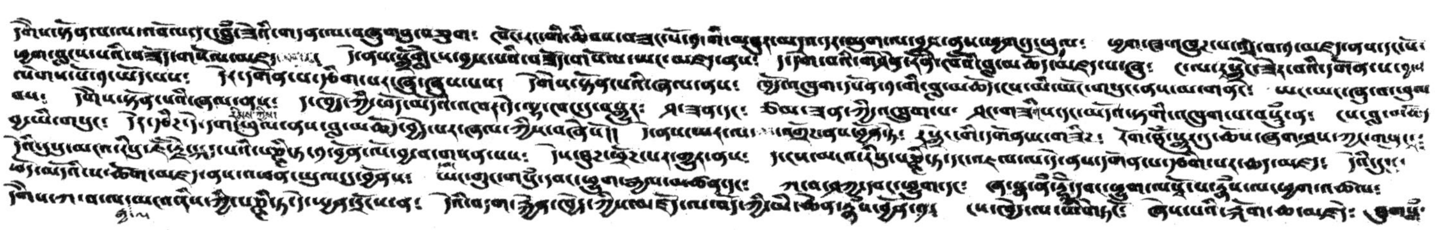

fol. 11

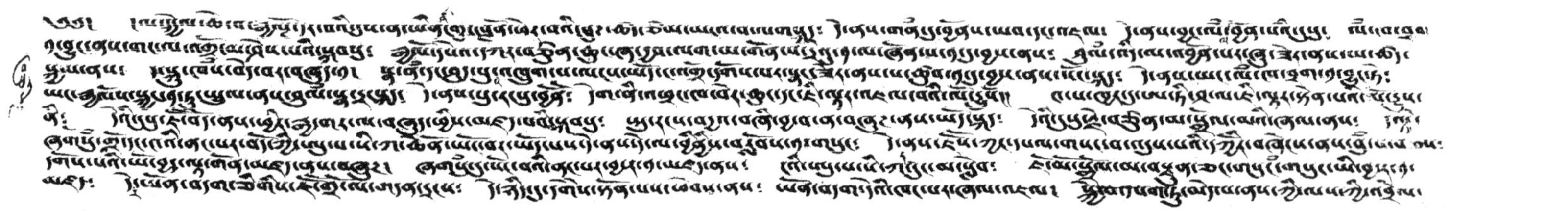

fol. 12

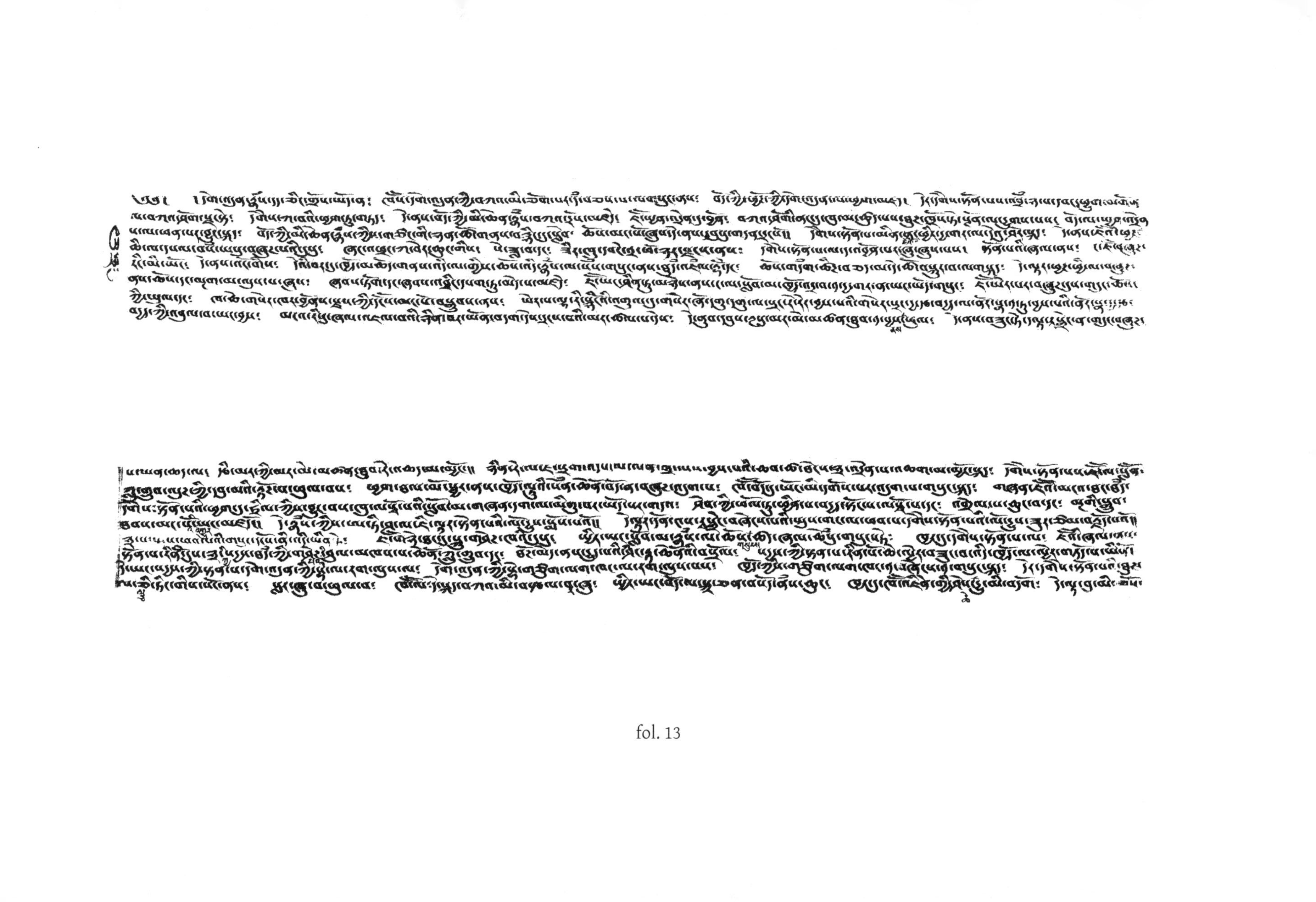

fol. 13

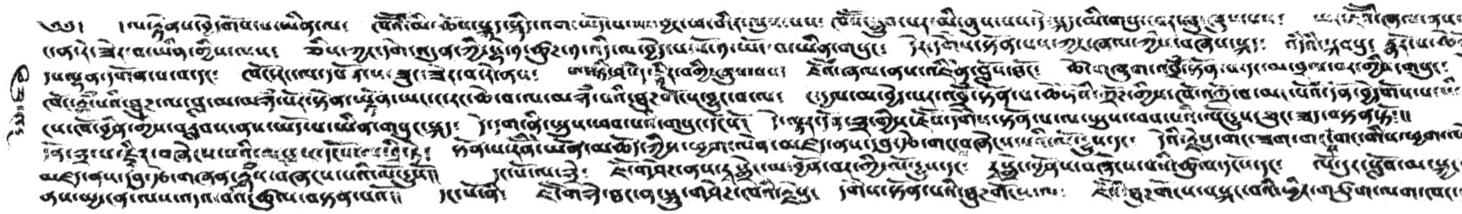

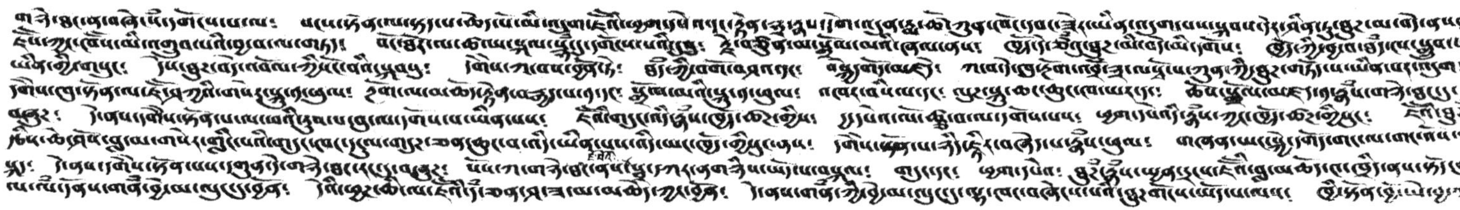

fol. 14

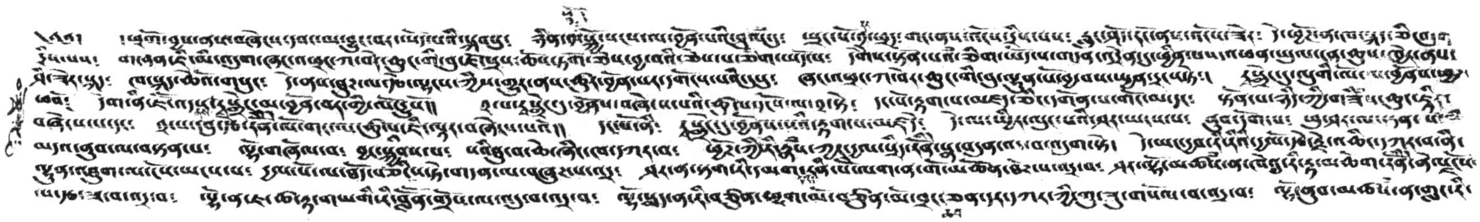

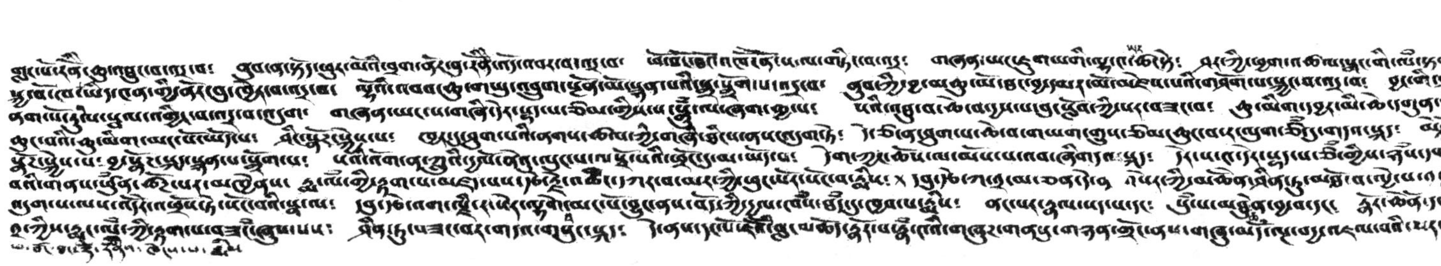

fol. 15

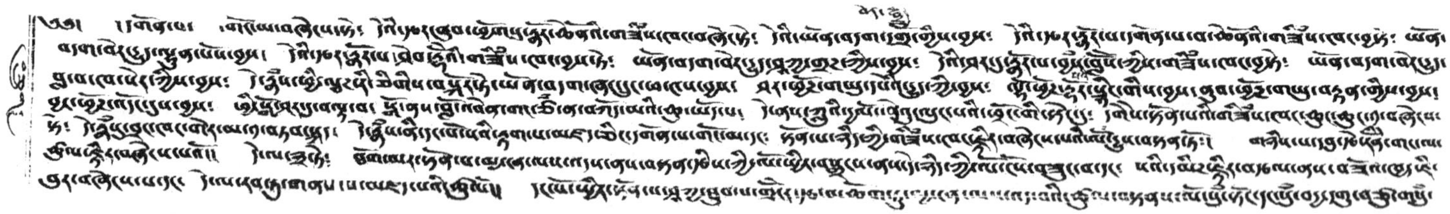

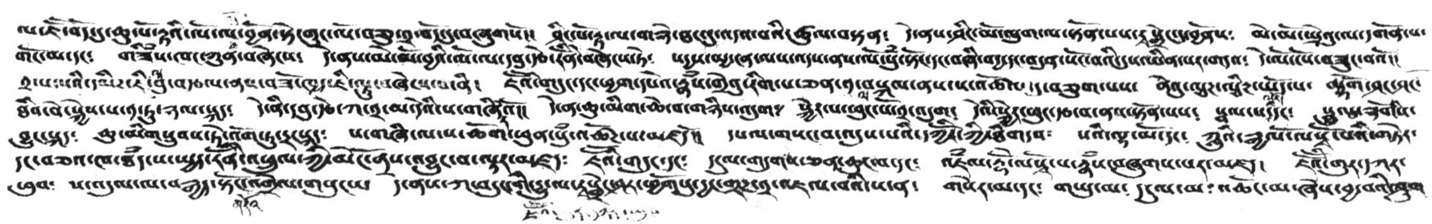

fol. 16

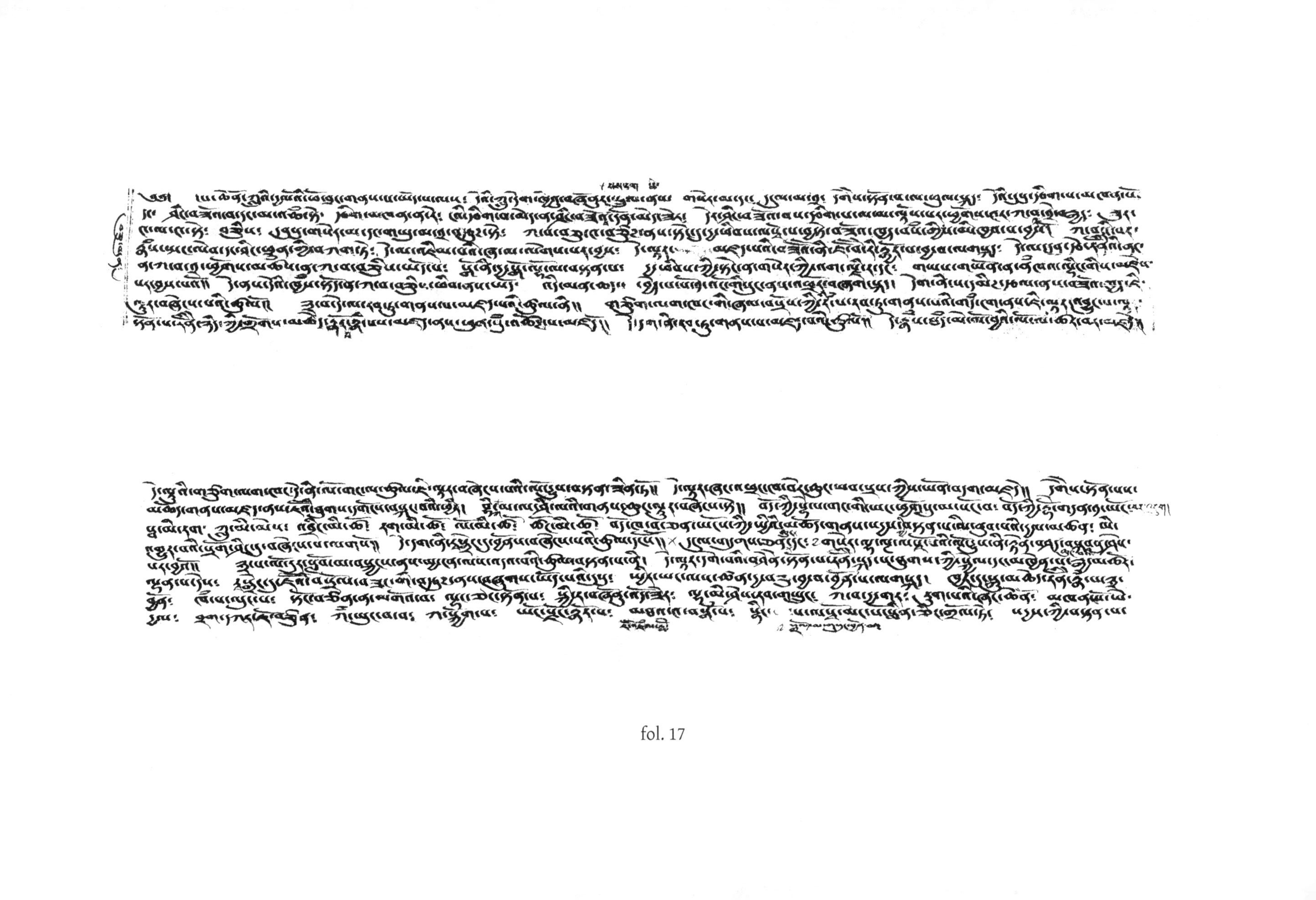

fol. 17

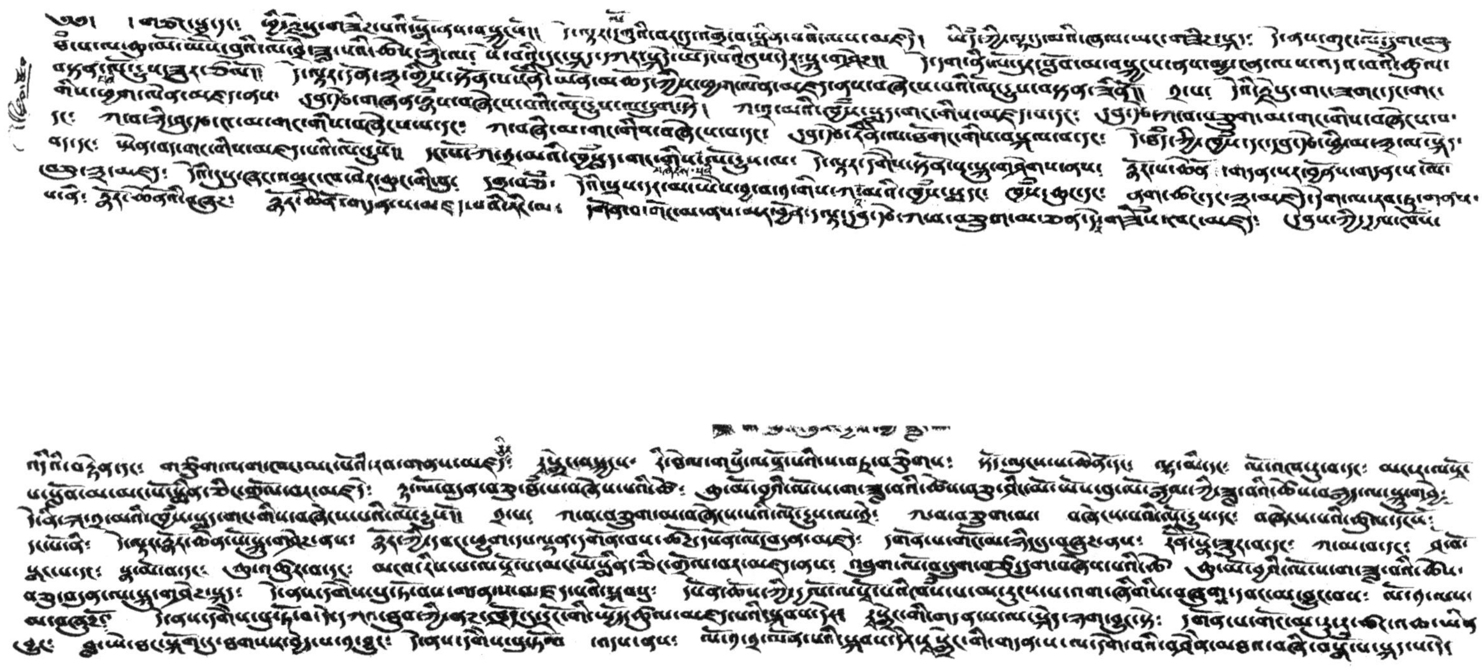

fol. 18

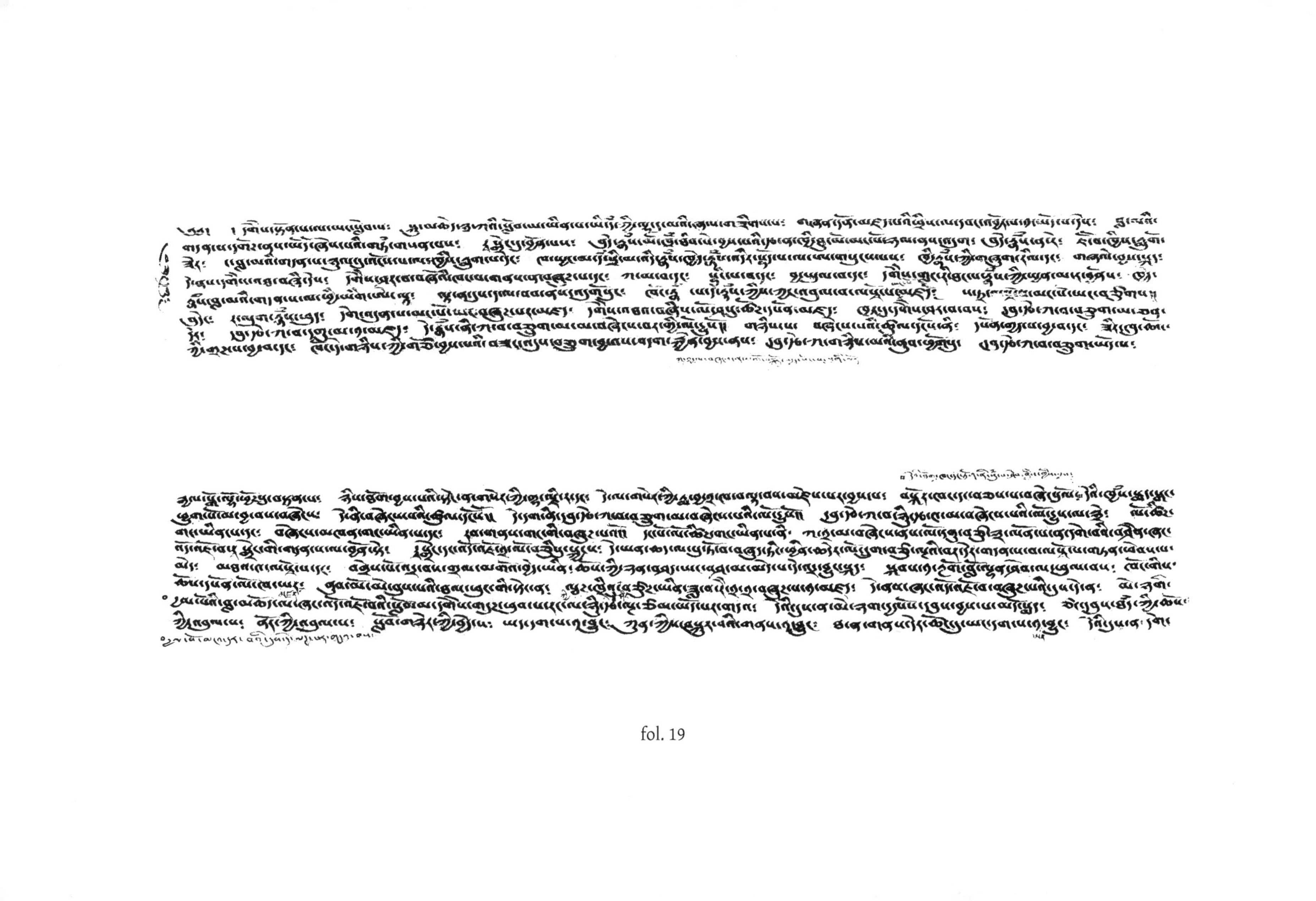

fol. 19

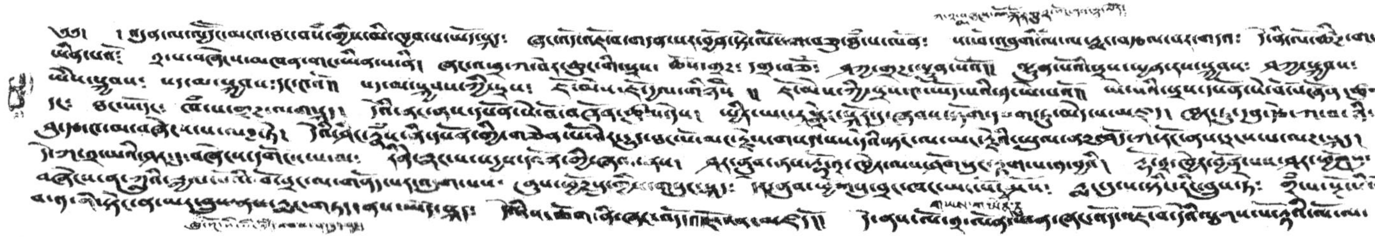

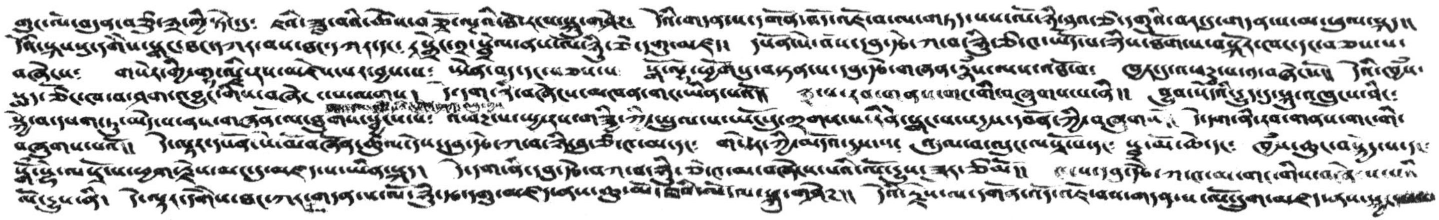

fol. 20

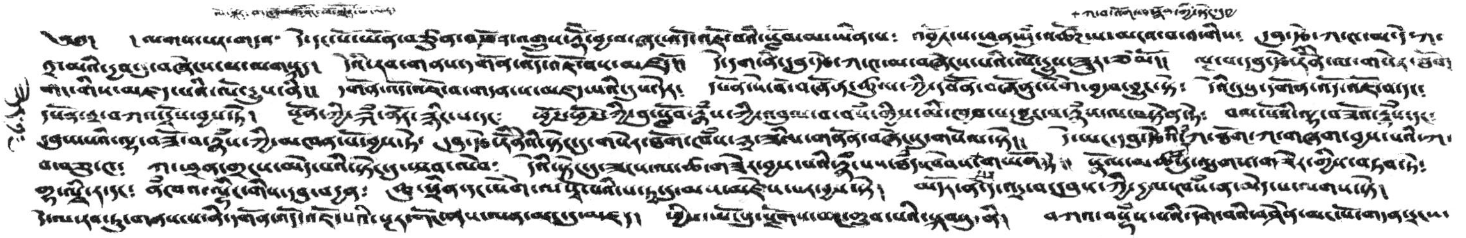

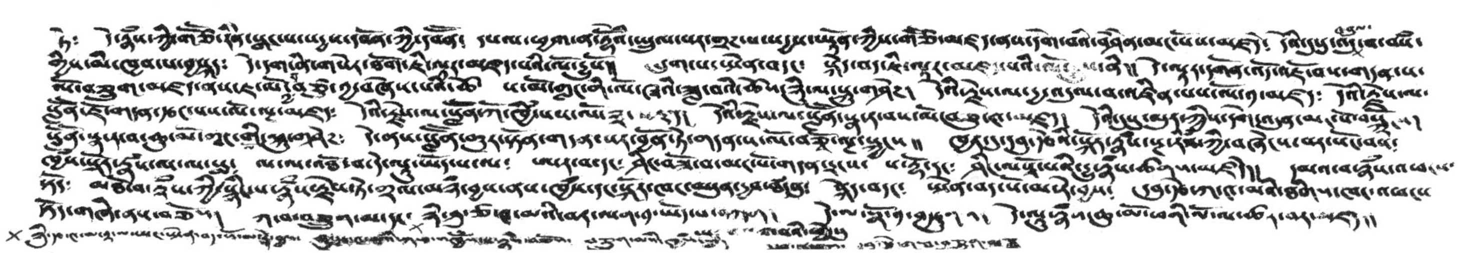

fol. 21

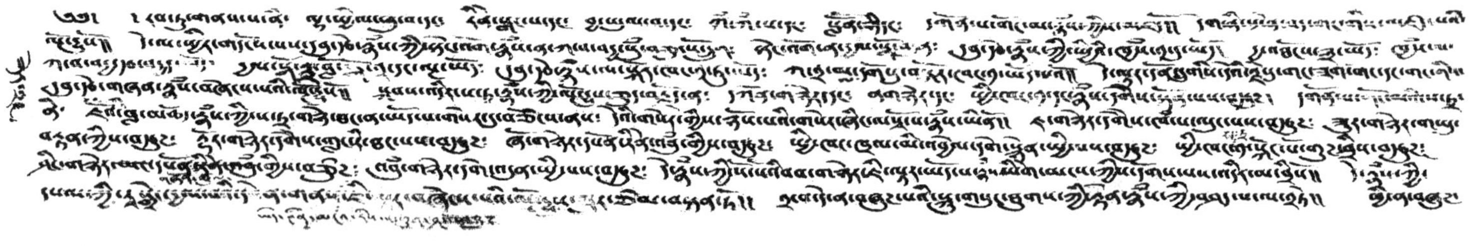

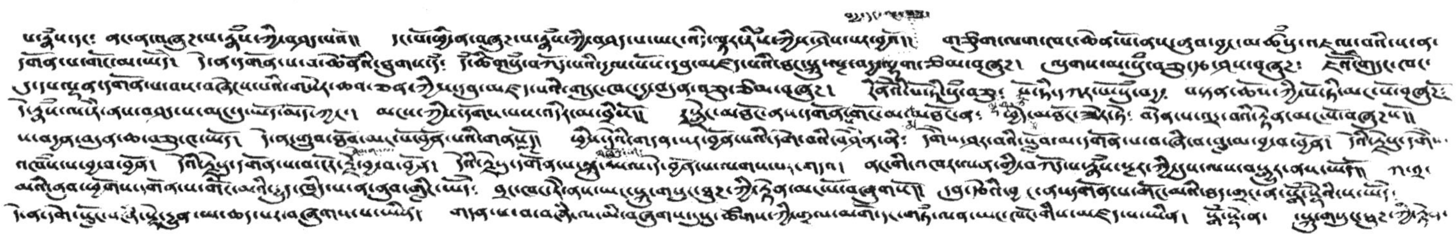

fol. 22

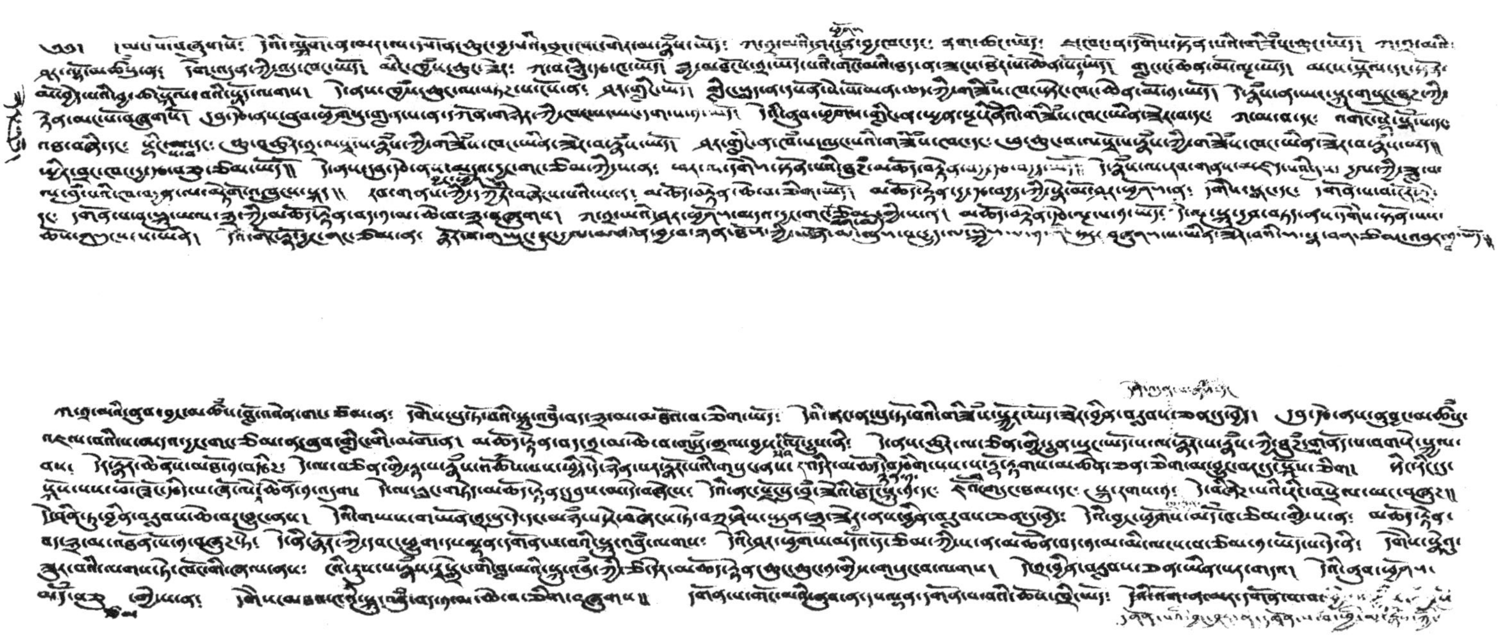

fol. 23

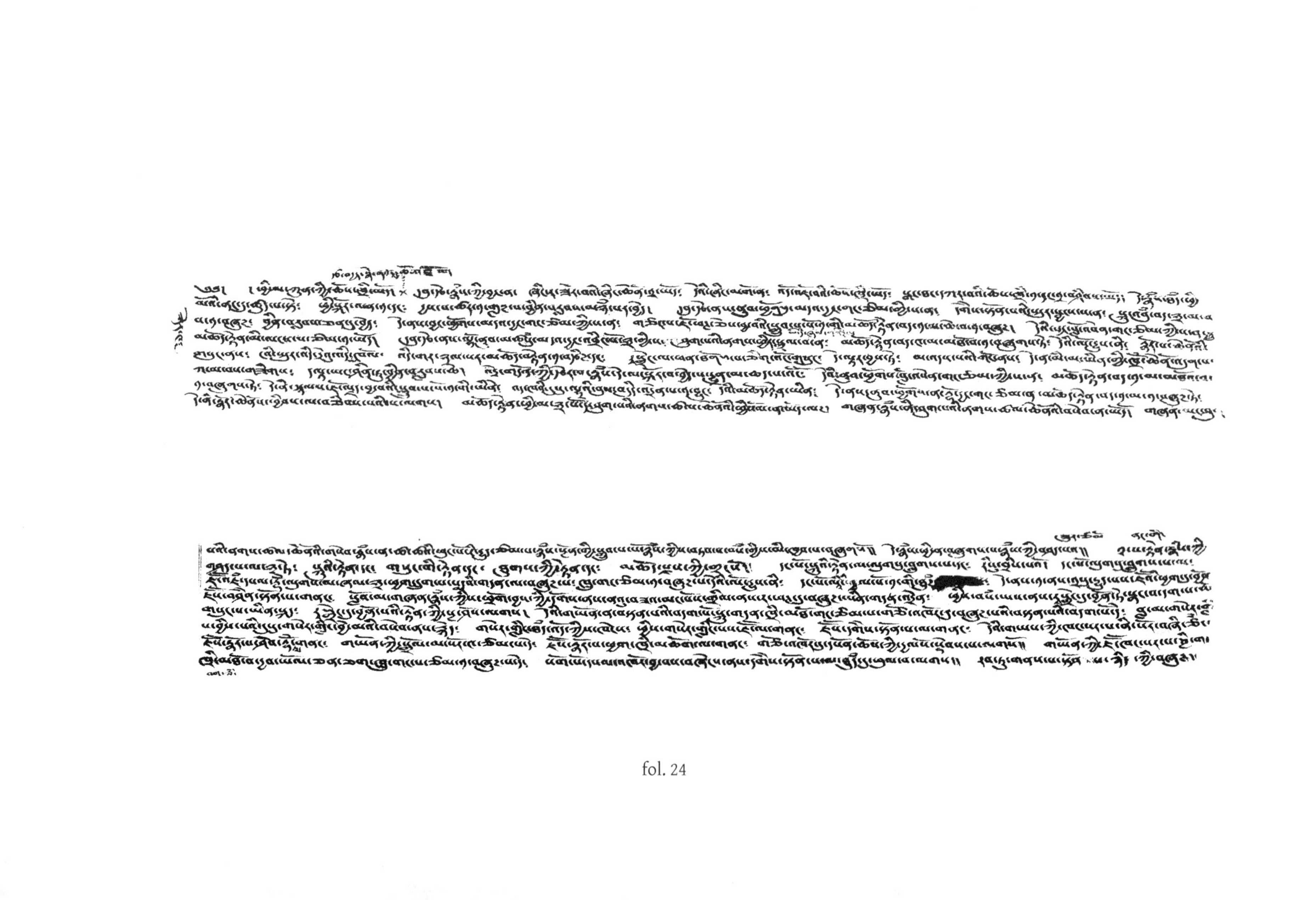

fol. 24

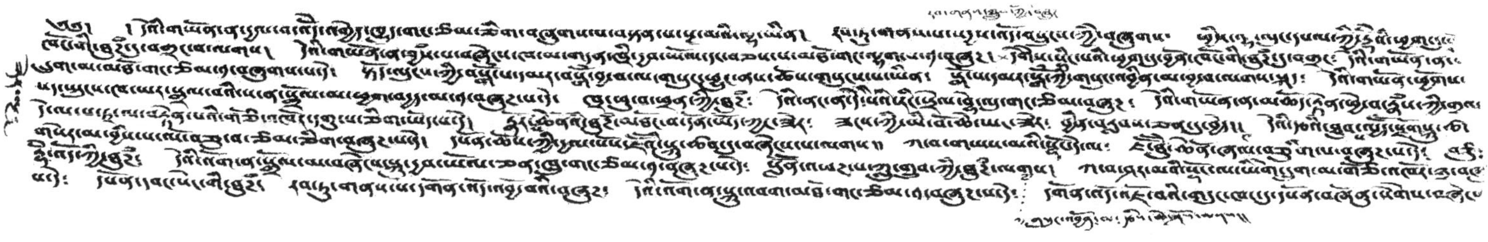

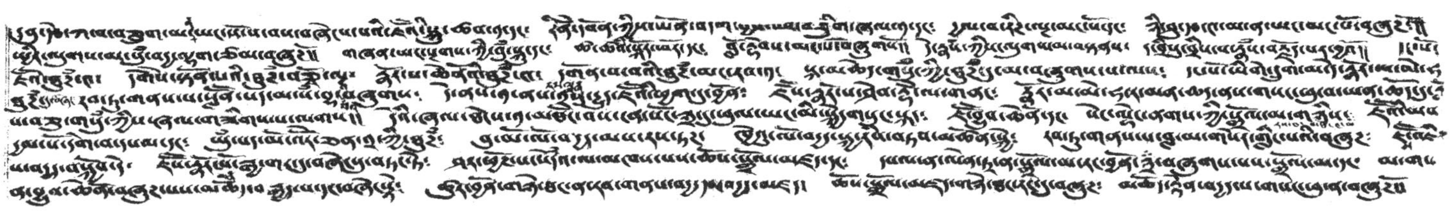

fol. 25

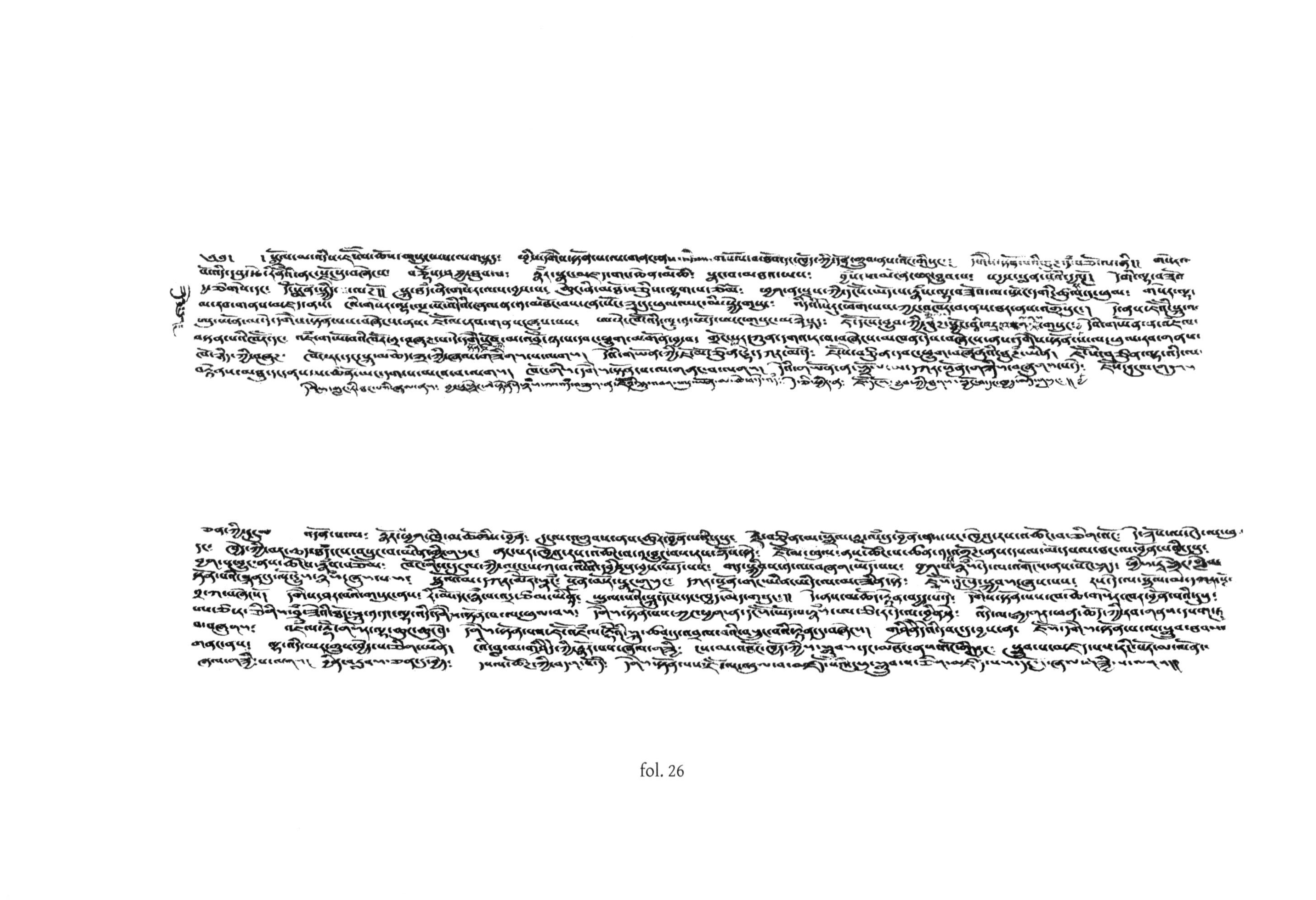

fol. 26

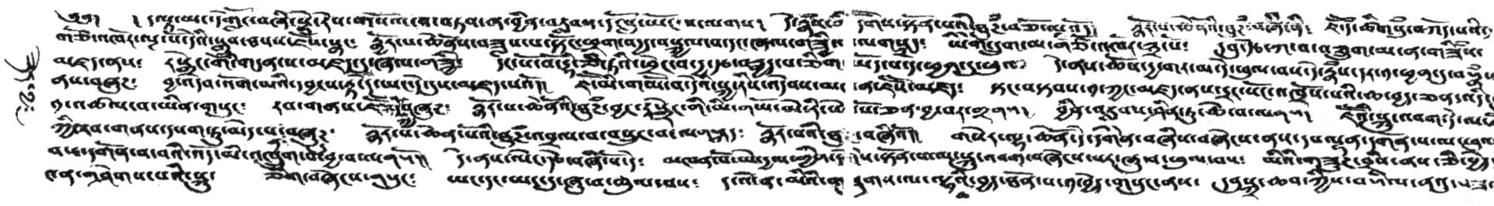

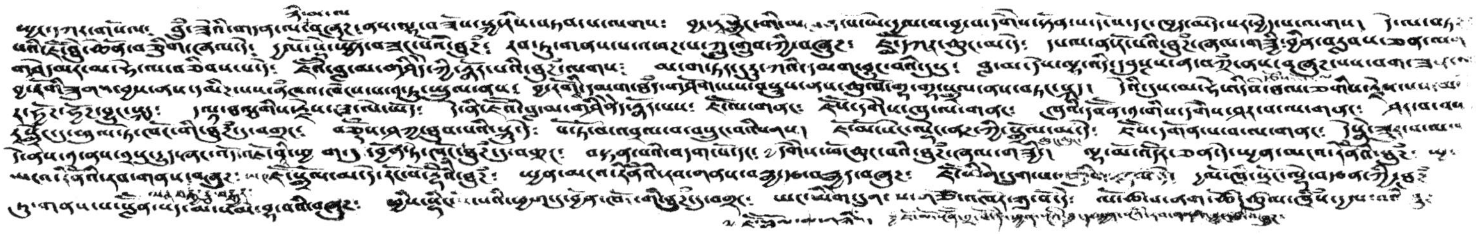

fol. 27

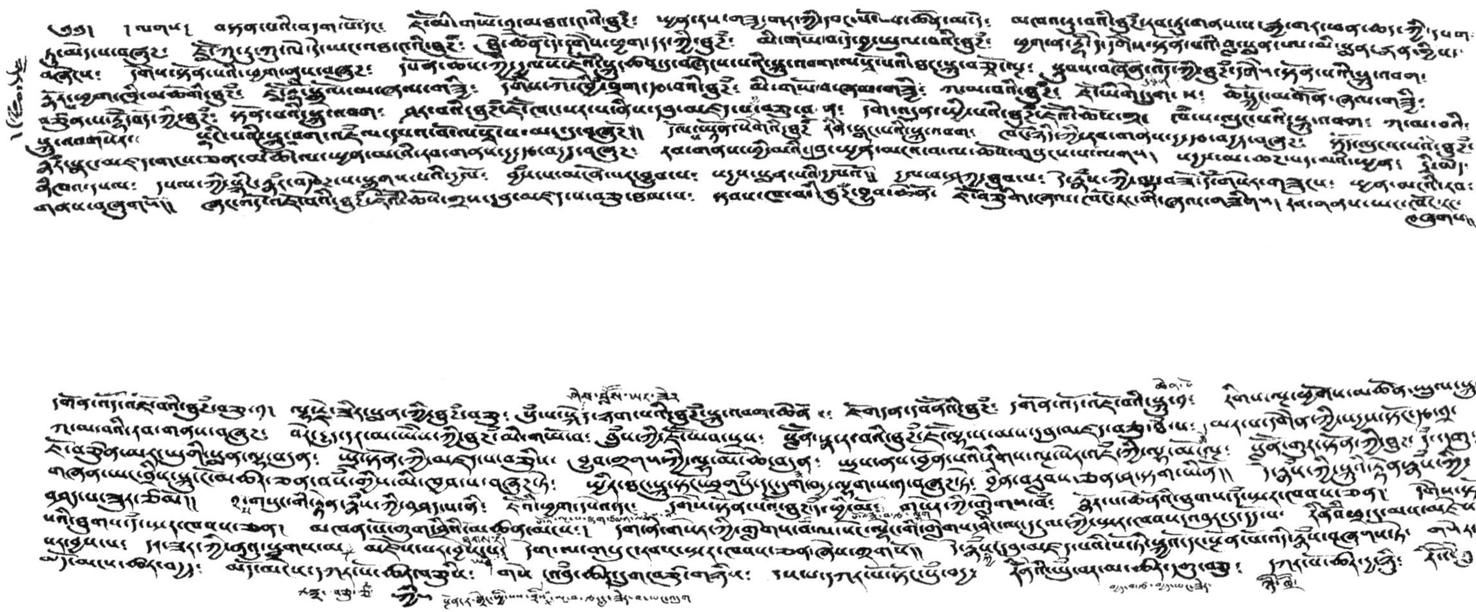

fol. 28

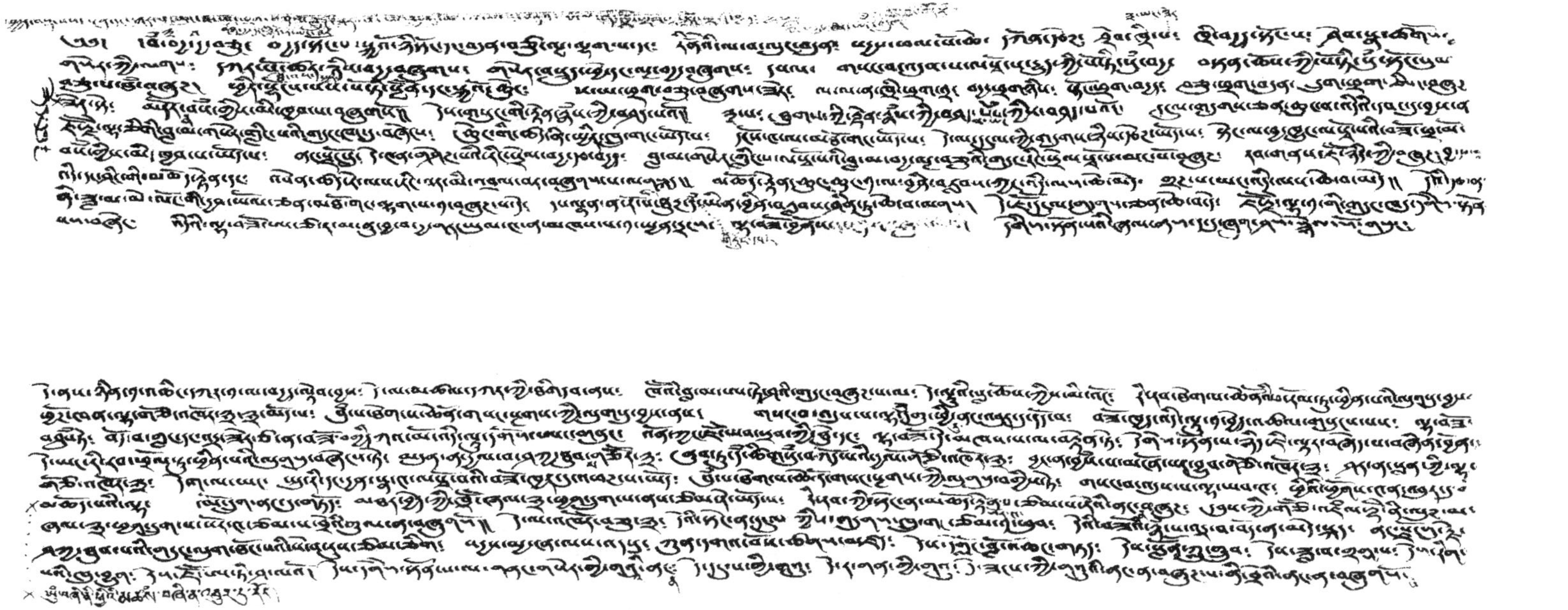

fol. 29

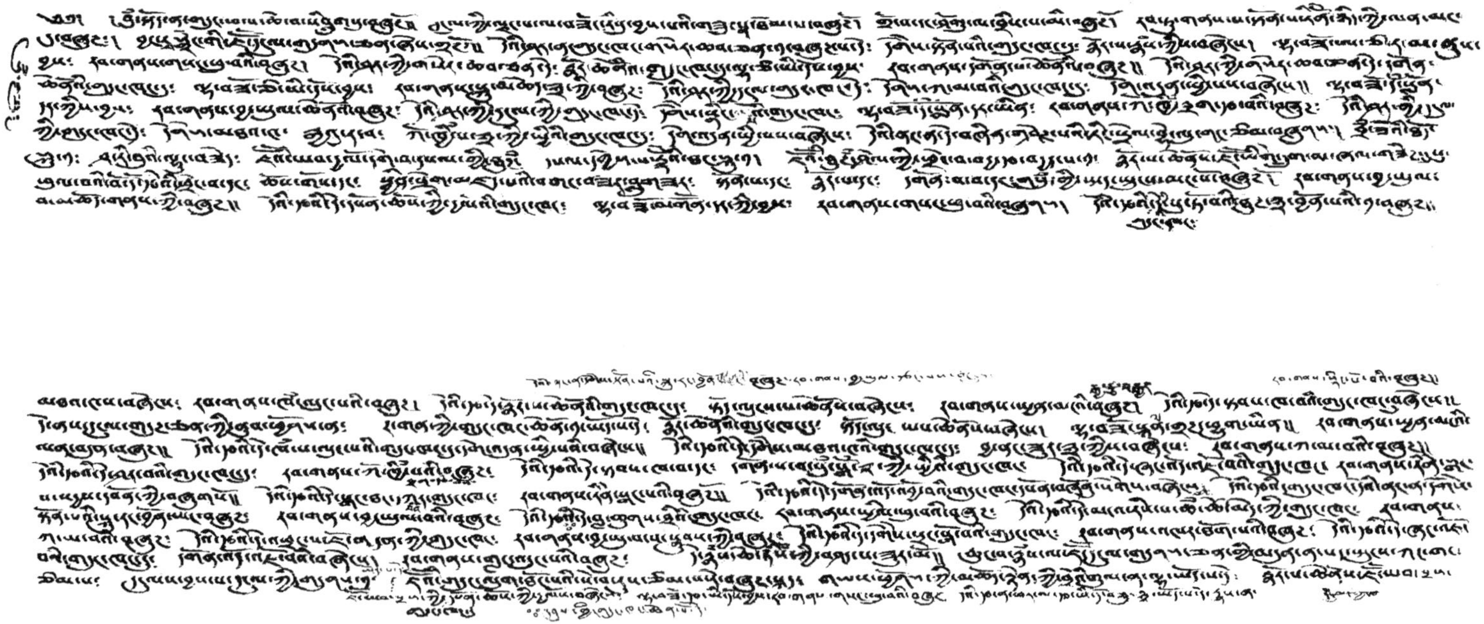

fol. 30

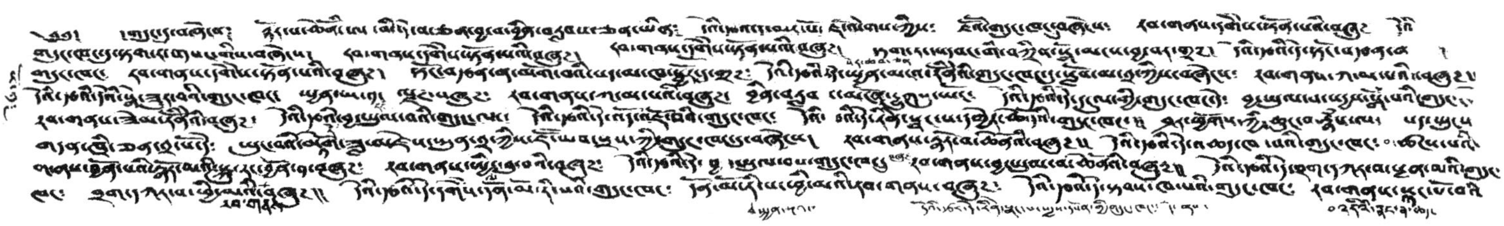

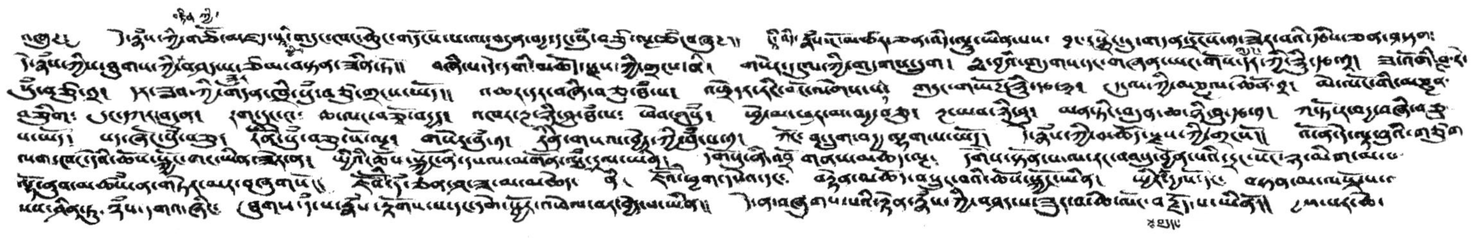

fol. 31

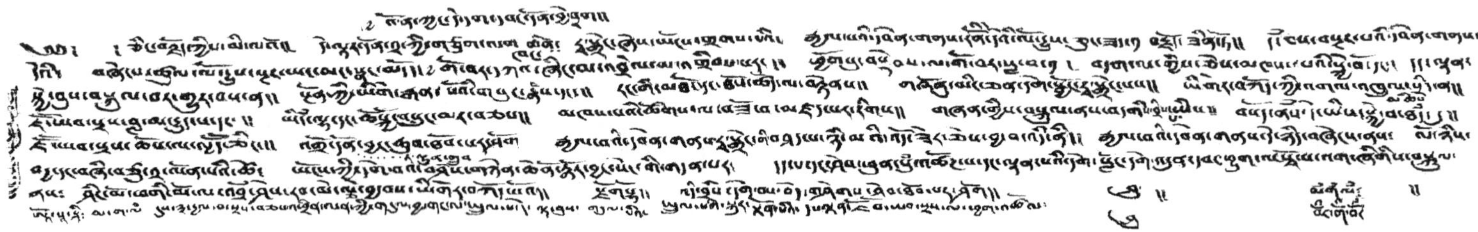

fol. 32